Grassroots Initiatives Shape an International Movement

United Ways Since 1876

GRASSROOTS INITIATIVES

Shape an International Movement

United Ways Since 1876

RICHARD N. AFT, PH.D. AND MARY LU AFT

Philanthropic Leadership

10   9   8   7   6   5   4   3   2   1

Library of Congress Cataloging-in-Publication Data

Aft, Richard N., Ph.D. and Mary Lu Aft
  Grassroots initiatives shape an international movement, united ways since 1876 / by Richard N. Aft, Ph.D. and Mary Lu Aft.—1st ed.
     p.   cm.
  Includes bibliographical references and index.
  ISBN 0-9676382-1-6
  1. SOC033000 SOCIAL SCIENCE/Philanthropy & Charity. 2. SOC035000 SOCIAL SCIENCE/Volunteer Work. 3. SOC016000 SOCIAL SCIENCE/Human Service. 4. SOC025000 SOCIAL SCIENCE/Social Work. 5. HIS037000 HISTORY/World. 6. HIS036010 HISTORY/United States/State & Local. 7. HIS036060 HISTORY/United States/Twentieth Century. 8. HIS037030 HISTORY/Modern/General. I. Title.

Library of Congress Control Number: 2004091000

DEDICATION

To all of the caring people whose local community creations have added up to define a global United Way movement.

"Never doubt that a small group of thoughtful, committed people can change the world. Indeed, it is the only thing that ever has."

—MARGARET MEAD

ACKNOWLEDGMENTS

In 2001, United Way Retiree Association Board members and Betty Beene, President of the United Way of America, asked the authors to research and record United Way history from the perspective of local community organizations whose leadership and innovations defined an international philanthropic movement. No group of friends or colleagues could have been more supportive during conceptualization, research, writing, and editing of this presentation.

Because of the extensive editorial review and contributions of United Way Retiree Association members and active United Way leaders, readers can be confident that any inaccuracies in this record are so commonly accepted that they will be remembered as fact.

Encouragement, anecdotes, and corrections were graciously shared by: Eric Aft, Bob Beggan, Gordon Berg, Jordan "Bud" Biscardo, Virgil Carr, Viney Chandler, Jim Colville, Chuck Devine, Ralph Dickerson, Elizabeth Gower, Jon Hall, Bernie Hyman, H. Allen Larsen, Dan MacDonald, Francis X. McNamara, Bill Mills, Peter Poulos, Don Sanders, Henry M. Smith, Maria Chavez Wilcox, George Wilkinson, and Jim Yu.

Information, editorial review, and advice were offered in abundance by: David Aft, Rob Aft, Amos Burrows, Meg Baxter, Gene Berres, Chris James Brown, Rick Belous, Joe Calabrese, Susan Carpenter, Frank Cleaver, Leo Cornelius, Pat Coyle, Owen Davison, Jack Dillencourt, Joan Dixon, Mike Durkin, John Dyess, Richard Flores, Debbie Foster, Diane Grzyb-Soper, Joe Haggerty, Leslie Ann Howard, Anne Hunt, Ty Joubert, Bill Kerrigan, Susan Lewis, Nancy Mason, Don Mattise, Dennis McMillan, Bill McQueen, Julie Mercer, Harve Mogul, Don Morgan, Jim Morrison, Larry Norvell, Richard J. O'Brien, Rosa O'Neal, Dave Orrell, Gary Ostroske, Sunshine Overkamp, Ruth Ramsden-Wood, Dell Raudelunas, Rob Reifsnyder, Juliet Rowland, Lauren Segal, Susie Sigman, Brent Stewart, Russy Sumariwalla, Michele Thibedeau-DeGuire, Louise Schwan-Kekanovich, Nelda Thompson, A. Rowland Todd, Ray Unk, Joe Valentine, Maria Vizcarrondo-DeSoto, Phillip Walker, Carl Warmington, Doug Warns, Ed Wills, and Don Wingard.

Professional editorial assistance was provided by Karla Zimmerman, a regular contributor to *Lonely Planet*, Anne Hunt of the United Way Retiree Association staff, and David Klaassen, Director of the Social Welfare History Archives at the University of Minnesota.

Publication and design services were generously contributed by F + W Publications, Inc. and printing was done by RR Donnelley & Sons Company.

Special thanks go to the family of Bill and Joan Portman and to Rich and Jill Cross. Their generosity and personal leadership personify the highest qualities of philanthropic leadership and make it possible for all proceeds from the sale of this book to be invested in United Way endowment funds.

Dick and Mary Lu Aft

Cincinnati, Ohio
May 2004

ABOUT THE AUTHORS

Richard N. Aft, Ph.D., and Mary Lu Aft have worked as a United Way team since 1961 when "Dick" served as a graduate intern with the United Fund and Community Planning Council of Evanston, Illinois, and Mary Lu helped him edit the first *North Shore Social Service Directory*. They also married that year.

Dick's career took Mary Lu and their three sons to United Way organizations in Aurora, Illinois; Newark, Ohio; Louisville, Kentucky; Atlanta, Georgia; Memphis, Tennessee; and finally, to Cincinnati, Ohio. While Dick served as a chief professional officer, Mary Lu served as a volunteer whose agency and United Way experiences prepared her to become a training consultant for United Way of America, United Way International, the American National Red Cross, and numerous local United Way and community organizations.

Dick has chaired the United Way of America National Professional Council and a United Way of America Staff Leaders' Conference. Mary Lu served as Host City Chair of the United Way of America Volunteer Leaders' Conference and Cochair of the International Conference on Volunteer Administration and United Way of America's Staff Partners Program. Together, they have represented United Way International as volunteers in Hungary, Indonesia, Poland, Ireland, Kazakhstan, and Romania.

Painful Decisions, Positive Results, Dick's 310-page history of the United Way movement in Cincinnati, is available through Cincinnati's United Way Foundation.

TABLE OF CONTENTS

Innovation

The Breath of Organizational Life

E conomic institutions were created by civic leaders in cities and towns, often by chance. Religious, educational and charitable institutions were developed by citizen leaders, always by choice.

It has been called by many names: Community Chest, Health & Welfare Council, United Fund, Crusade of Mercy, Welfare Federation, United Appeal, and more.

Insiders have described it as community organization, social work, the business side of human services, community problem solving, fund-raising, community building, and more.

Critics have applied a variety of descriptors: centrist, elitist, establishment, monopoly, and more.

Elmer Tropman's grandmother called it "charity."[1] That's all.

For over 125 years, no humanitarian vision, goal, or result has better reflected the voluntary caring of North American people than their hundreds of local United Way organizations. These special groups truly mirror the neighborliness that North Americans have expressed and continue to express in nearly every city and town. And what better way to understand the people who shared a "united way" to prevent and alleviate human suffering than by looking at the tools and techniques they developed to meet the needs of their times—especially those that worked so well, that when shared, became common United Way practice in communities all over the world.

United Way grew from the seeds of a process that Alexis deTocqueville called "association."[2] The United Way movement was a locally developed, openly shared method by which concerned citizens expressed their caring for their neighbor's needs . . . one community at a time. Its past, present, and future are the sum of the best practices of hundreds of local community organizations who share an abiding passion to nurture children, strengthen families, prevent disease, enhance neighborhoods, and foster self-sufficiency in a *united way*.

How can we know whether the little things we do today make a difference? This collection of local innovations that became common United Way practice makes these points:

- Creative ideas that help us define work and carry them out were conceived by people individually and in small groups.
- When they worked and were well communicated, locally conceived approaches have shaped and reshaped common practices and procedures.

Malcomb Gladwell, in his national bestseller *The Tipping Point, How Little Things Can Make a Big Difference*, puts it this way: the "tipping point" is that magic moment when an idea, trend, or social behavior crosses a threshold, tips, and spreads like wildfire. "Just as a single sick person can start an epidemic of the flu, so too can a small but precisely targeted push cause a fashion trend, the popularity of a new product, or a drop in the crime rate."[3]

Just as organisms change in response to epidemics, organizations change in response to ideas that become shared as "best practices." They change. They grow.

Unlike human organisms, successful organizations continually cycle and regenerate. Following a life cycle from birth, through adolescence, and into maturity, organizations need an occasional "epidemic" of innovation to sustain their value to stakeholders. Judith Sharken Simon and J. Terence Donovan give perspective on these cycles in *The Five Life Stages of Nonprofit Organizations: Where You Are, Where You're Going, and What to Expect When You Get There.*

STAGE ONE: Imagine and Inspire ("Can the dream be realized?")

STAGE TWO: Found and Frame ("How are we going to pull this off?")

STAGE THREE: Ground and Grow ("How can we build this to be viable?")

STAGE FOUR: Produce and Sustain ("How can the momentum be sustained?")

STAGE FIVE: Review and Renew ("What do we need to redesign?")[4]

Thanks to the talent and creativity of United Way volunteers and staff, local innovation continues. Life cycles go on; continuous improvement overwhelms resistance to change. Best practices are shared. Better ways are found. Efficiency and effectiveness are increased.

And thanks to the commitment of generous stakeholders, innovations that have benefited United Way organizations have served their local communities as well as the entire movement.

---

[1] Tropman, John E., ed. *Grandma Called It Charity. The Collected Writings of Elmer J. Tropman on Community Development and Organization.* Pittsburgh: the Pittsburgh Foundation, 2001.

[2] deTocqueville, Alexis. *Democracy in America,* 1835. (Henry Reeve Translation, revised and corrected, 1839.)

[3] Gladwell, Malcomb. *The Tipping Point, How Little Things Can Make a Big Difference.* San Francisco: Back Bay Books, 2000.

[4] Simon, Judith Sharken and J. Terence Donovan. *The Five Life Stages of Nonprofit Organizations: Where You Are, Where You're Going, and What to Expect When You Get There.* St. Paul: Wilder Foundation, 2001.

Creating Community Organizations

B rian A. Gallagher, President of United Way of America, brought United Way's history and reason for being into clear focus when he addressed the 2002 Community Leaders' Conference:

> *"Uniting is how we began. It's our history. If I look back in every community, it's the same story. It started because the Industrial Revolution created wealth and opportunity, along with social need that communities had never seen before. Thousands of people were moving from rural areas into the cities for jobs; communities were faced with issues related to health and education and housing and juvenile delinquency that they had never seen before. There was no way they could effectively respond to those issues only as families or just individual institutions.*
>
> *"United Way didn't begin as a fund-raising federation. It began as a planning organization. And the reason that the fund-raising focus worked is that it created impact at a community level that had never been seen before. It changed people's lives and the condition of communities.*
>
> *"In my mind, true community impact begins with being very clear that it's our core business. Community impact is not a department in United Way. Community impact and trying to change the condition of life at a community level is the reason that we exist."*[1]

Everything happens for a reason. Everything happens in its own time. How many times have we heard those expressions?

United Way history is filled with examples of actions and reactions on local, state, national, and international levels. They reflect the environment, conditions, milieu, and people of their times. In retrospect, those are the factors that comprise social history. In the present, those are the realities that shape actions.

United Way history is also filled with examples of innovations that were adopted by many communities because they were developed at just the right time, and they worked. Many of these inventions, or sometimes accommodations, became common practice. They grew from United Way's grass roots, from the hundreds of local communities that are the United Way.

Even before United Ways had a national association, its leaders met to share their dreams, experiences, and best practices. Like all colleagues, they also joked about their worst practices. They learned from one another. They learned to apply the best and to avoid the worst.

A long-time United Way colleague, Dan Ransohoff, who served as Cincinnati's Special Projects Director for over 40 years and whose photos of children served as national campaign posters in the 1960s, always asked people where they were from. Once he heard their answer, he told them why their city was located where it is. "It's on a river where a port was needed," he'd say. Or, "That's where the trail ended." Or, "Ships could land there." He knew that almost every city is located where it is for a reason.

United Way, where are you from? Spokane? Montreal? Anniston? Somerset? San Antonio? Tallahassee? Vancouver? United Way is there for a reason: community, which is the cause, the site, and the laboratory of United Way. It is the soil from which "community organization social work" grew. It is home for people who, whether they like to admit it or not, share neighborhoods and newspapers, successes and scandals, triumphs and tears. It is also the home of people and organizations who voluntarily give their time, talents, and money because they care about their fellow human beings. In almost every community, they have done so in a united way—a united way known by many names.

Organizations' Names Described Functions

No one questioned what the first Social Service Exchange did in 1872. Its name called it what it was. Community Funds and Councils of Social Agencies were true to their names, too. Leaders in many communities developed unique names for the organizations that preceded United Way.

Those that did so wished to express the individualities of their organizations and communities and to differentiate their community organizations from those in other cities.

Individuality in name, however, did not mean difference in function. There were similarities. Those with names that included "Council" were the *planners*. They convened people to understand human needs and services, to identify gaps and overlaps, and to plan and coordinate. Organizations with names including "Fund," "Chest," or "Appeal" were the *campaigners*. They organized people to raise money. Organizations with names including "Federated or Federation" often did both community planning and campaigning. Depending on time and place, funds raised were allocated by one or more of these organizations.

As with all start-up organizations, communities' fund-raising, planning, and allocating groups struggled to find effective ways to carry out their day-to-day work. Early successes were communicated among cities by business and civic leaders as they traveled. News of community approaches to dealing with the agencies' needs made good topics of conversation with business associates, families, and friends. Charitable agencies also shared news of the best and worst practices of these new community organizations at their national forums.

In 1919, the social work professionals who headed Community Chests and Councils of Social Agencies formed the American Association for Community Organizations (AACO) to share their unique experiences and ideas to better serve their communities. Annual conferences and the monthly *Bulletin* provided platforms for sharing successes and failures. Often, *Bulletin* articles offered detailed descriptions of innovations that produced desired results.

Unlike many direct client service agencies whose local affiliates had been created by their national "parent" organization, Chests and Councils grew from local roots. High value was placed on the uniqueness of each community's needs and resources. For this reason, AACO affiliates insisted that membership in their national association be voluntary. They structured their national organization so that it focused on the needs of autonomous community organizations and their volunteers and professional leaders. The *Bulletin* regularly reported the experiences of individual members, but never suggested policies or programs that would impinge on their autonomy.

By the late 1920s, the Community Chest name was used by almost all cities' fund-raising and combined fund-raising/community planning organizations. "Council" was the common denominator in the names of Social Agency Councils, Community Planning Councils, and the other community organizations that focused on community planning. In keeping with these generally used names, the American Association for Community Organizations changed its name to Community Chests and Councils, Inc. (CCC or "Three Cs") in 1927. Responding to the needs of over 100 Canadian cities' Community Chests and Councils, a Canadian national organization known as Centraide Canada was formed in 1939.

Special Names for Special Needs

Use of the War Chest name during both world wars (1917–18 and 1941–1945) reflected the special needs of these periods. The 1950s saw the separate Red Cross and Community Chest campaigns combine into united appeals in most communities. This change brought common use of the "United" prefix to a variety of Community Chest or Chest/Council organizations. Community Chests and Councils, Inc. changed its name to United Community Funds and Councils of America (UCFCA) in 1956 to reflect the names used by the majority of its members.

The turmoil surrounding the social changes of the 1960s prompted further changes in the name of many communities' "united" organizations. Critics of existing organizations that were trying to keep pace with human needs placed most community organizations into a category they labeled "the establishment." For them, "the establishment" was a term that signified the failure of lofty goals such as the elimination of poverty and racism. United Appeals, Health and Welfare Councils, United Crusades, United Community Services—most communities' successors to Community Chests and Councils were on "the establishment" list.

In 1964, the federal government took unprecedented action. Under the aegis of the Economic Opportunity Act of 1964, federal tax dollars were passed directly to local nonprofit organizations. State and local governments, for the first time in history, were bypassed by federal officials.

4

"Establishment" organizations like the affiliates of UCFCA were, for the most part, bypassed as well.

Very quickly, the community-level planning was replaced by agency and neighborhood-level planning, and the community organization role that United Way groups had performed dissolved. Few separate community planning organizations survived the reorganizations of Funds and Councils in the early 1970s. For the most part, Council staff members became the staff of planning or planning and allocations divisions of the combined organizations.

Multiple Names for the New Organizations Confused People

The number of localized names for organizations with similar functions confused people whose jobs took them from city to city or gave them responsibility for working with a number of cities. They might support the United Fund of one community, the Crusade of Mercy in another, and the United Appeal in yet another. Late in the '60s, United Community Funds and Councils of America (UCFCA) took a hard look at itself and its services to nearly 2,100 local United Way organizations that chose to be its members. "Name" was among the subjects it examined. For nearly two years, a national "blue-ribbon committee," consisting of local community representatives and the leaders of a number of major American corporations, worked with Peat, Marwick, Mitchell, and Company consultants. They looked at the role and functions of UCFCA. They looked at the needs of the member communities. Their deliberation and dialogue produced general support for changing the name and functions of the national association to United Way of America. It also led to the 1972 introduction of a logo and graphically bold presentation of the United Way name by Saul Bass, a nationally prominent artist and brand designer.

United Way Name and Logo Introduced

"Vibrant, exciting, colorful, positive, and changing" were the adjectives Bass used as he dramatically unveiled "the sun-like rainbow growing out of the hand" to those who attended the 1972 United Way Volunteer

Leaders' Conference.[2] The logo and presentation of the United Way brand were well received, and before long, most local communities had adopted it. Centraide Canada's 120-plus members did the same. And, as was inevitable, community leaders personalized the name with city, county, or other geographical designations, such as The United Way *of Lincoln County, Tri-State* United Way, or The United Way *of the Central & South Okanagan/Similkameen* (Kelowna, British Columbia).

Many names used by United Way and predecessor organizations appear at the end of this Introduction.[3]

Regardless of name, these organizations brought people together to work for their communities in a "united" way. Together. For people in need. For one another. For the community.

A Movement

For people who are new to United Way, it may just be an organization, a charity, or an office building. But for those who know more, it is the sum of more than 125 years of learning by the leaders of hundreds of local community organizations. Their words were often as different as their dialects, yet they shared a commitment to community. They strove for efficiency and effectiveness. They searched for outcomes that they were certain flowed from the teamwork of their contributors, agencies, volunteers, and staff. They believed that they were reasonably impartial. They knew enough to bring broadly representative groups of people to a "community table" to solve community problems. They were confident in their skills in problem identification, planning, priority setting, program evaluation, fund-raising, accounting, and stewardship. They believed in collaboration. They wanted to prevent and alleviate human suffering. They were all about a community approach to improving the quality of life for all of their residents. They believed, with good reason, that the organizations they nurtured and sustained, while far from perfect, were among the best voluntary institutions ever developed.

Above all, these movers in the United Way movement were relentlessly determined that, in their communities, every child would succeed, every adult would be self-sufficient, every family would be strong, every older person would be independent, every individual would be healthy, and every neighborhood would be safe.

Together, their words transcended organizations. Their concepts comprised a movement.

What has come to be called the United Way began as local community experiments in collaboration, charity, philanthropy, social work, and community organization. United Way organizations have persevered as voluntary nonprofit organizations that increase people's capacity to care for one another. In some communities they are more a *place* than an organization. They serve as a place where people can come together to find ways to deal with the problems that are synonymous with living together in a community.

Names have changed, including those of the organizations and those of their leaders. But the dreams have not. They are what American communities are all about:

- neighbor helping neighbor
- enabling each person to develop to his/her fullest capacity
- enhancing the quality of life
- contributing to making communities a good place to live, work, and raise a family
- people helping people

A movement!

An Invitation to Become Part of This History

The pages that follow give a history of the local community inventions and innovations that have become the tools and techniques of the United Way field. They are presented in the context of the times in which they were developed.

Peter F. Drucker, a scholar whom the Harvard Business Review calls "the father of modern management," validated the need for people to continue to contribute to a United Way history. He shared his perspective at the Drucker Foundation's 2002 Organization of the Future Conference:

"We are in the midst of a transition period," he said. "These periods create enormous opportunities and enormous dislocations and challenges. I see the next five or ten years of tremendous opportunity for the community-based nonprofits. You may have a national organization. . . . But the work has to be done in the community by people who know and are known in the community. They will need to be innovative, because the problems are not the same as the problems of yesterday. I think we are just at the beginning of the most important period for the American nonprofit."[4]

Drucker's words invite us all to add to the rich history of Caring People . . . Building Communities that has been United Way since 1876.

---

[1] Gallagher, Brian A., President, United Way of America. "Keynote Address: 2002 United Way of America Community Leaders' Conference." Indianapolis: April 26, 2002.

[2] Bass, Saul. "A Positive Symbol of United Way." Presentation at the 1972 United Way Leaders' Conference. Washington, DC: May 2, 1972.

[3] Many of the community names used by local United Way predecessors included:

Social Service Exchange (Boston, MA)	1876
Charity Organization Society (Buffalo, NY)	1877
Associated Charities (Boston, MA)	1879
Charity Organization Society (Denver, CO)	1887
Council of Social Agencies (Pittsburgh, PA)	1908
Federated Charities (Elmira, NY)	1910
Federation of Charity and Philanthropy (Cleveland, OH)	1913
War Council (Cincinnati, OH)	1915
Welfare Council (Dallas, TX)	1916
War Chest (Cleveland, OH)	1917
Community Chest (Rochester, NY)	1918
Health & Welfare Council (Louisville, KY)	1945
United Foundation Torch Drive (Detroit, MI)	1949
United Community Chest (Niagara Falls, NY)	1954
United Medical Research Foundation (Durham, NC)	1955
United Health Foundation	1961

then, United Appeal, United Fund, United Neighbors, United Good Neighbors, United Torch Services, United Crusade, Crusade of Mercy, United Givers Fund, and United Community Services

State organizations began in Ohio:

Institute for Public Efficiency (Columbus)	1913

National association names over the years were:

American Association for Community Organizations	1919
Association of Community Chests and Councils	1927
(Mobilization for Human Needs of the American Association of Community Chests and Councils)	1932
Community Chests and Councils	1933
(National Budget Committee for War Appeals of the Community Chests and Councils)	1942
(National Budget Committee of Community Chests and Councils)	1946

Canadian Welfare Council	1935
Centraide Canada	1939
Community Chests and Councils of America	1948
(United Red Feather Campaigns of America of the Community	
Chests and Councils of America)	1951
United Community Funds and Councils of America	1956
United Way of America	1970
United Way of Canada	1972
United Way International began as a division of United Way of	
America and incorporated separately	1992

[4] Drucker, Peter F. "Keynote Address: 2002 Organization of the Future Conference." New York: Peter F. Drucker Foundation, February 28, 2002.

CHAPTER ONE

Roots of Community Organization

1876—1886

Science Comes to the Art of Charity

T he United States was 100 years old. Canada was just nine. "Westward ho" was on the lips and in the hearts of young families, many headed by teenagers. The Civil War, just 10 years past, was more personal than historical. The abolition of slavery was difficult for many Americans to grasp. Men of African ancestry couldn't vote. Nor could women of any race.

Immigration of poor and non-English-speaking people from Europe to America's east coast increased each year. Northbound migration of poor and often illiterate former slaves in search of work began to accelerate. The conditions of crowding slums, poverty, crime, and disease were being addressed more each day in houses of worship, and their budgets for programs to assist the poor became depleted. Concern grew about the number of destitute people who repeatedly returned for help and those who sought help from more than one institution.

The day had arrived when those who practiced the "art of charity" reached out for help from people who could apply science to the management of care. Americans began to develop programs and procedures that brought together individuals and organizations to help people in need, and they began to work in a "united way." The manner in which they worked together and the tools they developed to facilitate their increased effectiveness reflected the conscience of their times.

People have always cared about their neighbors. But in 1876, it seemed that orphans were as numerous as horses in the streets of our cities. In the wisdom of the times, those neighbors were relegated to orphanages. Women whispered, "There but for the grace of God go I," as they passed the poor in the markets. Those neighbors were sent to poorhouses. Workers' guilt diminished as they dropped pennies into the outstretched hands of beggars. Those neighbors were placed in workhouses.

"Anticipate charity by preventing poverty."
—MIAMONIDES

Just a few years earlier, Charles Dickens had popularized Christmastime giving to the poor. Seasons' Greetings took shape in gifts of food.

For some, the orphanages were safe havens. For others, county homes or "poor farms" were the only alternatives to starvation. Still others found themselves sharing filthy berths in sanitaria, the last resort for those suffering mental and physical illnesses.

Death. Desertion. Disease. Divorce. Drug abuse. Disability. Depression. Displacement. Destitution. Despair. Dan Ransohoff's staccato recitation of his "10 Ds" opened every presentation of "A History of Social Work,"[1] his narrative of the development of health and social services in Western civilization. As America approached her second century, people who were unable to help themselves were increasingly able to find humane places to receive help. While the life-sustaining measures of the 1870s and 1880s offered little more than stairways leading to early graves for some beneficiaries, many others drew strength from the increasing acts of kindness being offered and gained self-sufficiency.

Look at the environment in which people lived during these years. Feel the context in which humanitarian leaders acted on the values rooted in their religions to care for people who could not care for themselves.

Signs of the Times

GLOBAL/NATIONAL EVENTS

1876–1886   Wars continued to be waged throughout Europe and Africa.

1877   Rutherford Hayes, behind by 19 electoral votes, disputed and won over 20 members of the Electoral College to become 19th President.

IN THE NEWS

1876   The Intercolonial Railway linked central Canada and the Maritimes.

1881   President James Garfield was assassinated.

1886   The capture of Apache Chief Geronimo brought an end to Indian Wars.

1878   An amendment to extend voting rights (suffrage) to women was introduced in Congress.

ECONOMY/BUSINESS CYCLES AND THE WORKPLACE

1876–1886   Private enterprise boomed; business monopolies began to take form.

1876–1886   Migrant and immigrant men, women, and children comprised an inexpensive labor pool.

1886   The American Federation of Labor was founded.

SCIENCE AND TECHNOLOGY

1876   Alexander Graham Bell patented the telephone.

1879   Thomas Alva Edison perfected the electric light bulb.

1880   Canned fruits and meats appeared on store shelves.

FAMILY/HOUSEHOLD STRUCTURE

1876–1886   Wealth, work, and poverty: income stratification defined upper, middle, and lower social classes.

HUMAN NEEDS

1876   The first North American juvenile reformatory was founded.

1876–1886   Urban public health continuously dealt with communicable diseases harbored in flood plains and slums.

1881   The concept of regulating occupational safety was discussed in the U.S. Senate.

Leadership Characteristics

BEGINNINGS

The beginnings of the movement that came to be called the "United Way" can be seen as early as 1876. Men and women stepped forward to lead the community-level/community-organization social work they saw as necessary. Their work crossed the geographic and religious boundaries that had previously described humane services. Their actions were motivated by a desire to identify and meet needs that were more common to communities than they were to individuals within communities. Understanding their characteristics enhances our appreciation of their actions.

THE PROFESSIONALS

"You can't do the Lord's work if you're broke," Ransohoff would remind twentieth century audiences of social work history.[2] Clergy of the 1880s preached a gospel of responsibility to help the less fortunate and to love others as one's self. On the Sabbath, they had the attention of businessmen in their congregations. On weekdays, they reached out to the businessmen's wives, the "ladies bountiful." The messages were powerful. Jews' *tzedakah* made aid, assistance, and money an obligation. Christians' *Golden Rule* encouraged love of others. When the clergy reached out to businessmen, they said, "We can't do the Lord's work without your money." To their wives, they said, "We can't do the Lord's work without your help—specifically, your time to assist our efforts."

These were the people who shaped modern health and human services. Roy Lubove, in *The Professional Altruist, the Emergence of Social Work as a Career 1880–1930*, sketched them in the context of their times. "In the early twentieth century the anatomy of contemporary private social work took shape: a compound of national health and welfare agencies and, in the larger cities, a host of specialized agencies involved in casework, group work, community organization and social reform. . . . A professional subculture sought to nurture a group consciousness and channel career opportunities. These widened the chasm between paid workers and volunteers or, more generally, between agency-centered, professional social work[ers] and average citizen[s]."[3]

*"An institution or reform movement that is not selfish must origi-
nate in the recognition of some evil that is adding to the sum of
human suffering, or diminishing the sum of happiness. I support
it as a philanthropic movement to try to reverse the process."*

—CLARA BARTON, *Founder, American Red Cross*

THE VOLUNTEERS

Members of these congregations were moved by fresh memories of Clara
Barton's selfless nursing on Civil War battlefields. They were inspired by
stories of happy endings for orphans placed in adoptive homes by New
York's Children's Aid Society. They followed the Judeo-Christian teach-
ings of their clergy. They gave money. They gave time.

But needs outweighed resources, and there was not enough money, not
enough time. Something had to be done, something that would enable
professionals and volunteers to better manage scarce resources. Collaboration and cooperation emerged as means to use limited assets more wisely.

Traditionally, the clergy and those who supported them had worked in
congregational or denominational groups, independent from one another.
The tools to stretch resources emerged as they came together to share
their perceptions of needs and assets.

How Approaches Reflected the Needs and the Times

SCHEMERS PROMPTED THE CREATION
OF THE SOCIAL SERVICE EXCHANGE

It was the schemers whom we might thank for fostering cooperation
among their benefactors. It began in 1876, in Boston, Massachusetts.
Many people "double dipped" at the doors of several agencies, which
quickly depleted already strained resources. Agencies decided something
had to be done, so they got together and created the first "social service
exchange." Its stated purpose was "to prevent duplication in relief-
giving."[4] Its charter was "to facilitate interagency communication
through maintenance of a central confidential file of families and individuals known to social agencies."[5] Agencies could now thwart schemers' efforts to get more than a fair share of assistance.

Some students of social work history might ask if the people who stood in more than their share of lines were taking advantage of free enterprise. Other students might ask if this earliest form of managed care increased or perpetuated the dependency of people whose share of charity was regulated by this new invention. But these questions were not on the minds of the creators of the first social service exchange. They wanted to stretch the soup and to turn away the schemers.

The mechanics of the first social service exchange were straightforward. "A member agency, upon receipt of an application for service, clears the names of the family with the exchange, which searches its files to determine whether the family has been known to other agencies. The exchange then provides this information to the inquiring agency. This enables the agency, in its judgment of the probable significance of earlier contacts, to initiate consultation with appropriate agencies."[6]

Social Service Exchanges increased in number well into the twentieth century. Boston's 1876 invention was replicated in hundreds of cities. But times changed. In a commentary titled "The Social Service Exchange—Yes or No?" Elmer Tropman observed, "[Social Service Exchange organizations] increased in number with the growth of social welfare, and came to be accepted as an essential instrument in preventing duplication of services and furthering cooperation among agencies. By 1946 there were 320 Social Service Exchanges."[7] When Tropman's commentary appeared in 1965, the number of Social Service Exchanges had fallen to 175. "This trend," he said, "was very disturbing to Social Service Exchange people and to others interested in furthering and improving cooperation and coordination in the increasingly complicated social welfare field. But unfortunately no instrument exists which would enable a community to study and evaluate objectively the effectiveness of its SSE."[8]

Tropman's lament rang true for all but the handful of Social Service Exchanges that operated at the end of this century. "There is no question that the need for teamwork and coordination among health and social welfare agencies is greater today than ever before. The vast, complex, growing, and specialized health and welfare service program requires much greater integration and interrelationship of our services than we have yet been able to achieve. Someone has said that future progress in

15

the health and social welfare field will be due more to improvement in our ability to integrate and coordinate present services than to the development of new skills and new services."[9] Elmer Tropman's epitaph for Boston's invention, however, pointed toward new creations that would be built on the foundation whose cornerstone was laid in 1886.

CHRISTMAS BUREAU CREATED TO MEET
SPECIALIZED SEASONAL NEEDS

It is ironic that in a season characterized by love, the Christmas Bureau was developed for quite another purpose—to stop abuse of holiday giving programs. The people of Boston were the first to create a Bureau. They used the science of the Social Service Exchange to put together a central repository of the names and addresses of people seeking Christmastime assistance to "deal with frauds and cheaters."[10]

The Christmas Bureau idea spread to other cities on the heels of the Social Service Exchange. Unlike the dollar-stretching goals of the Exchange, however, Christmas Bureaus were organized specifically to prevent holiday program misuse. Organizations preregistered the people they planned to help with gift baskets or food, clothing, and toys. Bureau clerks screened lists for duplication before baskets were delivered.

 "The whole idea of living in the city instead of the country is that your neighbors are close enough to bring soup if you need it, and it's hot when you get it."
—MARK TWAIN

Recollections of a Chicago Christmas Bureau pioneer, Elizabeth A. Hughes, painted the sad truth: "We have unfortunately not yet passed onto the plane where indiscriminate Christmas giving to socially dependant families is not full of menace."[11] Years after the creation of the first Christmas Bureau, the American Association of Social Service Exchanges interviewed its founder, Laura Woodbury. She was critical about the policing role it served in its early years. "Miss Woodbury speaks very severely about the Christmas basket registration which in her opinion creates uncertainty about social work, for it is not social work."[12]

Social work or not, this 1876 invention continues by more ecumenical names such as Holiday Clearing House in most communities. Well beyond its founders' purpose—preventing client fraud—this nineteenth century invention has grown to spread limited holiday charity as far as it will go. The Christmas Bureau has outlived its Social Service Exchange parent, but it still uses its recipe to "thin the soup."

SERVICE AND FUND-RAISING COORDINATED AMONG
SMALL GROUPS OF SIMILAR AGENCIES

Human needs grew between 1876 and 1886 more quickly than the human service agencies created to respond to them. Building on the values of exchanging client information, agencies began to develop associations to coordinate their responses to community service needs.

Agency leaders in Buffalo, New York, were the first to come together as a Charity Organization Society, according to *The Greenwood Encyclopedia of American Institutions.*[13] In 1887, they met to confront the reality that clients often needed services other than those individual agencies could supply. Few agencies could afford to meet every service need of every client. By comparing programs of service and client characteristics, agency professionals were able to coordinate areas of specialization and arrange systems of client referral. No record exists of their success in this regard. Logic dictates, however, that the clients of the Buffalo agencies benefited from the insights these human service pioneers had of their clients' multiple needs.

"We accept the seed, but grow the plant to make the next seed a better one."
—BOOKER T. WASHINGTON

In Boston, just two years later, agency volunteers convened a meeting to discuss the fund-raising difficulties they were causing for one another. Edward Jenkins, in *Philanthropy in America*, reports that their 1879 efforts resulted in an annual sharing of fund-raising campaign schedules.[14] In subsequent years, the Boston scheduling model was adopted by United Way predecessor organizations in most cities. It came to be called a "campaign clearing house" by many. However, increasing numbers of nonprofit organizations and campaigns made it more and more difficult for United Way organizations to continue this function during the second half of the twentieth century. United Way's impartiality as coordinator of a community schedule was brought into question. Some cities placed the scheduling function with their Chambers of Commerce. Others legislated governmental coordination of fund-raising schedules. Neither approach prevailed as the number of requests for exclusive campaign dates has been surpassed by the number of campaigns. What's more, no organization—United Way, business, or government—has wanted to regulate the growth of free enterprise in charitable fund-raising.

While towns and cities locally addressed their unique needs, the people of one state found value in sharing information about their local problems on a statewide basis. In 1881, according to Amos Warner's *American Charities*,[15] the first statewide Conference of Charities was convened in Wisconsin as the Wisconsin Conference of Charities and Corrections. With service and fund-raising coordination as their mission, those present pledged to share information with one another at continuing annual meetings. The idea was to take root in many forms over the years ahead: local, national, and international workshops, seminars, and conferences to share best practices, outcomes, and ideas. The values of service and fund-raising coordination and information sharing had been demonstrated and warranted long life.

Key Innovations in the United Way of Serving
Communities Between 1876 and 1886

1876	Centralized agency client registration	Boston, MA
1876	Christmas Clearing House (i.e., Christmas Bureau)	Boston, MA
1877	Centralized agency service coordination	Buffalo, NY
1879	Agency fund-raising coordination	Boston, MA

---

[1]   Ransohoff, Daniel J., Ph.D. Cincinnati speeches, 1974–1993.

[2]   Ransohoff.

[3]   Lubove, Roy. *The Professional Altruist, the Emergence of Social Work as a Career 1880–1930.* Boston: Harvard University Press, 1965, pp. 202-203.

4   Lurie, Harry L., ed. *Encyclopedia of Social Work*, Fifteenth Issue. National Association of Social Workers, 1965, p. 731.
5   Lurie, p. 732.
6   Lurie, p. 732.
7   Tropman, Elmer J. "The Social Service Exchange - Yes or No?" *Community Magazine*, United Community Funds & Councils of America, June 1959, p. 164.
8   Tropman, p. 164.
9   Tropman, p. 165.
10 Street, Elwood. "The United Way, A History." Unpublished memoirs on file at the University of Minnesota Social Welfare History Archives, 1958, p. 833a.
11 Street, p. 833a.
12 Woodbury, Laura. Annual review published by the American Association of Social Service Exchanges, 1923.
13 Romanofsky, Peter, Editor-in-chief. *The Greenwood Encyclopedia of American Institutions: Social Service Organizations*. Boston: Greenwood Press, 1978, p. 741.
14 Jenkins, Edward C. *Philanthropy in America*. Chicago: Association Press, 1950, p. 177.
15 Warner, Amos G. et al. *American Charities*, Fourth Edition. New York: Thomas Y. Crowell Co., 1930, pp. 132-133.

CHAPTER TWO

Uniting Communities

1887—1929

Industrialization, Immigration, Urbanization

[I] nvention, mass production, economic boom—these are words that many Americans of the era took to the bank. But disease, workplace accidents and birth defects took others to the poorhouse or to early graves. Six-day workweeks and 10-hour workdays were the norm. Electricity and running water in homes were luxuries. Peoples' concerns for one another led them to create an increasing number of charitable organizations. Pressing human needs always outweighed available charitable resources.

The action the people of Denver took to deal with this dilemma in 1887 illustrated "necessity as the mother of invention." Their need for money to support philanthropic enterprises led them to create a fund-raising campaign that would come to be replicated time and again. Their leadership united their community in a way that had never before been done. Their example did far more than raise money. It demonstrated a way for caring people to reach beyond single agency interests to unite their compassion on behalf of their entire community.

COMMUNITY-WIDE APPROACHES BEGIN

The birth of community-wide fund-raising for multiple charities gave life to far more than federated fund-raising. In 1887, the citizens of Denver applied the principles of federated fund-raising that had been developed by the leaders of Jewish agencies in New York City earlier in the century. Instead of making use of this social device for a limited group of agencies, the people who initiated the Denver initiative showed that volunteers and professionals could unite their efforts to prevent and alleviate human suffering on behalf of their total community. The power of Denver's pioneering example was to be replicated in cities throughout the United States, Canada, and 41 countries around the world.[1]

REMEMBER THIS WARNING –

Give no money to a stranger in the street, at the door, or in your office. Give no money until you have personally investigated the case. Give no clothing unless you know the applicant, or have made a thorough investigation.

Do not give anything to beggars, but send their names and addresses to the Secretary of the Charity Organization Society, 1420 Champa Street, and an investigation will be promptly made.

This notice appeared from 1887 until 1902, in each of the first 15 Annual Reports of Denver's Charity Organization Society.

Communities quickly followed Denver's example of community organization. Long before Cleveland conducted the first modern day "united" campaign in 1913, agency volunteers and professionals experimented with a variety of approaches to stretching precious health and social service budgets. Publication of social service directories became commonplace before the end of the nineteenth century, sparked by Chicago's successful publication of such a volume in 1891. Meetings of human service agency representatives were convened in dozens of cities following Pittsburgh's 1908 example: an assembly on the subject of social work, the first citywide "health and social service planning council." These early councils met community and agency needs for communication and coordination among volunteer and professional leaders. They also served as the incubators in which ideas for new agencies, programs, and configurations of services were conceived and nurtured.

The zeal of professionals to consider total community needs and resources caught the attention of civic leaders. By 1900, traditional theories of private charity were being challenged. A retrospective of the period published by President Herbert Hoover's Research Committee on Social Trends noted that, "Early in the twentieth century, appreciation of the distinction between charity and philanthropy became more general; all efforts to alleviate human suffering were termed charity, while philanthropy carried the idea of prevention of distress and the positive promotion of human welfare. In general, the period (1900–1920) was one of great expansion of philanthropic interest manifested both in range of enterprises and in volume of funds."[2]

FORM OF BEQUEST.

I hereby devise and bequeath to THE CHARITY ORGANIZATION SOCIETY OF DENVER, for the purpose or promoting its objects, the property described as follows, to-wit: _____

At the turn of the century, two groups were organized in Cincinnati: "The Business Men's Benevolent Advisory Association, which inquired into the merits of fund appeals, and the Monday Evening Club, where people interested in social work talked over problems."[3]

Best Practices Shared Nationally

Before long, the need for a national means of sharing developments in community organization was recognized. In 1918, United Way's first professional, William J. Norton, then heading Detroit's Associated Charities, along with his Cincinnati protégé, C.M. Bookman, invited nine professional colleagues to meet with them in Chicago. They shared the tools and techniques that were working best in local social planning and community fund-raising and created the American Association for Community Organization (AACO) to continue what they had begun. Its initial purpose was "to encourage and stimulate collective community planning, and the development of better standards of community organization for social work."[4]

Needs and ideas spawned a torrent of approaches in two distinct streams of early community organization. Social planning organizations and processes gave attention to ways of identifying, coordinating and prioritizing the many aspects of human suffering and efforts to help. Fund-raising organizations and techniques reflected perspectives that focused on resources. In some communities, social planning organizations created joint fund-raising programs; in others, community fund-raising organizations created social planning bodies. As would be the case over the decades to come, community organization was practiced within two prevalent structures. One combined social planning and fund-raising work in one organization; in the other, separate organizations carried out planning and fund-raising.

The number of organizations involved with financing and delivering health and social services differed greatly in each community and state/province. Many orphanages and adoption agencies, counseling services, vocational training, and emergency assistance agencies were established under the auspices of the religious institutions that had founded them. In general, local governments carried responsibility for operating poorhouses, the service of last resort for destitute older people and young women. Some state and provincial governments operated institutions for people who were presumed to be permanently dependent because of mental illnesses or developmental disabilities.

In homes, neighborhoods, and cities, Americans took part in what seemed to President Herbert Hoover to be "a period of change so rapid and complex that it is likely never to occur again."[5] So it was with efforts to create community organizations that could plan, coordinate, and raise funds for services that would meet human needs for total communities—community organizations that could cross social, religious, and geographic boundaries. And like other efforts throughout history that depended on the coordination of a variety of people, institutions, and organizations, the work of community organization pioneers was done within the context of the times. Understanding the environment in which they worked is helpful.

Signs of the Times

GLOBAL/NATIONAL EVENTS

1898   Spanish American War began on April 20 and ended eight months later on December 10.

1907   Austria approved suffrage for all citizens, becoming the first country to allow women to vote.

1914   World War I began; it ended four years later in 1918 (U.S. and Canada entered in 1917).

1917   Canada enacted a federal income tax as a temporary wartime measure.

1919   The League of Nations was created.

IN THE NEWS

1896   Gold was discovered in the Klondike.

1901   President McKinley was assassinated.

1906   An earthquake devastated San Francisco.

1914   Panama Canal was opened.

SOCIAL MOVEMENTS/GOVERNMENTAL POLICIES & PROGRAMS

1893   Colorado became the first state to enfranchise women.

1905   Carnegie created the first foundation for humanitarian purposes.

1920   U.S. Congress ratified the 19th Amendment to the Constitution giving women the right to vote.

1925   Newfoundland women receive the right to vote.

ECONOMY/BUSINESS CYCLES AND THE WORKPLACE

1892   Henry Ford built his first gasoline-powered car.

1910   The "weekend" for workers was adopted as common business practice.

1929   The stock market crash triggered the Great Depression.

SCIENCE AND TECHNOLOGY

1889   Hollerith developed the first punch card system to automate manufacturing processes.

1895   Marconi invented the radio.

1903   Wright brothers made their first airplane flight.

1916   Blood for transfusion was first refrigerated.

DEMOGRAPHY

1887   U.S. population estimated to be over 50 million.

1915   U.S. population passes 100 million.

1908   Urban public sanitation standards were adopted to deal with overcrowding in urban slums.

1887   Poverty brought common needs for food, shelter, clothing, and safety.

1916   The first birth control clinic was opened.

1918   World war increases numbers of widows, orphans, and disabled men.

Leadership Characteristics

THE PROFESSIONALS

Women's suffrage was accompanied by increased involvement of women in work outside the home. Work as volunteers prepared a small but growing number for professional employment. Male professionals, as traditional breadwinners, found increased employment in which religious conviction could be translated into services for children and families. A 1908 review of *American Charities and Social Work* described professionals as "people of the '90s who assumed an ideal state of society which ought to be brought about, and measured the needs of their beneficiaries by their deviation from normal."[6]

"New perspectives emerged as groups of agency professionals came together to look at total community needs," the 1908 review continued. "The social workers of the '20s approach their clients and their communities somewhat after this fashion: What is the trouble here? How did all this come about? What would you like to do about it?"[7]

In 1913, the Cincinnati Council of Social Agencies employed William J. Norton as its director, according to Elwood Street, a United Way executive/historian of the twentieth century's first half, and ". . . thus the Cincinnati Council became the first [United Way] to have a full-time paid professional executive."[8] Norton and his generation raised questions that couldn't be answered by cause-focused agencies nearly so well as the new wave of community organizations.

THE VOLUNTEERS

Since the majority of health and social service programs grew out of sectarian auspices, it is understandable that their volunteers came largely from the religious congregations. Personal wealth was a common attribute of the volunteer leaders of the movements. Their actions founded and fostered agencies for immigrants, the poor, children, and those suffering disability and disease.

Many volunteers expressed sympathy for individuals and families by serving need-specific causes. They served on the boards and committees of agencies, and represented them in the community. Women worked on-site, serving as paraprofessionals and office volunteers. Men raised money for them.

How Approaches Reflected the Needs and the Times

AGENCIES JOIN SOCIAL SERVICE PLANNING EFFORTS

Buffalo, New York's Charity Organization Society painted a picture of poverty in 1888 with data provided by local agencies:

Causes of Poverty in Buffalo, 1878–1887[9]

	Number	Percent
Lack of employment.	1,873	30.2
Sickness	1,268	20.5
Accident.	208	3.4
Insanity of bread-winner	51	.8
Insufficient earnings.	451	7.3
No male support	397	6.4
Imprisonment of bread-winner	108	1.7
Intemperance.	700	11.3
Shiftlessness	440	7.1
Physical defects	525	8.4
No cause	176	2.9
Total number of causes . . .	6,197	100.0

Individually, Buffalo's agencies knew the problems with which they were dealing, but they didn't know who else was dealing with similar problems. Most were too busy serving their clients to take the time to find out. A helpful solution was in the making hundreds of miles away in Chicago.

THE FIRST SOCIAL SERVICE DIRECTORY

In 1890, Chicago business owners met with the leaders of the city's social service agencies to share a common concern. They had no uniform basis on which to make judgments about the many charitable organizations that asked for their personal support. Within a year, working through a newly formed Charity Organization Society, the agencies published the *Handbook of Chicago's Charities*. Its introduction was responsive to the concern business leaders had presented to them. Street wrote, "This handbook is issued to put in permanent form a list and directory of the charitable societies of Chicago and the State institutions, and to give as nearly as possible such data as will enable a business man to form an intelligent opinion on the relative scope and value of each organization."[10] By listing 450 societies and institutions, the first directory clearly illustrated the growing multiplicity of agencies.

A COMMUNITY-WIDE PERSPECTIVE OF SOCIAL PROBLEMS

Community-based social planning began with the organization of Pittsburgh's Council of Social Agencies in 1908. Building upon attempts of the Civic Club of Pittsburgh, civic leaders brought Pittsburgh's social agencies together to discuss the *Pittsburgh Survey* that had been conducted under the auspices of the Russell Sage Foundation.[11] The survey shocked the community. "In the midst of depression [the first industrial depression of 1907–1908], workers are paid in scrip instead of $20 gold pieces or bank checks. The community suffers high accident rates in the mills, lack of injury compensation, poor housing, poor water supply and poor sanitation." An outbreak of typhoid fever added weight to the report.

It continued, "Of even more significance to philanthropy was the discovery that existing agencies were crossing themselves every step of the way. We found that six private agencies were giving material relief to families, nine were providing visiting nurse services and 40 institutions were providing care for dependent children."[12] The issues identified in the Pittsburgh study fired the engines of community-based planning for the social work of agencies and the philanthropy that supported them.

As Pittsburgh's leaders did their work, Cincinnati's agency representatives met to form a Conference of Charities and Philanthropies. It was to consider jointly services to support recovery from the Great Miami Valley flood of 1913. Cincinnati's C.M. Bookman wrote, "It assumed responsibility not only for immediate, but for subsequent reconstruction of Cincinnati social work. Soon after its organization, the Conference recognized the need for the help of business leaders and voted to reorganize and change its name to the Council of Social Agencies. It sought the help of business owner Frederick A. Geier to head a Managing Committee and set about organizing programs of coordinated relief to families left destitute by the flood."[13]

Learning from Pittsburgh's *volunteer-driven* Council and Cincinnati's *professional-driven* social service planning, Dallas volunteers and professionals joined together in 1916 to create a *joint volunteer/professional* approach to coordinating services and fund-raising. In 1919, the Louisville Social Planning Council divided their organizational structure and grouped agencies into one of three categories: health, education, or welfare. Councils around the country adopted standard three-part divisional structures based on the Louisville model. Soon thereafter, many divided their work within the areas of health, education, and welfare based on client needs.[14] Groups such as maternal health councils and child welfare councils brought agency leaders together in ways that fostered acquaintance and allowed for coordination and cooperation.

SOCIAL PLANNING ROLES DEFINED

In 1921, the New York City Central Council of Social Agencies categorized 13 roles for their Central Council of Social Agencies.[15] These roles became the industry standard for United Way community planning/problem solving for much of the remainder of the century:

1. Education as related to its member societies.
2. Approval or disapproval of new undertakings in the social field.
3. Development of new activities.
4. Reorganization of old agencies.
5. Abandonment or combination of any agencies unnecessary or superfluous or ineffective.
6. Improvement and intensive development of cooperative relationships between agencies.
7. Development of standards of work.

8. [Dissemination of information on] developments in public departments.

9. Program of legislative development.

10. Specific cooperative activities [central services] carried on by the council itself.

11. Joint consultation regarding budgets and mutually agreed upon changes.

12. Arrangement [of the] sequence of financial campaigns.

13. Advise agencies as to the right kind of publicity.

As councils of agencies were created in America's cities, each carried out one or more of the roles identified in New York. These early standards also helped agency groups in many cities take a next step: consolidating their agency fund-raising.

FEDERATED FUND-RAISING TOOK SHAPE

The number of independent fund-raising appeals grew with the increasing number of agencies. "In many cities, it was found that a handful of well-to-do and generous folks were being solicited over and over again by a host of organizations of every description," according to Amos Warner's *American Charities and Social Work*. "Many people who were quite able to contribute were giving little or nothing to any social agency. Still others confined their donations to their own 'pet' charity."[16] The leaders of Denver's largest agencies did something about it. They designed the first coordinated, community-wide fund-raising approach. Using a model of federated giving first tried in Liverpool, England in 1873, they planned a common effort that would allow their agencies to meet critical human needs.[17]

In 2000, Mike Durkin, president of the Mile High United Way, spoke about this history: "Join me in thinking for a moment what Denver was like in 1887. Mining booms and busts; people with broken bones and broken dreams seemed to abound. And the role of government was applied very little to providing for the welfare of families; it seemed to fall largely on the shoulders of churches and a few organized charities. At that time, Denver was just an overgrown village. It had a population of 83,000 people; 50,000 of them had arrived during the preceding decade. Thousands had come following the discovery of gold and silver in nearby mountains. . . . Many others had come in search of health, for the report had spread through the East that the cool, dry climate of this Mile High City was a sure cure for tuberculosis."[18]

The following excerpt from *Pioneers, Peddlers, & Tsadikim*, by Ida Libert Uchill, shows how civic leaders first responded to the city's needs:[19]

Denver's charity work, although early begun, had not achieved its first charitable institution until 1872, with the Denver Orphan's Home, the city's first non-sectarian relief organization. The Jewish women had formed the Hebrew Benevolent Ladies Aid Society that year. As its president, possibly the second one, Mrs. (Frances) Jacobs found not only that the problems were too vast for one organization, but also that they were not Jewish problems. She believed that charity was to come from everyone and to be given to any who needed it. While retaining her interest in the Jewish group, she began to work at all levels of civic charity, from the top, where her 'elocutionary powers made her an attraction' and loosened the purse strings of the community, to the 'bottoms,' where she assumed the menial responsibility of disbursing the funds.

The Ladies Relief Society (formed in 1874) was an important force by the time it held its fourth public meeting at the Tabor Grand Opera House in 1887. More than 2000 came to the meeting, and many were turned away from the overflowing opera house. The 22 different charities were considered, and the idea already in the minds of some of them was formulated by Rev. Martin Reed and Father William O'Brien. The two men discussed their idea and 'sought and found Mrs. Frances Jacobs, first vice-president of the Ladies' Relief Society, and a woman who shared their ideas. . . . The three formed a tri-unity, and started toward the organization of Denver's charity.' They were joined by Dean Martin Hart and another Catholic priest. Hart, who was from London, had some background in the English idea of federation (John C. Fleming, 'Golden Anniversary of the Community Chest,' 1887–1937). Together these five achieved the first federation in Denver, The Charity Organization Society of 1887, and possibly, despite other claims (Abraham Cronback, "Jewish Pioneering in American Social Welfare," American Jewish Archives, June, 1951, p. 51), the first successful plan for financing a federated charitable organization, through which teams of workers solicited men in different lines of business and other citizens to raise a set sum.

For 50 years, others than these five have been honored as the founders of the Community Chest in Denver. The most popular and recurring acknowledgment is to 'two Protestant ministers, a Catholic priest, and a Jewish rabbi.' There was no rabbi in the group. Frances Jacobs was the 'Queen of the Charities' and the founder of the forerunner of the Community Chest. The C.O.S. (Charity Organization Society), as it was called, became a federation of most of the philanthropic societies and institutions of the city.

The federation's fund-raising methods and outcomes were described as such:

"The short, intensive technique of the modern campaign had not yet been developed. The 1888 campaign, their first, did have a campaign set-up, however, composed of 67 different teams of about six members each, organized on trade lines—doctors, grocers, barbers, blacksmiths, lawyers, livery stable owners, state officials, milliners, etc., to solicit those in the same trade or profession. There were no report meetings and no time limits. Ten agencies participated and received a total of $17,880.03 of the $21,700 raised."[20] However, Denver's community-wide campaign was not destined to thrive much beyond the end of the century. Business and bank failures plagued Denver when Congress declared that silver would no longer serve as a standard for U.S. currency. Flaws were identified within the charter of the Charity Organization Society, under whose auspices the campaign had been conducted. "[It] had its roots almost exclusively in a desire for economy and the saving of the giving public from annoyance. It did not sufficiently stress cooperation, community planning, and high standards of work,"[21] according to a 1924 retrospective published by Chicago's Council of Social Agencies.

ENDORSEMENT OF CHARITIES LEADS TO
NEXT STEP IN FEDERATED FUND-RAISING

Elsewhere, the number of charitable organizations seeking support from business leaders grew each year. At the request of its members, the Cleveland Chamber of Commerce, in 1900, initiated two new programs: a Charities Endorsement Committee to review the merit of agency appeals for funds, and a Committee on Benevolent Associations to advise agencies of community needs as seen by Chamber members. By judging the merits of agency appeals and advising agencies of perceived needs, the business leaders of Cleveland laid the groundwork for the creation of what has come to be called "the first modern Community Chest."[22]

Debate between agency and business leaders about structure and procedures went on for nearly a year. Why would donors support a campaign that did not have the personal appeal that individual agencies possessed? How could donors continue to support agencies of particular meaning to family and friends? Debates ended as business leaders pressed for action. Finally, the first campaign of the Cleveland Federation of Charity and Philanthropy was conducted in 1913. It produced a net of $33,715 for 53 agencies. Its success was so persuasive that the debate between agency and business leaders was lost in celebration, only to be raised again and again in succeeding decades.

United Way of America's 1977 publication, *People & Events*, reported that "Cleveland avoided two mistakes made in Denver. They recognized the necessity for an able staff and the need for a steady campaign of public education and interpretation. A speaker's bureau was formed. Much resistance was avoided by letting contributors designate gifts if they wished. Membership was limited to organizations receiving endorsement from the Chamber of Commerce."[23]

Cleveland's experience proved helpful to a number of communities whose agency leaders were searching for answers to fund-raising and service coordination problems. *The Financial Federation Movement*, a dissertation written by University of Chicago graduate student Harvey Leebron, provides a 1916 snapshot of United Way development:

"[After its first three years of success,] the efforts of the Denver cross between a Charity Organization Society and a Council of Social Agencies continued to eke out a precarious and little-noticed existence. In 1907–08, Washington, DC, tried out a new experience in cooperative financing among three large agencies. They employed a publicity agent for a general newspaper campaign. And they sent out 13,000 appeals, personally addressed, with follow-up on behalf of the three organizations."[24] Results were too few to warrant continuation of this collaborative effort.

Leebron continued: "The federated plan was reborn in Cleveland and made three major contributions to the principles of federation: (1) co-operative welfare promotion as an integral part of the Welfare Federation and Community Fund, (2) continuous, year-round educational activities, supplementary to the separate educational activities of individual agencies, and (3) the practice of including a considerable sum for unforeseen emergencies in the community fund budget.

"Cincinnati's Council of Social Agencies initiated three of the major principles of federation: (1) Central budgetary control, (2) The intensive—time limited—annual campaign, and (3) the encouragement of designations of contributions."[25]

"Social advance depends as much upon the process through which it is secured as upon the result itself."

—Jane Addams, *Founder, Hull House*

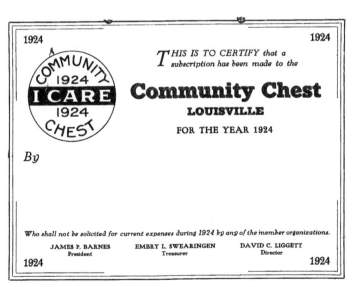

*Community Chest agencies in Louisville were
prohibited from asking contributors to do more.*

CONCEPT OF COMMUNITY-WIDE CAMPAIGN SPREADS

Leebron continued with his campaign description: "By 1916, 20 cities had adopted central financing of one sort or another for their social agencies; five cities had abandoned the practice; and the movement was assuming national proportions. In a considerable number of other cities, the merchants' organizations were considering, planning, or promoting the adoption of financial federations. Of considerable interest is the provision adopted in Elmira, New York, that campaign contributors earn an exemption from further solicitation."[26]

Finally, Leebron observed, "The development [of the federation movement as of 1916] had completed the major contributions to present day principles of the American federation movement: (1) centralized collection and distribution of current operating funds—Denver, (2) immunity of federation contributors from individual solicitation by member agencies for current expenses for maintenance—Elmira, (3) social betterment promotion as an integral part of the organization and work of the federation—Cincinnati, (4) continuous year-round central educational publicity supplementary to the separate educational activities of individual agencies—Cleveland, (5) contingency or emergency funds as part of the campaign goal—Cleveland, (6) central budget making, (7) annual campaigns, and (8) the encouragement of designated contributions—Cincinnati."[27]

Each early campaign experimented with new ways for collecting and distributing contributions to meet health and social service needs. They illustrated what President Hoover's Committee on Social Trends called "a possible substitute for the church in dispensing funds." But they were also criticized by the President's Committee for "yielding valuable experience, though attempting no clear cut enunciation of principles for giving."[28] The criticism was accepted as good counsel and was used to further develop emerging models of fund distribution.

MULTIPLE CAMPAIGN MODELS DEFINED

The President's Committee also pointed out that not all cities adopted the model established in Cleveland. During the 15 years that followed Cleveland's innovative approach, nine distinct models of community-wide campaigns were identified:[29]

1. The first Cleveland plan provided for joint control by givers, agencies, and the Chamber of Commerce.
2. In Cincinnati, a council of social agencies created a financial federation within itself.
3. Under the Kansas City plan, a department of the Chamber of Commerce undertook to raise and distribute money.
4. The second Cleveland approach, taken in 1917, found contributors and the Chamber of Commerce seeking to require all charitable fund-raising to be conducted under a single auspice.
5. The war chest, initiated in 1917 by three cities in New York (Syracuse, Ilion, and Mohawk), was described by President Hoover's Committee as a limited corporation of a few men who set out to raise money from the public and to distribute that money on the basis of their own best judgment.
6. Detroit's community fund, initiated in 1918, created a board of citizens who raised and distributed money to agencies.
7. Rochester, New York, instituted a service planning and fund-raising partnership of citizens and agencies in 1918.
8. Ohio formed a state-level united campaign in 1919 for smaller communities who pooled their operations under a single operating staff and board, but reserved the right to make local decisions on distribution of campaign contributions.
9. In 1925, New York suburbs conducted independent campaigns, but used common dates and campaign materials.

A tenth approach, not identified by the President's Committee, began in 1919 in Portland, Oregon, when Community Fund leaders contracted with the American City Bureau to staff their annual campaign. Contract staff began in July to help recruit a campaign chair and to organize the campaign.[30]

As a founding participant in many community campaigns, the Salvation Army's perspective of early campaigns may be representative of most agencies. In *Marching to Glory, the History of the Salvation Army*, Edward McKinley observed, "Regardless of its many forms and structures, its convenience and practicality, combined with its appeal to bumptious community loyalty and the boosterism of the decade (1910–1920), has caused the Community Chest to spread rapidly. They have made it possible for many corps to survive by providing funds that the soldiers hadn't contributed."[31]

The editors of *Community*, the monthly "Bulletin of Community Chests and Councils, Inc.," saw the War Chest campaigns emerge from World War I with a common, clear purpose. "Out of the competitive and chaotic war appeals of 1918, the Community Chest was born. It was desperately needed and warmly welcomed. It suited the American mood and temperament. For the first time, voluntary health and welfare services could present a united front: inclusive, comprehensive, flexible enough to cope with the ever changing needs of people."[32]

PUBLICITY AND PUBLIC RELATIONS TECHNIQUES
WERE ADAPTED FROM BUSINESS

It followed that the business leaders involved with community campaigns brought business publicity and public relations tools and techniques with them. Rochester, New York, introduced *contributor recognition pins* in 1918: red, white, and blue with a bold WAR CHEST. Workers who were solicited on street corners were pleased to receive recognition in the form of the very same lapel pins the leaders of their companies wore.

Campaign progress in Savannah, Georgia, was posted by Girl Scouts on an *outdoor campaign thermometer* in 1919. Just seven years earlier, Savannah civic leader Juliette Gordon Low had established Girl Scouts in the United States. Des Moines is reported to have conducted the first community campaign *public report meeting* in 1923.

In 1924, the Motion Picture Producers and Distributors Association of America wrote to the members of the American Association for Community Organization (AACO) offering to develop a motion picture film "to help Community Chests of the country in their effort to raise funds for community work."[33] The offer was published in AACO's newsletter, the *AACO News Bulletin*. The Philadelphia Welfare Federation stepped forward and, with the help of a New York production firm, prepared a combined animated cartoon and photographic film. In 1925, it was made available to other Community Chest organizations as a *national campaign film*.[34]

MORE INNOVATIONS INITIATED TO PUBLICIZE CAMPAIGNS

The first *campaign poster contest* was conducted among Cleveland artists by the Cleveland Community Fund. The poster, to be used in Cleveland's 1926 campaign, attracted the interest of a number of successful artists and was made an assignment in Cleveland art classes.[35] In 1927, the seeds of a *national campaign poster* were sown as "45 cities used Cleveland's campaign prize-poster and 33 borrowed Philadelphia's poster."[36] The *AACO News Bulletin* that described these posters also included a proposal made by Tulsa's executive Charles Lee. Based on his observation that most communities were using the Community Chest name, he proposed "that a national symbol be adopted for the Community Chests and a national contest be conducted to secure the symbol."[37] *News Bulletin* editors sought opinions from their readers, but did not report on the results of their survey for nearly a decade.

Car cards were created in Cincinnati in 1927 in response to an agency volunteer who owned the local transit firm. "The Cincinnati Street Railway Company," the *News Bulletin* reported, "has just afforded the Cincinnati Community Chest and its agencies a splendid opportunity for publicity. The company will display two cards per week in 800 street cars, each card to be devoted to the work of some agency or the Community Chest itself. The company will not only offer space, but will pay the cost for the printing, amounting to $1,600."[38]

Putting the various elements of their public relations programs together, the staff of the Cleveland Federation appears to have developed the first "systematic" approach to public relations. In *The Professional Altruist*, Roy Lubove cited references suggesting that "The Federation used every possible medium, including newspapers, window and bulletin board posters, stereopticon slides, bulletins, yearbooks, exhibits, and a speakers' bureau,"[39] in a well-ordered approach. "Cleveland's emphasis upon publicity and education," he continued, "had a 'profound influence' upon the federation movement."[40]

CONTRIBUTORS SOUGHT ACCOUNTABILITY, OFFERED GUIDANCE, CREATED BUDGET COMMITTEES

Raising money in community-wide campaigns may have been the easier of the early United Way organizations' two primary tasks. Distributing the money seemed far more difficult. To make matters more complex, perceptions of need and priority held by the budget volunteers were always subject to the evaluations of donors, agencies, and the press.

Regardless, campaign proceeds in hand, or promised, procedures had to be established to allocate, or "budget," funds. In some communities, the Council of Social Agencies was given this responsibility. In others, the fund-raising organization allocated the funds raised. Procedures varied widely. Agency professionals and their volunteer advocates knew the needs for service with which each agency was confronted. But groups of agency representatives found it difficult to raise the penetrating budget questions of one another that others might have raised. Groups responsible for distributing funds raised in every community struggled to find ways to stretch available dollars to meet needs. Procedures needed to be developed to understand agencies' budgetary needs and to bring rationality to allocation decisions.

A model was identified. In 1913, prior to Cleveland's reintroduction of Denver's community approach to federated fund-raising, Columbus, Ohio's Institute of Public Efficiency started an orderly examination of health and social service budgets. Their purpose was quite different, but it was a start.

THE FIRST STATE UNITED WAY

In Columbus, according to former Ohio Citizens' Council/Ohio United Way executive Wilson Posey, people had come together to "understand the imperfections and shortcomings of state and local government as compared with [their] voluntary social agencies."[41] The organization they created was to become the model for future state United Way organizations. At its core, the 1913 Institute was a taxpayers' watchdog organization. In that capacity, an approach had been developed to obtaining line-by-line financial information from the accounts of governmental units and voluntary social agencies. This was the approach that could be applied by the Community Chest and Council budget committees.

MINIMUM STANDARDS FOR AGENCY SERVICES AND
ADMINISTRATIVE PRACTICES WERE ESTABLISHED

Leaders of the St. Louis Central Council found a way to bring more order to agency information. In 1915, they introduced "the St. Louis Plan" for holding societies (agencies) receiving campaign funds to *minimum standards.* According to *People & Events,* standards were adopted by the Council, "with the backing of the Business Men's League, the local endorsing agency, which agreed not to endorse campaigns by societies with unapproved standards . . . the St. Louis plan featured detailed questionnaires, tabulation of replies, formulation of tentative standards by each group [of agencies] and revision by the Executive Committee."[42]

C.M. Hubbard, Secretary and General Manager of the St. Louis Provident Association, shared the objectives of agency standards with those who attended the 1916 National Conference on Social Welfare: "To tell how the welfare of a child should be safe-guarded by a placing-out agency; to prescribe the proper medical supervision for a day nursery, to describe in detail the points that should be included in a proper investigation by a society engaged in relief and social service."[43]

Hubbard went on to caution, "They [standards] would be of secondary importance in comparison with good business administration and reliable management." Then, he elaborated, "There is a lack of time on the part of competent paid workers to make the necessary detailed study of the subject." And, he concluded, "It is feared that some societies would withdraw their membership in the councils if an attempt should be made to interfere with the way they do their work. It would be embarrassing for social workers to act as critics of their fellow workers."[44]

"Community Chest budget committees were designed on the model of American governance. The United States is a representative republic in which citizens elect others to make decisions for them. Were our country a democracy, every citizen would vote on every issue; if each of us did what we alone wished, we would be an anarchy, instead of a country."

—RALPH BLANCHARD, *Community Chests & Councils of America*

Hubbard's words were helpful to communities in which volunteers not affiliated with agencies were asked to take part in the distribution of funds raised. Cincinnati was the first. "The Cincinnati Council of Social Agencies . . . requested the social agencies to conform to a budgetary procedure. The first time, I believe," said C.M. Bookman to the 1921

National Conference on Social Welfare, "that [an impartial] budgetary procedure on a large scale was introduced into social work. The budgets that were received were open to the inspection of the general public and were discussed in open meetings by representatives of the agencies themselves, *plus* general community representatives."[45]

With public budget disclosure, community leaders saw evidence that allocations to agencies were not enough to meet agencies' needs. In 1924, Bookman shared his community's perspective that agencies share responsibility for their financial support. His words were charged with his conviction that every citizen share responsibility for his/her community:

"The complexity of modern community life makes each individual dependent upon the welfare of every other individual; be he Catholic, Jew, or Protestant, white or black, he must be concerned with the social conditions under which he lives. New sources of revenue must be explored [by agencies], such as taxation, earning power, and endowments. The fact scarcely needs statement that social agencies will not develop such sources of revenue to the fullest extent if expanded budgets are allowed [by the Community Chest] year after year."[46]

The need for annual review of agency income from all sources became commonly accepted. Attention turned to what Cleveland leaders termed "the total amount of money being spent on all public and private social work."[47] That city's pioneer work on their *expenditure study* was cited by AACO in 1925 as a model whose standard formats should be considered by other communities."[48]

DECISIONMAKERS BEGAN TO CONSIDER
FORMAL SOCIAL RESEARCH

Increasingly, community leaders became aware of the importance of the factual data they were collecting. In 1929, the Pittsburgh Federation of Social Agencies, with funding from the Buhl Foundation, established a Bureau of Social Research. "It became a national and local force, helping to cement the concept that sound research is basic to meaningful human service planning. The Bureau's analysis of census data, trends and emerging problems was the forerunner of what today is called 'forecasting' or 'the environmental scan,' "[49] according to Mary Bower's history of the

Pittsburgh Health and Welfare Planning Association. Another subject, agency staff salaries, became a subject for study in Denver in 1927.[50]

More and more innovations helped define accountability and support for the work of budget committees. Monthly agency finance and budget forms were developed in Minneapolis in 1928.[51] Memphis followed with annual agency budget forms in 1929.[52] And Milwaukee introduced a mechanical data recording system to the United Way field in 1929 to organize the volumes of data that were beginning to accumulate.[53]

AN EYE TO THE FUTURE ADDED VALUE

As the public accountability of Community Chests and Councils increased, and data became available to help them understand their work, their learning from one another increased. Leaders began to take time from daily business to look to the future.

In 1924, while Toronto leaders planned the National Conference of Social Work, they decided that professionals from the various fields of service might find time to give thought to the future of their work if they were housed together, instead of being assigned to hotels on a first-come, first-served basis. By grouping registrants with similar responsibilities in designated hotels, Toronto's conference hosts advanced the value of bringing *all* similarly employed professionals together outside the formal conference programs. "The experiment was so successful," according to AACO's *News Bulletin,* that "Community Chest people will be quartered in the same hotel again at the next national conference."[54]

It was at the 1924 conference that representatives from Dayton, Ohio, shared information on their look at future methods and strategies to achieve their goals. Arch Mandel, director of the Dayton Research Association, called for all Community Chests and Councils to look ahead. "[The] evolution in the support of social service has brought social work to the point where it must be subjected to the searching analysis of what it is doing and where it is going; how much of the work is necessary, and how much is merely desirable. This should be done through continual self-surveys by the local organization, calling in specialists, if necessary, primarily to direct planning for future strategies. Whatever is done ought to

The 1919 Minneapolis campaign featured this depiction
of the Community Chest during war years.

be tied up closely to a local organization which has its roots in the community and which understands thoroughly local conditions."[55]

The professionals raised another question about the future: Would
these new organizations reach a day when cash contributions would not
be enough? The February 1925 issue of *News Bulletin* carried an article
describing what may well have been the first *solicitation of in-kind gifts*. "I
ran across something new at Newport News during their [last] campaign,"
wrote John F. Hall, executive secretary of the Norfolk Community Fund.
"They secure donations of foodstuffs from wholesale firms which would
not make cash subscriptions. They are looking ahead to years in which
we can't raise enough money."[56]

ACCOUNTING PRACTICES ENHANCED CONTRIBUTORS'
ACCEPTANCE OF SOCIAL WORK

In 1925, the Federated Budget Board of Winnipeg took a different view
of the years ahead. They anticipated future growth in campaign pledges

and accounts receivable and expressed concern about the capacity of their federation to account for its finances in the future. So office staff "worked out a system of handling Community Chest pledges and accounts which has greatly simplified office work, reduced the possibility of error in contributors' accounts, and thus helped to promote a good feeling between the Community Chest office and contributors," they reported in AACO's *News Bulletin*.[57] Winnipeg leaders had adopted many of the innovations that other cities had developed and now had a new approach that would become adopted by all similar organizations.

The report of Winnipeg's contribution was followed with the editor's statement, "Mr. Walker [Secretary of the Federated Budget Board] says he will be very glad to furnish copies of the study and the forms he has worked out to any Community Chest executive interested." Dozens of Community Chest professionals wrote for the materials Mr. Walker had offered and applied them in their communities. Word of the transferability of Winnipeg's approach spread quickly, and, typical of local United Way leaders' willingness

---

THANK YOU!

We acknowledge with thanks your subscription of $............................ for carrying on the work of the organizations affiliated in the Community Chest in 1924.

You are not to be solicited for current expense gifts during 1924 by any of the following agencies, members of the Community Chest:

Boy Scouts of America—Louisville Council.
Central Purchasing Bureau.
Children's Bureau.
Children's Free Hospital.
Children's Protective Association.
Colored Orphans' Home.
Consumers' League of Kentucky.
East End Day Nursery.
Eleanor Tarrant Little Foundation.
Family Service Organization.
Girl Scouts—Louisville Council.
Health and Hospital Council.
Home of the Innocents.
Hospital Social Service Association.
Inter-Racial Commission.
Jennie Casseday Rest Cottage.
Jewish Welfare Federation.
Kentucky Animal Rescue League.
Kentucky Child Labor Association.
Kentucky Humane Society.
King's Daughters' Home for Incurables.
Legal Aid Society.

Louisville Fresh Air Home.
Louisville Safety Council.
Louisville School of Social Work.
Louisville Tuberculosis Association.
Louisville Urban League.
Neighborhood House.
Orphanage of the Good Shepherd.
Plymouth Settlement House.
Presbyterian Colored Missions.
Protestant Episcopal Orphan Asylum.
Psychological Clinic.
Public Dental Clinic.
Public Health Nursing Association.
Salvation Army Citadel.
Salvation Army Susan Speed Davis Home and Hospital.
Social Service Exchange.
Union Gospel Mission.
Wesley Community House.
Young Men's Hebrew Association.
Young Women's Christian Association.
Y. W. C. A.—Phyllis Wheatley Branch.

If any individual appeals to you for help, direct him as follows:

Homeless woman, wanting food and shelter, to the Salvation Army Citadel, 216 West Chestnut Street. Phone Main 2097 or City 9024.

Homeless man, wanting food and shelter, to the Salvation Army Industrial Home, 328 East Chestnut Street. Phone Main 2260 or City 8518.

Person with home or family in Louisville, wanting help of any kind, to Family Service Organization, 215 East Walnut Street. Phone Main 882 or City 8825.

Homeless man or woman wanting transportation to another city, clothing or guidance, to Family Service Organization, 215 East Walnut Street. Phone Main 882 or City 8825.

If you want to know what to do with any solicitor on the street, call us.

COMMUNITY CHEST

658 South Fourth Street   Phones: Main or City 1993
LOUISVILLE, KENTUCKY

---

to share their innovations, the product of one community's approach became standard operating procedure among most United Way organizations.

THE SEEDS OF THE FUTURE WERE SOWN

Another look to the future came from Rochester, New York. "How One Memorial Gift Inspired a Far-Sighted Plan" was the headline for a 1946 retrospective *Community* article on Rochester's Trust Fund.[59] "A memorial gift of $50,000, totally unsolicited and unexpected, dropped into the lap of the Rochester Community Chest during its annual campaign in May 1927. . . . That first gift, Rochester realized, might set precedent for other similar gifts." It did, for Rochester and hundreds of other communities. Unfortunately, actions to endow the ongoing capacity of local Community Chest organizations were limited to Rochester and very few other cities until much later in the twentieth century. A few communities had followed Cleveland's example of reserving a portion of campaign results for emergencies. Even more sought individuals who would provide trust funds similar to that established in Rochester, but to little avail.

In a *Community* magazine review of the history of Volunteer Bureaus, Ann Jacobson quoted a founder: "If we are to step up to the needs of charities in the future [and] to have the manpower to do their work, we must take a more businesslike approach to using the services of the good people who choose to volunteer." The speaker's name wasn't reported, but her/his message lived on. "Since the organization of the first *volunteer bureau* in Boston 45 years ago [1926]," Jacobson wrote, "they have been established in most of the major cities of the United States and Canada. They were created to bring unity to a larger-scale use of volunteers into civic, education, health, and welfare organizations."[58] Boston's leaders foresaw a need and opportunity that would touch the lives of nearly every American family. At its zenith in the 1970s, the number of Volunteer Bureaus reached 1,970.

More visionary thinking was needed. How might the leaders of pioneering community organizations do more brainstorming about ways to improve future services? Coming together at the Black Mountain, North Carolina conference grounds of the YMCA in 1927, social work executives in the southeast United States founded the first of a quartet of regional *interdisciplinary think tanks*. What came to be called the Blue Ridge Institute was open to "social service executives and potential executives in agency administration and community organization. . . . The discussion method of conducting the Institute was used, rather than lectures. All attending were urged to participate and get to know one another," according to AACO.[60] It was reported that "executives led by Community Chest professionals and Black Mountain YMCA leaders improved the quality of social work in the South."

Think tanks were just one of several techniques developed during this period to prepare professionals and their organizations for the future. In 1927, the Ohio State University in Columbus and the University of Chicago initiated year round *university training programs* for Community Chest executives. Ohio State's College of Commerce and Journalism received funds from the Ohio legislature to develop several short lectures at the university. The University of Chicago established a chair of community organization in the graduate School of Social Service Administration. Courses were described in *News About Community Chests from AACO*. Course titles were "General Community Organization, Financial Federations, Administration of Social Agencies, and Methods of Marshalling Communities Behind Community Projects."[61]

Two years later, in 1929, the St. Louis Community Chest identified the need to develop professional expertise in its minority community comparable to that in the nonminority community. With that commitment to the future, a course of *Training for Minority Professionals* was established at the Community Chest office.[62]

Perhaps a premonition of the hard times ahead led the New Orleans Community Chest, in 1929, to establish "Professional Standards for Council and Chest Executives."[63] The days and years that would begin with that October's economic catastrophe would bring many unprepared and unqualified people into consideration for positions of community trust. Irene Conrad, Executive Secretary of the New Orleans Central Council of Social Agencies, shared her organization's standards at the National Conference on Social Work. They included at least two years of training in social work, background work, and personal and financial integrity. She closed her presentation noting that "A limited number of well chosen social work executives can, at present, afford no ill charges, since good salaries and limited opportunities make our positions attractive

Before cartoonist John Hix created the syndicated feature "Strange As It Seems," he worked for the Greenville (SC) News. *His concept for a 1920's cartoon was found in the attic of a past Board President by his niece and past Council executive, Elizabeth Gower.*

to many who are not qualified by experience or behavior to bear the mantles of trust given to us by our communities."

STOCK MARKET CRASH BROUGHT
CAMPAIGNS TO THE WORKPLACE

The most-used word in the October 24, 1929 evening newspapers accurately dramatized the events that day on Wall Street—"Crash."

The months of headlines that followed sounded a call to Community Chest leaders in every city: "American Tragedy," "Unemployment," "Poverty," and "Soup Kitchens."

When record losses shattered the financial ability of many mainstay contributors to continue their gifts to agencies and Community Chests, the leaders of community campaigns scrambled to find replacements. In

Cincinnati, the Community Chest founder F.A. Geier was approached by a foreman from his milling machine shop with a request that reshaped fund-raising.

According to C.M. Bookman's recollections, recorded in *The First Twenty Years, 1915–1935*, the foreman told his employer that he and his fellow shop workers wanted to share their blessing of continued wages with people who had not been so fortunate. He asked if he could stand at the pay clerk's window that Friday to ask his fellow employees give something from their wages.[64] The enthusiastic and generous response of Geier's employees led him to offer a regular payday place for an employee representative to receive Community Chest donations from fellow employees. Geier suggested to fellow business and community leaders Barney Kroger and William Cooper Procter that they do the same. Others soon followed.

Employee workplace giving to the Community Chest was born. The 1929 *Social Work Yearbook* reported, "The Cincinnati Chest developed 'industrial solicitation' in over 500 factories, departing radically from its previous practice of only soliciting employees of stores and factories at their homes."[65]

In Memphis, Jacksonville, and Indianapolis, the local Community Chest organizations took Cincinnati's approach to the workplace one step further. The 1929 *Social Work Yearbook* reported that " . . . in their industrial programs [these cities] emphasized 'employee fellowships'—permanent organizations of employee groups. The Indianapolis Chest also used fellowships for publicity and policy-making purposes."[66] The fellowships were asked to determine the particular interests of workers as a means of both encouraging giving and providing directions to the Community Chest on how to use their contributions.

Reports of more innovations in the way people were asked for money quickly followed. Harrisburg, Pennsylvania, volunteers adopted *standards of giving*: " . . . employees were asked to give at least $5. Those unable to do so were 'frankly excused.' "[67]

In Hartford, Connecticut, company shareholders, in a special community-wide appeal, were asked to support *corporate gifts* to the Community Chest for the first time.[68] In Dayton, Ohio, "the Foreman's Club of 1,100 members was utilized in organizing industrial solicitation."[69] And in Saginaw, Michigan, the local Welfare League included agency capital construction needs in its annual campaign goal.[70]

A SCHOLAR SUMMARIZED THE ROLE OF UNITED
WAY DURING ITS GREATEST PERIOD OF GROWTH

Addressing the 1928 Conference on Social Welfare, Rowland Haynes, Secretary of the University of Chicago, explored the theme of "uniting people."[71] He reviewed the contributions he saw Community Chests making and their "ways of getting people to think harmoniously and to act unitedly in matters of community welfare.

"We do not realize the contribution Community Chests are making to the renaissance of community spirit," he said. "The growth of cities has revealed the divisive power of sheer size and deadening inertia of numbers who do not know each other. Twenty-five years ago, Jane Addams pointed out that, in a big city, neighborhood feeling is often weak or nonexistent. Group or class feeling is often strong. On the other hand, the Community Chest has counteracted this divisive tendency by bringing back a consciousness of common interests of the *whole* community."[72]

The dramatic changes in every agency and household in the country that were brought about by the Great Depression required huge changes in the emerging United Way movement. No longer could local volunteers and professionals take time to work through the growing pains of their fledgling movement. The country needed bold thinking and decisive action to meet the needs of people whose lives had been drastically changed. For the first time, the attention of community planning and fund-raising organizations, now in hundreds of cities, reached beyond the poor and disenfranchised. All Americans felt the pain of Wall Street's crash and organizations that could unite communities were needed more than ever.

Innovations in the United Way of Serving
Communities Between 1887 and 1929

1887	The first federated fund-raising campaign	Denver, CO
1891	Social services directory developed	Chicago, IL
1908	Collective social agency planning	Pittsburgh, PA

1913	Community-needs-driven fund-raising for agencies	Cleveland, OH
1913	Campaign speakers' bureau created	Cleveland, OH
1913	Community-based service planning by agency representatives	Cincinnati, OH
1913	State-based service advocacy	Columbus, OH
1913	Campaign allows designated gifts to agencies	Cincinnati, OH
1915	Member agency standards developed	St. Louis, MO
1916	Inclusion of emergency funds in campaign goal	Cleveland, OH
1916	Community-based service planning by agencies and citizens	Dallas, TX
1916	Central budget committee formed	Cincinnati, OH
1916	Year-round promotion	Cleveland, OH
1916	Time-limited annual campaign	Cincinnati, OH
1917	Consolidation of all charitable appeals	Cleveland, OH
1917	War Chests bring war appeals together	Syracuse, NY, Ilion, NY, and Mohawk, NY
1918	Service planning and fund-raising partnership of citizens and agencies	Rochester, NY
1918	Federation of agency campaigns	Detroit, MI
1918	Contributor recognition pins given	Rochester, NY
1919	Social planning councils divide duties into health, education, and welfare	Louisville, KY
1919	Campaign thermometer developed	Savannah, GA
1919	State United Way formed	Ohio
1919	Private fund-raising counsel hired	Portland, OR
1920	Agency capital needs included in campaign goal	Saginaw, MI
1921	Agency budgets made public	Cincinnati, OH
1921	Thirteen roles of councils defined	New York, NY
1923	Public report meeting held	Des Moines, IA
1924	In-kind gifts solicited	Newport News, RI
1924	Agency self-support encouraged	Cincinnati, OH

1924	International Community Chest conference	Toronto, ON
1924	Strategic planning	Dayton, OH
1925	Motion picture used for fund-raising	San Francisco, CA
1925	Social service expenditures studied	Cleveland, OH
1925	Accounts receivable systematized	Winnipeg, MB
1925	Simultaneous campaigns	Suburbs, New York, NY
1926	Volunteer bureau created	Boston, MA
1926	Campaign poster contest	Cleveland, OH
1927	Streetcar card advertising	Cincinnati, OH
1927	University training for professionals	Chicago, IL and Columbus, OH
1927	Interdisciplinary think tank founded	Black Mountain, NC
1927	National campaign poster developed	Philadelphia, PA and Cleveland, OH
1927	Agency staff salaries studied	Denver, CO
1928	United Way endowment established	Rochester, NY
1928	Standard monthly agency budget forms devised	Minneapolis, MN
1928	Systematic public relations introduced	Cleveland, OH
1929	Social research centers created at United Way	Pittsburgh, PA
1929	Training for minority professionals	St. Louis, MO
1929	Corporate gifts solicited	Hartford, CT
1929	Workplace employee solicitation tried	Cincinnati, OH
1929	Giving standard encouraged	Harrisburg, PA
1929	In-plant federation promoted	Memphis, TN, Jacksonville, FL and Indianapolis, IN
1929	Foremen solicit employees	Dayton, OH
1929	Standards for professional staff developed	New Orleans, LA
1929	Combined annual/monthly budget forms created	Memphis, TN
1929	Mechanical accounting and billing system introduced	Milwaukee, WI

1   United Way International, 2001 Annual Report.

2   Hoover, President Herbert. *Recent Social Trends in the United States, Report of the President's Research Committee on Social Trends.* Boston: Whittlesey House, 1934, p. 1168.

3   Thompson, Guy. "Fifty Years of Federated Campaigning in Cincinnati." *Community Magazine,* United Community Funds and Councils of America, Spring 1965, p. 20.

4   Romanofsky, Peter. *The Greenwood Encyclopedia of American Institutions: Social Service Organizations.* Boston: Greenwood Press, 1978, p. 742.

5   Hoover. Foreword, p. i.

6   Warner, Amos Griswold, Stuart Alfred Queen, and Ernest Bouldin Harper. *American Charities and Social Work,* Fourth Edition. Boston: Thomas Crowell Company, 1930, p. 26.

7   Warner, p. 26.

8   Street, Elwood. "The United Way, A History." Unpublished memoirs on file at the University of Minnesota Social Welfare History Archives, 1958, p. 110.

9   Warner, p. 47. Citing a 1888 Buffalo, NY, study by the Charity Organization Society.

10   Street, p. 268.

11   McLean, Francis H. *The Pittsburgh Survey.* Pittsburgh: The Russell Sage Foundation, 1907, pp. 166-167.

12   McClean, p. 167.

13   Bookman, C.M. *The First Twenty Years, 1915–1935.* Cincinnati: Ruter Press, 1935, p.8.

14   *Social Work Year Book 1929.* New York: Russell Sage Foundation, 1930, p. 97.

15   McClean, Francis H. *The Central Council of Social Agencies—Actual Accomplishments.* New York: American Association for Organizing Family Social Work, 1921.

16   Warner, p. 540.

17   Trattner, Walter I. *From Poor Law to Welfare State, A History of Social Welfare in America.* New York: Free Press, 1974, p.216.

18   Durkin, Michael K. "Remarks at the September 24, 2000 St. John's Evensong." Denver.

19   Uchill, Ida Libert. *Pioneers, Peddlers & Tsadikim, The Story of Jews in Colorado.* Denver: University Press in Colorado, 2000, pp.120-121.

20   Justis, Guy T. "After Fifty Years Denver Looks at Federated Financing." *CCCs, Inc. News Bulletin,* September 1937, p. 8.

21   *The Financing of Social Agencies, a Fact-Finding Report.* Chicago Council of Social Agencies, 1924, p. 113.

22   *People & Events, A History of the United Way.* United Way of America, 1977, p.28.

23   People & Events, p. 29.

24   Leebron, Harvey. *The Financial Federation Movement.* Chicago: University of Chicago Press, 1924, p. 112.

25   Leebron, p. 114.

26   Leebron, p. 114.

27   Leebron, pp. 112-118.

28   Hoover, p. 1168.

29   Warner, pp. 542-543.

30   Devine, Chuck. Conversation with author, May 2002.

31   McKinley, Edward H. *Marching to Glory, The History of The Salvation Army in the United States.* New York: Harper & Rowe, 1980, pp. 145-146.

32   *Community,* Bulletin of Community Chests and Councils, Inc. New York: June 1946.

33   Street, p. 59.

[34] *News Bulletin*, American Association for Community Organization, September 1925.

[35] *News Bulletin*, July 1926.

[36] *News Bulletin*, March 1927.

[37] *News Bulletin*, March 1927.

[38] *News Bulletin*, March 1927.

[39] Lubove, citing a letter from Sherman Kingsley to Pierce Williams, July 7, 1928. Held in the Cleveland, Ohio, Folder of the United Community Funds and Councils of America archives.

[40] Lubove, Roy. *The Professional Altruist, the Emergence of Social Work as a Career 1880–1930*. Boston: Harvard University Press, 1965, citing William J. Norton's *Cooperative Movement in Social Work*, p. 279.

[41] Posey, Wilson H. *A History of the Ohio Citizens' Council for Health and Welfare*. Unpublished, 1971, p.2.

[42] *People & Events*, p. 37.

[43] Hubbard, C.M. "Formulation and Improvement of Standards by Central Councils of Social Agencies." *Proceedings of the 1916 National Conference of Social Work*. Chicago: University of Chicago Press, 1916, p. 326.

[44] Hubbard, p. 327.

[45] Bookman, C.M. "From a Federation Secretary's Point of View." *Proceedings of the 1921 National Conference of Social Work*, 1921, p. 415.

[46] Bookman, C.M. "The Community Chest Movement—An Interpretation." *Proceedings of the 1924 National Conference of Social Work*, 1924, p. 25.

[47] Bookman, p. 26.

[48] *News Bulletin*, March 21, 1925.

[49] Bower, Mary A. with John G. McCormick and Elmer Tropman. *Impact, A History of the Health and Welfare Planning Association, 1922–1991*. Pittsburgh: Health and Welfare Planning Association, 1992, p. 6.

[50] *News Bulletin*, March 21, 1925.

[51] *News Bulletin*, October 6, 1928.

[52] *News Bulletin*, February 19, 1929.

[53] *News Bulletin*, February 19, 1929.

[54] *News Bulletin*, January 1924.

[55] Mandel, Arch. "How Much Use Can or Should Be Made of the Survey Method?" *Proceedings of the 1924 National Conference of Social Work*, 1924, pp. 492-493.

[56] Hall, John F. In a letter to the *News Bulletin*, February 1925.

[57] *News Bulletin*, September 1925.

[58] Jacobson, Ann. "Volunteer Bureaus—a link between needs and people." *Community*, March-April 1971, p. 3.

[59] *Community*, May 1946, p. 178.

[60] "Proposal for Southern Institute." *News about Community Chest from the AACO*, American Association for Community Organization, 1927, p. 269.

[61] "Report on Year Round Course of Training." *News about Community Chest from the AACO*, American Association for Community Organization, 1927, p. 245.

[62] *Social Work Year Book 1929*, p. 99.

[63] Conrad, Irene Farnham. "Professional Standards for Council and Chest Executives." *Proceedings of the 1929 National Conference of Social Work*, 1929, p. 580.

[64] Bookman, p. 91.

[65]   *Social Work Year Book 1929*, p. 98.
[66]   *Social Work Year Book 1929*, p. 98.
[67]   *Social Work Year Book 1929*, p. 98.
[68]   Street, p. 1043.
[69]   *Social Work Year Book 1929*, p. 98.
[70]   *News Bulletin*, December 1933, p. 4.
[71]   Haynes, Rowland. "The Contribution of the Community Chest to Community Welfare Planning." *Proceedings of the 1928 National Conference of Social Work*, 1928, p. 404.
[72]   Haynes, p. 405.

CHAPTER THREE

Neighbors Helping Neighbors

1930—1940

Responding to Economic Depression and Natural Disasters

S andwiched between the "Black Tuesday" of the Great Depression and the bombing of Pearl Harbor, the 1930s were years of unparalleled complexity and contradiction. The economy was down and spending was up. Unemployment reached record levels, and the federal government became the nation's largest employer. Middle income households experienced economic poverty. Farmers moved from rural to urban areas. Americans endured economic crisis after crisis while they witnessed the creation of the monuments and national parks that symbolized a cultural golden age.

The period began with the echo of President Herbert Hoover's words, "We have reached a higher degree of comfort and security than ever existed before in the history of the world."[1] It neared its end with President Franklin Roosevelt's observation, "I see one-third of the nation ill-housed, ill-clad, ill-nourished . . . the test of our progress is not whether we add more to the abundance of those who have much; it is whether we provide enough for those who have too little."[2]

President Hoover believed that the restoration of Americans' confidence in their economy would reverse the impact of the Great Depression. He opposed the creation of a national program of public welfare or direct relief, leaving that role to private charities and local governments. When President Roosevelt took office, one-third of the population was unemployed. He believed that hungry and unemployed Americans could not have confidence in the economy. It was this belief that led the White House to refocus "from pure preoccupation with relief needs to a concern with an all-around social welfare program."[3] President Roosevelt's "New Deal" established the national Social Security and Public Works Administrations in partnership with local governments and private charities.

"The equivalent word for charity *in classic Hebrew is* tzedaka, *but it does not actually mean charity. It means righteousness; that is, the poor have righteous claim upon the rest of us."*
—Rabbi Arthur Hertzberg, *New York University*

In nearly every large city, and in a number of states, the ancestors of United Way organizations found common roles as conveners of social workers and leaders of health and social service agencies. The voices of these Community Chest and Council volunteers and professionals spoke to every human need. Their sharing of experiences and "best practices" through regular national meetings and publications brought a high degree of similarity to their own programs and those of their local and state governments.

Local fund-raising campaigns continued within the frameworks established before the Great Depression. But the reasons some people gave to Community Chest campaigns and others did not prompted researchers to ask "why?" They wanted information that could make the dream of a common campaign theme, *"Everybody Gives, Everybody Benefits,"* become a reality.

In 1930 the Red Feather was introduced as a campaign symbol in two communities: Duluth, Minnesota, and New Orleans, Louisiana. By 1940, it became a nearly universal symbol of local community campaigns. Operational economy became recognized as a source of funds that could also be applied to increase agency services.

Signs of the Times

GLOBAL/NATIONAL EVENTS

1930	Bread lines and soup kitchens opened to millions of new urban poor.
1931	Severe drought hit Midwestern and Southern U.S. plains.
1934	Drought covered 75 percent of U.S.; 27 states form "dust bowl."
1935	Nuremberg Laws deprived German Jews of citizenship.
1936	German troops occupied the Rhineland; Hitler won 99 percent of the German vote.
1938	Franklin D. Roosevelt became the first U.S. president to make an official visit to Canada.

IN THE NEWS

1930	Hull House founder Jane Addams won the Nobel Peace Prize.
1931	Canada was granted full legislative authority by British Parliament.
1932	President Roosevelt declared four-day bank holiday; Congress stabilized the banking industry.
1937	U.S. Supreme Court ruled that the minimum wage law applied to women, as well as men.
1938	Supreme Court ordered the University of Missouri to "admit Negroes."
1940	U.S. enacted a peacetime military draft.

SOCIAL MOVEMENTS/GOVERNMENTAL POLICIES & PROGRAMS

1932	America's first unemployment insurance program was enacted in Wisconsin.
1935	The Social Security Act was signed into law by President Roosevelt.
1939	Richard Wright published *Native Son*, the first major novel about the "black experience" in America.
1940	The Canadian Unemployment Insurance Commission was introduced.

ECONOMY/BUSINESS CYCLES AND THE WORKPLACE

1930	Business failures displaced millions of American workers.

1932   One of every four families in U.S. was on relief.

1938   The economy rebounded as prewar industrial growth occurred.

SCIENCE AND TECHNOLOGY

1930   Vannevar Bush introduced the computer with his invention of the differential analyzer.

1936   Artificial heart was developed by Alexis Carrel.

1937   Insulin was first used to control diabetes.

DEMOGRAPHY

1930s   Migrants moved from America's rural South to industrial Midwest and Northeast in search of employment. Drought forced more farmers to leave barren fields.

1940   Census reported 7.3 percent population growth for 1930s, the smallest increase in U.S. history.

FAMILY/HOUSEHOLD STRUCTURE

1930s   Extended, multigenerational families shared housing to cope with unemployment/poverty.

1934   Half of the homes in the U.S. had radios.

HUMAN NEEDS

1933   Social worker Harry Hopkins was appointed to head President Roosevelt's "New Deal" Civil Works Administration (CWA) and Federal Emergency Relief Administration (FERA) with a three-year, $2 billion budget for doles and work relief.

1935   Civilian Conservation Corps (CCC) employment reached 2.5 million young men on conservation and reforestation projects.

1935   The Works Progress Administration (WPA) was created by Congress; at its peaks, this "New Deal" program employed more than 3 million people building more than 2,500 hospitals, 5,900 school buildings, and nearly 13,000 playgrounds.

Leadership Characteristics

"Movers and shakers gathered at the Community Chest today to find solutions for the critical unemployment that plagues our community," read a 1930 headline in the *Indianapolis Star*.[4] Leaders who worked with social work professionals to find local answers for problems that gripped the country represented the companies and families whose wealth and wisdom helped them survive the "crash." These were the people who urged the 1932 White House to create a nationwide initiative to put all charitable organizations under one banner. "They persevered, even though they met with little success, until the national government became directly involved in broad reaching programs of assistance to businesses, families, children, and youth. They were leaders who wouldn't quit until a problem was solved," wrote Elwood Street in his reflections in *The United Way, a History*.[5]

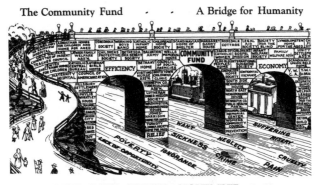

Typical of 1930s local campaign posters, this drawing depicts Community Fund agencies and attributes as the bridge over troubled waters.

How Approaches Reflected the Needs and the Times

LOCAL LEADERS UNITED IN A NATIONAL MOBILIZATION

Local community philanthropy in the years following the Great Depression reflected the financial losses suffered by local employers, their executives, and their workers.

"At first, private family agencies received extensive new amounts of philanthropic funds to distribute as relief to the poor, particularly in 1931," said Eleanor Brilliant in her narrative of "Changing Roles" in *The United Way, Dilemmas of Organized Charity*.[6]

"These agencies, however, rapidly depleted their resources, and as the depression continued, they proved unable to cope with the enormity of the pressures caused by the distribution of [limited] public funds. Thereafter, there was a loss of confidence in what private social welfare agencies could or should do, in light of expanding public sector activity."

1934 MOBILIZATION FOR HUMAN NEEDS

Administrative Agency
COMMUNITY CHESTS AND COUNCILS, INC.

NEWS BULLETIN — JULY 1934

REBUILD

INTENSIVE MOBILIZATION PERIOD — OCTOBER 21 TO NOVEMBER 11

In many cities, Community Chest budget committees raised their own questions about what they could do to make up for losses in family income. They moved money from all other programs into relief budgets, but there still wasn't enough money available to meet the needs of agencies' clients. Community Councils brought agency and civic leaders together to look for ways to find enough money for communities to meet needs for both the "remediation" of general relief problems and "prevention" of further human suffering. It became clear that solutions were beyond the financial capacities of local campaigns for contributions. The answer to their problem was a new approach to government/nonprofit teamwork.

In the fall of 1932, Cleveland's Newton D. Baker convened a national meeting of community leaders identified by their local Community Chests and Councils. He asked them to join him as members of a National Citizens' Committee for the "Welfare and Relief Mobilization of 1932."[7] Each name, as it appeared in Baker's announcement of mobilization leaders, was prominent in local and national philanthropy.

CHAIRMAN
NEWTON D. BAKER
VICE-CHAIRMEN
WILLIAM COOPER PROCTER   DR. GEORGE E. VINCENT

CHARLES E. ADAMS, Cleveland, Ohio	HOWARD HEINZ, Pittsburgh, Pa.
JULIUS H. BARNES, Duluth, Minn.	FRED HOKE, Indianapolis, Ind.
MRS. AUGUST BELMONT, New York, N. Y.	LOUIS E. KIRSTEIN, Boston, Mass.
FRED R. BIGELOW, St. Paul, Minn.	HARRY C. KNIGHT, New Haven, Conn.
CORNELIUS N. BLISS, New York, N. Y.	THOMAS W. LAMONT, New York, N. Y.
MRS. NICHOLAS F. BRADY, New York, N. Y.	JOSEPH LEE, Boston, Mass.
HOWARD BRAUCHER, New York, N. Y.	BISHOP FRANCIS J. McCONNELL,
FRANK J. BRUNO, St. Louis, Mo.	New York, N. Y.
JOHN STEWART BRYAN, Richmond, Va.	TRACY W. McGREGOR, Detroit, Mich.
CHARLES C. BURLINGHAM, New York, N. Y.	FREDERICK B. PATTERSON. Dayton, Ohio
E. L. CARPENTER, Minneapolis, Minn.	HON. JOHN BARTON PAYNE,
HON. ROY D. CHAPIN, Washington, D. C.	Washington, D. C.
W. L. CLAYTON, Houston, Tex.	GEORGE WHARTON PEPPER,
HON. CHANNING H. COX, Boston, Mass.	Philadelphia, Pa.
WINTHROP M. CRANE. Jr., Dalton, Mass.	F. W. RAMSEY, Cleveland, Ohio
FREDERIC A. DELANO. Washington, D. C.	RUSH RHEES, Rochester, N. Y.
WILLIAM H. CROCKER, San Francisco, Cal.	EDWARD L. RYERSON, Jr., Chicago, Ill.
EDWARD D. DUFFIELD, Newark, N. J.	JOHN D. RYAN, New York, N. Y.
FRED W. ELLSWORTH, New Orleans, La.	ALFRED H. SCHOELLKOPF, Buffalo, N. Y.
GENERAL OTTO H. FALK, Milwaukee, Wis.	JOSEPH SCOTT, Los Angeles, Cal.
RUSSELL G. FESSENDEN, Boston, Mass.	RABBI A. H. SILVER, Cleveland, Ohio
MORTIMER FLEISHHACKER,	HON. ALFRED E. SMITH, New York, N. Y.
San Francisco, Cal.	TOM K. SMITH, St. Louis, Mo.
RT. REV. JAMES E. FREEMAN, -	MRS. ROBERT E. SPEER, New York, N. Y.
Washington, D. C.	MISS LILLIAN WALD, New York. N. Y.
HARVEY D. GIBSON, New York, N. Y.	FELIX M. WARBURG, New York, N. Y.
WALTER S. GIFFORD, New York, N. Y.	J. F. WELBORN, Denver, Col.
MRS. JOHN M. GLENN, New York, N. Y.	OSCAR WELLS, Birmingham, Ala.
WILLIAM GREEN, Washington, D. C.	ROBERT W. WOODRUFF, Atlanta, Ga.
WARREN S. HAYDEN, Cleveland, Ohio	COL. ARTHUR WOODS, New York, N. Y.
MOST REV. EDWARD J. HANNA.	C. S. WOOLWORTH. Scranton, Pa.
San Francisco. Cal.	OWEN D. YOUNG, New York. N. Y.

In addition to these leaders, he asked 29 national relief-giving agencies that were affiliates of local Chests and Councils to join together in an unprecedented program of cooperation under the aegis of the Association of Community Chests and Councils. Together, these individuals led Community Chest campaigns out of the doldrums of failing post-Depression campaigns. In most cities, the 1932 campaigns exceeded 1930 and 1931 results.

BUT WELFARE AND RELIEF MOBILIZATION WASN'T ENOUGH

Even with the success of local campaigns, states and cities could not carry the financial load of public relief. Baker's national committee of citizens and agencies reached out to newly elected President Roosevelt for help. They presented their design for an even broader national mobilization that included significant financial and program participation by the federal government. They proposed the infusion of large sums of federal income taxes into services that they believed would help get people back to work. Their plan anticipated the reshaping of the traditional roles of nonprofit and governmental agencies.

It worked! Chests and Councils made their case that responsibilities for public relief for impoverished and unemployed people had to be

---

On September 8, 1933, President Franklin D. Roosevelt called together the leaders of America's local Community Chest and Councils. He invited them to build upon the Welfare and Relief Mobilization and help him mount a national "Mobilization for Human Needs":

"All of this Community Chest work, all of this uniting in the cause of meeting human needs, is based on that old word 'cooperation.' Your work has a two-fold purpose. You are meeting the emergency and at the same time you are building for the future. Community Chests are going to keep on just as long as any of us are alive—and a mighty good thing they are too.

"I tell you very simply that you have a great responsibility on your shoulders and I know that you are going to fulfill it. You are going back to your States and your communities and give them this message from me: this work is an essential part of the Government's program, the program of the people of the United States to bring us back to where this country has a right to be. So, go to it, and make a record not only of money but a record of service of which we shall all be very proud."[8]

---

delineated from responsibilities for individuals and families with other needs. Within two years, the lion's share of financial responsibility for public welfare services was shifted from voluntary philanthropic contributions to the national government. Tax funds were committed to provide subsistence-level grants to people who had nothing, and voluntary contributions could be applied to grants to agencies for services that help people deal with and prevent dependence on "welfare." John Seely reviewed this fundamental change in his case study of philanthropy titled *Community Chest*: "As the needs of the unemployed outran the resources of private, local, and state authorities, the national government assumed more and more responsibility for the provision of relief. By [the end of] 1933, public funds supplied nearly 95 percent of total relief expenditures, and the pattern of increasing federal responsibility, thus clearly set during the early New Deal days, has not yet been reversed."[9]

Most communities integrated the Mobilization for Human Need's eagle into campaign and year-round graphics.

The mobilization designed by representatives of local United Way organizations and agencies proved effective. In 1935, national efforts to fight unemployment and poverty, as represented by the Mobilization for Human Needs, became incorporated into the Social Security Act. "About 150 years after the founding of the republic, Americans developed their first set of national social welfare programs," according to Bruce Jansson, in *The Reluctant Welfare State*. "These efforts culminated in the passage of the Social Security Act, a remarkable policy breakthrough for the United States."[10]

A NATIONAL ASSOCIATION FOR CANADA

"That same year," as reported in United Way of America's *People & Events*, "Canada formed its own organization for Dominion-wide health and welfare planning. . . . Similarly affected by the depression, Canada had become all too familiar with unemployment, bread lines, and inadequate relief measures. . . . The Canadian Welfare Council took a leading role in meeting those needs, making surveys, calling conferences, making recommendations, and running Canada's first national publicity program for Community Chest campaigns."[11]

"What the heart gives away is never lost because it stays in the hearts of others."
—DAVID LAM, *Lieutenant Governor, British Columbia*

COMMUNITY COUNCILS' COORDINATION
DEMONSTRATED BENEFITS OF COOPERATION

As the numbers of employment and financial relief programs increased, concern grew about possible duplication and overlap of programs and their clients. In 1932, Detroit's Community Council initiated a program of systematically recording the names and birth dates of all members of families served by charitable organizations. The description of this innovation presented to the National Conference of Social Work included this reflection: "With so many agencies involved in giving relief, the Community Council found it necessary to create a specialized social service exchange. As Wayne County [government] gradually assumed responsibility for dispensing state and federal relief funds, the Community Council gave each donor and taxpayer impartial assurance that fraudulent actions by people portending destitution were held to a minimum."[12]

NEIGHBORHOOD COUNCILS TOOK ROOT

Taking a lesson from the operating principles of Jane Addams' Hull House, leaders of the Hartford Community Council hastened their city's recovery from economic devastation on a neighborhood by neighborhood basis. According to the *1936 Social Work Yearbook*, "In 1934, the *Hartford Survey* recommended the creation of four such [neighborhood] units under the Council of Social Agencies of the city. This tendency is likely to proceed as rapidly and as far as the staff and financial resources will permit."[13]

The staff and resources proved to be a worthwhile investment. By the end of the decade, the number of Hartford's neighborhood councils had doubled and the creation of similar neighborhood organizations was being practiced by several hundred Councils. These groups spoke for neighborhood constituents and made sure that services were utilized and program expenditures were monitored.

NEWS BULLETIN

Community Chests & Councils, Inc.

November, 1935

HUMAN NEED

Fitzpatrick in Collier's Weekly
November 2, 1935

IF UNCLE SAM LETS GO
WILL THE STATES TAKE UP THE RELIEF LOAD?

EDUCATING GOVERNMENT OFFICIALS
RESULTED IN MONEY FOR AGENCIES

Beginning with the Los Angeles Welfare Federation's employment of a "legislative education professional" in 1937, local Councils found that educational programs for elected officials and local governmental organizations could increase income for nonprofit agencies and save money for taxpayers.[14] By contracting with nonprofit organizations to provide skill-building services to public welfare clients, governmental agencies could reduce welfare rolls. In his retrospective of 25 years of service as executive secretary of Cincinnati's Community Chest, C.M. Bookman reflected that "The money we can obtain for needed agency services by skillfully educating local governmental officials does more good than the funds we raise in our campaign. Elected officials often need help to understand the capacity of voluntary agencies to carry out services at lower costs than agencies of government."[15]

COMMUNITY CHESTS and COUNCILS, Inc.

NEWS BULLETIN
NOVEMBER 1937

Find the Man Who Has Just Made His Contribution
(Printed by Special Permission from NEA Service, Inc.)

INFORMATION AND REFERRAL SERVICE INITIATED

The impact of the Mobilization for Human Needs and the Social Security Act of 1935 became evident by the end of 1935. As employment increased, needs for financial relief gradually decreased in most cities. With the benefits of these new federal initiatives came a confusing array of programs. The abbreviations that identified them, the so-called "alphabet soup," didn't help: WPA—the Works Progress Administration; FERA—the Federal Emergency Relief Administration; and CCC—the Civilian Conservation Corps were just a few.

People needed guidance to know where to turn for the help they needed. In 1936, the leaders of Boston's Community Council established an "Information and Referral Service." According to Hal Demone's *Community* magazine article titled "The Nucleus of a Human Needs Program," it was created "to provide the most expedient handling of social problems. Our task is divided into four parts: information and direction, referral, short-term counseling, and consultation with referral sources and resource agencies. Requests are received from individuals, social agencies, business firms, labor unions, civic organizations, churches, other professional workers, hospitals, and businessmen."[16]

The "I & R" not only provided help to those who called, Demone continued, "Such inquiries—thousands each year—provide an accurate test of felt needs and trends. To the degree that the needs are not effectively met, the inquiries offer information about program gaps. Finally, they give important information about the response of the care-giving system."

Similar services to coordinate increasing numbers of government and nonprofit agency services became commonplace in city after city. Following the lead of the Ohio Citizens' Council for Health and Welfare, the number of state associations of Community Councils grew as well. One of the most creative roles designed by these collaborative organizations was West Virginia's statewide social service exchange. This office provided a clearing house function for all government and nonprofit social welfare and employment agencies. It served as a center for data collection on human needs, and provided data that helped state legislators design public services. It also provided information that led to the development of state regulations and licensure requirements for health and social service agencies.

NEW APPROACHES TO FUND-RAISING

As needs increased, local agencies looked to Community Chest leaders to find ways to bolster the results of annual campaigns. Soliciting workers at their places of employment, as well as door-to-door campaigns in neighborhoods, were showing the effect of the faltering economy and increasing unemployment. The *News Bulletin* of the Association of Community Chests and Councils regularly carried descriptions of local innovations aimed at producing increased campaign contributions. A number of them were adopted by enough communities to be considered common Community

Chest practice. Four of the most significant included the first board member campaign, use of a continuous giving campaign pledge, creation of a leadership giving society, and the initiation of a separate women's campaign.

MONTREAL STAGED A BOARD MEMBER CAMPAIGN

"Unemployment has affected practically every agency in the Federation. [It has] affected the health and morale of the people, reduced the income of agencies and their ability to serve the increasing needs of our people." These were the words that greeted all Welfare Federation and agency board members when they opened personal letters written to them by the 1931 Montreal Campaign Chairman, according to the Association of Community Chests and Councils' *News Bulletin.* The story went on to describe "the cooperation of about 900 men and women serving on the boards of agencies who joined in an effort to increase giving to the 1931 campaign."[17]

The campaign exceeded its monetary goal. Moreover, it positioned the Welfare Federation as a unique local organization that could rally support from diverse constituencies for the good of the entire community. By successfully including board members from all affiliated agencies at a time of economic duress, the Welfare Federation realized three achievements that other communities were to emulate.

First, the campaign demonstrated that, by working together, community leaders could reach important goals, even in the most difficult of times. Second, the neighbor-to-neighbor social work of the Montreal Welfare Federation was something in which people believed. When convinced of the needs, people would support the approach generously. Third, the Chest/Council movement represented a means through which people could work together for the good of the total community. Rather than serving as *agency-driven organizations*, Community Chests and Councils were transforming themselves into *community organizations.*

CONTINUOUS GIVING COMMITTED

The Community Chest of Jacksonville, Florida, tried an approach in 1931 that swept the country. Campaign prospects were asked to sign a commitment card that promised monthly payments until the donor "cancelled, decreased, or increased" giving.[18] Just two years later, Grand Rapids Community Chest secretary Tom Devine shared "A Plan for Continuous Campaigning" in the *News Bulletin*.[19] His community had adopted "a new plan of campaign which will be primarily on a continuous basis, as opposed to the annual intensive appeal that crowded all fund-raising into too brief a schedule." Working year-round, campaign volunteers sought gifts from individuals with regular "tag days," pledges, and the creation of "Employee Fellowship" groups within each plant, firm and public service organization employing 20 or more people.

Jacksonville, Fla., Nov. _____1931

Five
Three
I PROMISE TO PAY Two **DOLLARS EACH MONTH**
One

BEGINNING DECEMBER 1, 1931, to the Community Chest, for the support of its agencies FOR THE YEAR 1932 and thereafter. These monthly payments will be continuous as long as I am a resident of Duval County, but may be cancelled, decreased or increased by my giving 30 days notice in writing of such change.

| SUBSCRIBER'S SIGNATURE | DATE _____ AMOUNT_____ 00 |
| SUBSCRIBER'S HOME ADDRESS | INITIAL _____ LEDGER _____ |

NAME OF SOLICITOR

IF UNABLE TO OBTAIN SUBSCRIPTION, SOLICITOR SHOULD WRITE EXPLANATION BELOW

While few communities adopted Jacksonville's tag day, many picked up on the idea of conducting parts of the campaign on a continuous, year-round basis. Jacksonville's ideas stimulated local experimentation with year-round publicity and education campaigns. The Jacksonville continuous giving pledge card was almost universally adopted by other cities' Community Chest organizations. Finally, while other cities did not copy Jacksonville's efforts to create employee fellowship groups, they saw in Jacksonville's work another illustration that asking people to "give where you work" could be a useful addition to the prevalent "give where you live" neighborhood/residential campaigns.

THE FIRST LEADERSHIP GIVING SOCIETY
The membership requirement for the first leadership giving society, as reported in the November 1936 *News Bulletin*, was simple: "Everybody

who gives more to the Yonkers Community Chest campaign than last year is entitled to membership in the mythical Legion of the Plus."[20]

"Give plus, Neighbor!" was the theme that challenged Yonkers citizens to "do more than duty and to give more than the minimum required for respectability."[21]

Leaders of the Yonkers campaign had hit upon an idea that was destined to be tried in hundreds of communities in almost as many variations. Early symbols of leadership giving reported in the *News Bulletin* reflected local culture and values. Yonkers' "mythical legion" wouldn't work in Youngstown, Ohio, a city with great pride in its public schools. There, the Community Fund established a giving "honor roll" for people who increased their annual campaign gifts. Birmingham, Alabama, witnessing a growing steel manufacturing industry, encouraged donors to become part of the community "girders club," while Little Rock, Arkansas, sought members of a group whose generosity reflected the architecture of its ante bellum homes, the Community Chest "pillars society."

A WOMEN'S CRUSADE
The Mobilization for Human Needs asked Cincinnati Community Chest leaders to design a campaign approach that would generate fund-raising interest among women. In the spring of 1933, the "Women's Crusade of Cincinnati" was unveiled. Its objectives were shared in the national *News Bulletin*:[22]

Objectives
- To bring to the women of Hamilton County a sense of partnership in the community's efforts to meet the general welfare responsibilities.

- To place upon the women a definite part of the responsibility to awaken all citizens to the seriousness of the social emergency and the vital necessity of continuing the success of the Community Chest.
- To unearth criticism based upon lack of understanding and let the criticism develop into support by presenting the real facts.
- To spread an understanding of the multiplicity of social work, and the community's dependence upon the whole well-rounded social work program.

Based on the success of Cincinnati's experiment, First Lady Eleanor Roosevelt accepted the Chairmanship of the Mobilization's National Women's Committee. In the October 20, 1933, issue of the Community Chests and Councils' *News Bulletin*, President Roosevelt joined Mobilization Chairman Baker and the First Lady in a request to support Community Chest or local welfare appeals (where no Community Chest existed).[23]

By the end of 1934, hundreds of Community Chest organizations had adopted the national Mobilization for Human Needs theme for their campaigns. The development of Women's Committees were regularly reported on a *News Bulletin* "scoreboard."

RESEARCH BECAME A CAMPAIGN TOOL

A graduate student at the University of Minnesota School of Social Work applied his social research training to squelch a rumor that troubled leaders of the St. Paul Community Chest. Carl Warmington, working as Secretary for Employee Solicitation at the St. Paul Community Chest, heard rumors that, after the Depression, pressure for workplace giving to the annual campaign resulted in some people losing their jobs because they did not give. He decided to devote his dissertation to finding out whether there was any truth to the rumors. Based on his research, Warmington reported that he could not find anyone in the St. Paul community whose experience substantiated the information that had been rumored.[24]

PRESSURE TO GIVE?

Regardless of Warmington's findings, it was generally accepted that employees in other cities had been required by their employers to give to

If people are hungry this winter, they will have food. If they are cold, they will have clothing and shelter. Federal and State funds are being appropriated to supplement your local efforts toward relieving actual hunger and physical distress.

Eating is not living; it is existing. If we are to justify our claim to civilization, we must think beyond primary needs of food and shelter. We must face our responsibility for human service, broader in conception, deeper in sympathy and understanding.

Care of the aged, service to demoralized families, hospitalization of the needy sick, home nursing, settlements, guidance of youth, care of the children without a chance—these and hundreds of other services are in the hands of your local welfare organizations. Some of these programs were overshadowed during the past year by the desperate fight to supply food and warmth to every one in need. But they must not be forgotten. Huge public appropriations only to maintain life necessitate your and my partnership in making that life worth while.

This year there are social needs created by the misery of the lean years we have gone through. These critical needs must be met by the local welfare agencies which you have maintained in the past and which must look to you for support again at this time.

I join Newton D. Baker, Chairman of the National Citizens' Committee, and Mrs. Roosevelt, Chairman of the National Women's Committee, in asking you to support your Community Chest or your local welfare appeals to the limit of your ability. It is a cause well designated by the title given it, "Mobilization for Human Needs."

Franklin D. Roosevelt

Community Chest campaigns as conditions of employment. Because of the inconsistency of the concept of "voluntary giving," with real or perceived "pressure to give," the St. Paul Community Chest began a practice that was adopted by many cities during the post-Depression years. Upon presentation of proof of payments made to Community Chest campaigns, refunds were discretely given to employees who felt that their employers had coerced them to give.

REASONS FOR GIVING AND REFUSING TO GIVE

In 1931, following the first campaign of the New Brunswick, New Jersey, Community Chest, 5,615 refusals to give were analyzed. The results were published in the *News Bulletin*. "Most could not afford to give, many were not interested, and a few just couldn't understand," was the summary of the analysis.[25]

COMMUNITY
CHESTS AND COUNCILS
Vol. 14   OCTOBER 1938   No. 2

Antonio Sotomayor of San Francisco catches a typical gesture of
Jose Iturbi who will conduct the Cincinnati Symphony Orchestra on
the nation wide broadcast of the Community Mobilization for Human
Needs on Friday evening, October 14, 10-10:30 E. S. T.

The following year, people who refused to give to campaigns in many communities were asked to complete unsigned cards used to help those who prepared Community Chest printed materials refine their messages to better reach those who "just couldn't understand."

Six years later, the *News Bulletin* carried a story titled "Columbus [Ohio] Studies Attitudes of Givers."[26] The survey sought answers to these questions: Do people give to the community fund because they care deeply about it? Or do they give from a vague feeling that on the whole it is a good thing, or because their employers expect them to?

One thousand of 47,000 contributors to the 1934 campaign and 200 noncontributors were personally interviewed by students of Ohio State University social work professor C.C. "Charlie" Stillman.

"FINDINGS: Made at a time when criticism of private welfare agencies was acute, when contributors were still feeling the pinch of the depression, and when all non-relief expenditures were under fire,

this study of the rank and file of contributors revealed a surprising amount of ignorance of the fund's purposes, affiliations, organization and financing; some intelligent and interested cooperation, but on the other hand, some antagonism; a considerable amount of misconception and misinformation, much of it traceable to gossip hoary with age; variation of adverse opinion with the amount of the contribution, opinion being least favorable among the large group of very small contributors."[27]

These survey results surprised Columbus' Community Fund leaders. They were proud that for a number of years they had carried on an active and varied campaign of public information. After thorough analysis of the responses, their conclusions signaled a change in attitude that forged the beginning of Chest and Council understanding of the values of citizen participation and ownership of their work.

"Persuasion, not pressure, is called for; more wide-spread participation in the privileges and responsibilities of agency direction; personal influence and face-to-face contacts with contributors, and more attention to the influence wielded by small givers. There are courses to be followed by every Chest which, like Columbus, faces honestly the way people feel about it and sets to work at winning a warmer, more understanding support."[28]

Professor Stillman made sure that his students shared the lesson learned by the Community Chest leaders. Their study became part of Ohio State University's graduate social work curriculum in "Community Chest Administration" for nearly two decades.

DATA DEVELOPED ON SERVICES RECEIVED BY BENEFICIARIES

The 1930s brought interest in learning about service recipients as well as contributors. Council leaders wanted to know more about the services received. Chest leaders wanted to know more about their contributors. Both groups wanted to know how much their services cost and who was paying the bills.

"It is easy enough to mass figures and believe that you have measured progress . . . but the measurement which we want is one which shall show whether enlarged expenditures have been matched by a corresponding increase in socially useful service. Unless, in the light of an audit, we have evidence that we are getting such returns, we may be called upon to revise our methods or change or objectives."

—C.M. BOOKMAN, *Past Executive Secretary, Community Chest and Council of Greater Cincinnati, Ohio*

In 1933, the New Haven, Connecticut, Community Chest and Council completed a "beneficiary study" that provided a format that could be copied by other cities. Their survey instruments were offered to other Chests and Councils. A graphical summary of their data appeared on the front page of the December 1933 *News Bulletin*. This innovative research formed the basis of regular studies of service beneficiaries and the sources of funds that made them possible. In 1934, New Haven added questions to their research about the places of employment of the parents and other family members of agency clients. The identity of individuals was kept confidential, but regular reports to employers were provided as part of the case of increased giving by corporations and their owners. The rationale of this request was the value returned to employers for services rendered to their beneficiaries.

Several years later, Milwaukee volunteer members of the community fund budget committee asked agencies to help them better understand their services by sharing *case histories* of clients. Before long, campaigners found that these stories, often presented by those who experienced them, served as excellent means of communicating the reason for which funds were being raised. The November 1939 edition of the *News Bulletin* reported Milwaukee's "excellent rapport with those who must make the difficult decisions about allocating campaign funds, as well as those who entrust us with that precious commodity."[29]

INNOVATIONS IN CAMPAIGN PROMOTION
The first use of television to broadcast a philanthropic message occurred in October of 1931 at the New York City studio of CBS, the Columbia

COMMUNITY CHESTS AND COUNCILS, INC.
1810 GRAYBAR BUILDING   420 LEXINGTON AVENUE
NEW YORK, N. Y.

NEWS BULLETIN
DECEMBER 20 1933

CHEST AGENCIES	FEDERAL	CITY & STATE
VETERAN'S RELIEF	$292,274 82.9%	$60,000 17.1%
WORK RELIEF	$3,000 1.2%	$124,884 50.6%	$117,770 7.46%
GENERAL FAMILY RELIEF*	$236,397 23.2%	$219,586 21.5%	$564,510 55.3%
HOSPITALS & DISPENSARY	$87,139 27.3%	$231,804 72.7%
CARE OF AGED	$53,113 48%	$57,648 52%
NURSING SERVICE	$140,762 69.4%	$62,275 30.6%
RECREATION PROJECTS	$228,172 78.5%	$62,501 21.5%
ORPHANS AND DEPENDENT CHILDREN	$406,149 89.7%	$46,827 10.3%
DAY NURSERIES	$29,235 100%	
CRIPPLED CHILDREN	$16,094 100%	

HOW CHEST AGENCIES, CITY AND NATION SHARE IN THE LOAD
From the 1934 Campaign Booklet
The New Haven Community Chest

Broadcasting System. Reporting on the progress of the New York and other Community Chest campaigns, Allen T. Burns, executive director of the National Association of Community Chests and Councils, said, "We realize that, in its present state of development, television reaches a very limited audience and consequently can be of but little actual service in our fund-raising efforts. . . . [This experience] served to give us a glimpse of the future, when television undoubtedly will play a great part, as radio is now doing, in education, philanthropy and public service."[30]

"Largest Ever Parade Heralds Campaign Start" was the 1935 *Newark Advocate* headline that announced the beginning of one of Ohio's oldest Community Fund campaigns. "In what is believed to be the first Community Fund campaign parade in the country, our city renewed its commitment to support services for the poor and unemployed. Organized by the Junior Chamber of Commerce, over two dozen businesses joined representatives of the Community Fund agencies to remind us all that we are responsible for our neighbors in need."[31]

NEWS BULLETIN

Community Chests & Councils, Inc.

March, 1935

Courtesy of the New Yorker

"First of All, There's the Community Fund"

A VARIETY OF APPROACHES TO COST
SAVINGS PROVED THEIR WORTH

Before the Depression, attention to cost saving measures was a necessary evil. After the Depression, cost saving became a way of life for nonprofit professionals and volunteers. Many agencies turned to Chests and Councils for help. In Minneapolis, the Community Fund documented its experience with central purchasing of automobiles.

James Rye, auditor for the Minneapolis Community Fund, documented the basis of agency charges for centralized vehicle purchase in a 1930 article in the *News Bulletin*. "An average mileage cost of $.05002 per mile is estimated as fair . . . with an average of 16,920 miles per car each year."[32] Combined annual capital and operating costs to agencies totaled $846.39.

In 1936, Dayton found more than cost savings when leaders merged their Chest and Council organizations. Helen Currier, associate secretary of the Dayton Council of Social Agencies, described anticipated benefits in the *News Bulletin*. "Integration of Council and Chest functions might result in more board member participation in money raising and interpre-

tation. A closer touch with the planning function and contact with professionals should allow more intelligent discharge of responsibility of Chest
board members."[33]

DONALD DUCK — THE 1940 ALL-AMERICAN
STAR COMMUNITY CHEST SOLICITOR

"The newly organized Flint [Michigan] Community Association . . .
represents a new venture in Chest history," stated the *News Bulletin*'s
description of an endeavor that sought to economize by increasing efficiency by "coordinating leadership in the social service, commercial, and
cultural fields of voluntary community effort."[34] Many benefits beyond
cost savings accrued to this ancestor of community leadership training
programs. Among them was Flint's coordinated approach to planning and
fund-raising for Community Chest, Allied Arts Council, and Chamber of
Commerce programs and services.

In Kansas City, Missouri, Jackson County Judge Harry S. Truman suggested a merger of the Kansas City and Independence, Missouri, Community Chests, along with the Kansas City, Kansas, organization to enable
greater efficiency, according to Owen Davison. He joined the staff of the
consolidated organization in 1942 and reports that "the staff didn't remember that it was Mr. Truman's idea."[35]

1930s NEEDS BROUGHT DIVERSE LEADERS TOGETHER
IN A SEARCH FOR PATHS BACK TO PROSPERITY

Nonprofit, civic, business, and government leaders struggled for most of the decade to find ways for individuals, families, and institutions to regain the enthusiasm of the years before the 1929 Wall Street crash. Social workers, represented by Councils of Social Agencies and Community Chests, worked side by side with leaders of business and industry as they attempted to reconstruct American society. Together, they decided that the national government had to use its taxing power to finance massive programs to treat health and social ills. Together, they shared dreams that voluntary agencies would prevent human problems so successfully that government programs would not be needed beyond the decade. Their planning never considered that the country would soon be involved in a war again whose costs in human sacrifice would require even more government spending than the Depression had.

Key Innovations in the United Way of Serving
Communities Between 1930 and 1940

1930	Central purchasing of autos studied	Minneapolis, MN
1930	Capital funds raised for agencies	Saginaw, MI
1930	Red Feather used as campaign symbol	Duluth, MN and New Orleans, LA
1931	Continuous giving pledges solicited	Jacksonville, FL
1931	Reasons for refusing to give studies conducted	New Brunswick, NJ
1931	Television used to promote campaign	New York, NY
1932	Public relief coordinated by a Community Council	Detroit, MI
1932	Agency board campaign conducted	Montreal, QU
1933	Women's Campaign Crusade begun	Cincinnati, OH
1933	Service beneficiary study conducted	New Haven, CT
1934	Year-round campaign initiated	Grand Rapids, MI
1934	Neighborhood councils created	Hartford, CT
1935	Street parade kicks off campaign	Newark, OH

1936	Fund-raising and community planning solidated under single board	Dayton, OH
1936	Information & referral service started	Boston, MA
1936	Leadership giving society created	Yonkers, NY
1936	Community leadership training initiated	Flint, MI
1937	Local public policy committee created	Los Angeles, CA
1937	Contributors' attitudes studied	Columbus, OH
1937	Agency case histories presented to United Way budget committee	Milwaukee, WI
1938	Area-wide merger proposed by Harry S. Truman	Kansas City, MO
1939	Statewide social service exchange created	West Virginia

1   Hoover, President Herbert C. Inaugural Address, 1929.
2   Roosevelt, President Franklin D. Second Inaugural Address, 1937.
3   Community Chest and Councils, Inc. *Yesterday and Today with Community Chests*, 1937, p. 28.
4   *Indianapolis Star*, March 13, 1930.
5   Street, Elwood. "The United Way, A History." Unpublished memoirs on file at the University of Minnesota Social Welfare History Archives, 1958, p. 128.
6   Brilliant, Eleanor L. *The United Way, Dilemmas of Organized Charity*. New York: Columbia University Press, 1990, p. 25.
7   Association of Community Chests and Councils. *Welfare and Relief Mobilization*, September 15, 1932.
8   Roosevelt, President Franklin D. *An Extemporaneous Address before the 1933 Conference on Mobilization for Human Needs*. Washington, DC: September 8, 1933.
9   Seeley, John R., with Buford H. Junker and R. Wallace Jones Jr. *Community Chest*. Toronto: University of Toronto Press, 1957, p. 22.
10   Jansson, Bruce S. *The Reluctant Welfare State*. Boston: Brooks/Cole, 1997, p. 10.
11   United Way of America. *People & Events, A History of the United Way*, 1977, p. 72.
12   Williams, John E. "Public Welfare Review." *Proceedings of the 1940 National Conference of Social Work*. 1940, p. 160-A.
13   *Social Work Yearbook 1936*. New York: Russell Sage Foundation, p. 104
14   Posey, Wilson H. *A History of the Ohio Citizens' Council for Health and Welfare*. Unpublished, 1971, p. 35.
15   Bookman, C.M. *The First Twenty-Five Years, 1915–1940*. Cincinnati: Ruter Press, 1940, p. 124.
16   Demone, Harold W., Ph.D. and David F. Long, M.S.W. "Information-Referral—The Nucleus of a Human-Needs Program." *Community*. United Community Funds and Councils of America, September-October 1969, p. 9.
17   *News Bulletin*, Association of Community Chests and Councils, Inc. New York: January 23, 1932, pp. 6-7.
18   *News Bulletin*, September 15, 1932, p. 12.

[19] *News Bulletin*, February 1934, p. 1.
[20] *News Bulletin*, November 1936, p. 8.
[21] ibid p. 8.
[22] *News Bulletin*, June 1933, p.4.
[23] *News Bulletin*, October 20, 1933, cover page.
[24] Warmington, Carl. "A Study of Industrial Giving to the St. Paul Community Chest, 1929–1937." University of Minnesota Graduate School of Social Work, unpublished.
[25] *News Bulletin*, "News About Community Chests—New Brunswick Analyzes Refusals to Give," April 20, 1931, p. 6.
[26] *News Bulletin*, "Columbus Studies Attitudes of Givers." December 1937, p. 8.
[27] *News Bulletin*, December 1937, p. 9.
[28] ibid p. 9.
[29] *News Bulletin*, "Case Stories Used in Milwaukee," November 1939, p. 14.
[30] *News Bulletin*, "Chests First in Television," November 18, 1931, p. 1.
[31] *Newark Advocate*, "Largest Ever Parade Heralds Campaign Start," September 5, 1938, p. 1.
[32] *News Bulletin*, "Minneapolis Studies Automobiles," April 1930.
[33] Currier, Helen M. "The New Type of Council Organization." *News Bulletin*, April 1936, p. 10.
[34] *News Bulletin*, "Flint Community Project," November 1936, p. 12.
[35] Davison, Owen R. Personal correspondence with the author. January 2002.

CHAPTER FOUR

Acting Locally, Serving Globally

1941—1945

Supporting National Defense and Victims of War

N ineteen forty-one. Countries that were not yet at war were getting ready. Community Chests and Councils which had just reached parity with post-Depression demands for increased local agency services already were receiving requests for money from war relief agencies around the world. Agencies served war refugees from more than a dozen countries. Others sought to relocate those in harm's way.

Local leaders, now schooled in both workplace and residential fund raising, as well as needs assessment, planning, and priority setting, were ready to meet new challenges. But, as the U.S. and Canada joined the world war, needs and challenges proved far more difficult than volunteers and staff had anticipated. Military service drained the predominantly male workforce of the contributors whose gifts had made it possible to reach aggressive goals during recent campaigns. Their female replacements found that their own service needs, such as child care, quickly depleted discretionary dollars. Plus, the needs presented by national defense programs and the war became unintentional competitors whose imperatives led employers to offer "payroll deductions" for the purchase of War Bonds.

Ralph Blanchard, executive director of "Three Cs" (Community Chests & Councils of America), described the landscape in which his local affiliates found themselves in the early 1940s in an article in *Community*. "Local needs became dominant. . . . and purely national and international programs suffered accordingly. By the end of the 1930s and very early in the 1940s, culminating in the April 1942 action of the Red Cross in withdrawing all their locals from the federation, national and international agencies had all but disappeared from local campaigns, except for the support given to local units. This was the condition which prevailed at the outbreak of World War II."[1]

"Then," Blanchard continued, "history began to repeat itself. One by one, war-related causes came into the picture."[2] Nearly every community confronted the same issues. The "War Chest" concept used during World War I was resurrected. It brought together Community Chests and Civil Defense Funds to provide a lens through which war-related services could be viewed together with local health and human needs and services so that communities could set priorities for the allocation of precious resources.

The need for contributions no longer grew incrementally; it grew geometrically as government and civic leaders throughout the country called upon their local War Chests and Councils to address global needs in addition to local agencies' needs. Appeals for contributions in support of local needs were combined with appeals to meet the needs of the war effort. Chest and Council allocations volunteers worked to balance the health and human service requirements at home with those of America's military personnel and the victims of the war.

Representing the consolidated needs of many more than the Community Chest family of agencies, War Chest Campaigns reached record levels of support. Even so, War Chests' contributions were falling short of needs. Families who lost sons and fathers in battle needed more than prewar levels of support. Adults and children scarred by war needed special services to cope with loss, disability, and the new realities of life.

The war brought new social issues to the Community Chest and Council agendas as women were asked to take their place beside the southern Blacks and Appalachians who had moved north to fill factory jobs in the war industry. Unusual demands of factory employment on women and minorities quickly changed definitions of family life. Employment of wives, mothers, and daughters in occupations traditionally held by men introduced lifestyle changes. The appearance of new faces, female and those of color, in military and civilian jobs previously filled by white men exposed smoldering questions of civil rights and equal opportunities.

Signs of the Times

GLOBAL/NATIONAL EVENTS

1942	The bombing of Pearl Harbor by Japanese war planes. Holocaust in Europe.
1942	Community Chests & Councils recommended that President Roosevelt create a National War Fund.
1945	United Nations Relief and Rehabilitation Administration attempted service consolidation for children, elderly and refugees.

IN THE NEWS

1941	U.S.-licensed TV began. Daily radio broadcasts and newspapers reported achievements and casualties, both local and global.
1945	U.S. dropped atomic bomb. War ended.
1945	United Nations was formed.

STATE/LOCAL COMMUNITIES & NEIGHBORHOODS

-	Population in industrial urban centers expanded as African American, Latino, and Appalachian people migrated to jobs.
-	Window hangings displayed the impact of military service and the loss of family members.
-	Families participated in metal and cloth scrap drives. Neighbors grew fruits and vegetables in communal Victory gardens.
-	Boy and Girl Scouts served as messengers on block civil defense teams.

SOCIAL MOVEMENTS/GOVERNMENTAL POLICIES & PROGRAMS

1940	Congress passed the Selective Services and Alien Registration Acts.
1944	National War Relief Control Board was appointed to review ap-

peals and establish nationwide priorities for the support of war-related appeals.

1944   Congress responded to educational, employment, and housing needs of returning troops by enacting a "GI Bill of Rights" that provided training, education, and loans.

ECONOMY/BUSINESS CYCLES AND THE WORKPLACE

- Fuel and food rationing were required to support war effort.
- Increased factory production created needs for more job training and raised industrial safety issues.
- Organized labor opened its ranks to new constituencies.
- Those still unemployed by the Great Depression entered military service or found work in war-related industries.

SCIENCE AND TECHNOLOGY

1940   Penicillin was developed and used to shorten illness, hasten healing, and cure disease. Emergency medicine was redefined through battlefield experience.

- Atomic energy, for better or worse, ushered in the "Nuclear Age," a new era for humankind.

DEMOGRAPHY

1943   Nearly half of the 132 million Americans were employed in military service or war-related jobs.

FAMILY/HOUSEHOLD STRUCTURE

- Mothers left their children in care of nonfamily members to work at war production jobs.
- Women assumed head-of-household responsibilities.
- Extended families continued to share households until heads of households returned from military service.

HUMAN NEEDS

- Families lost members to war and the Holocaust.
- Orphanages overflowed with children of the Depression and war refugees.
- Sexually transmitted/venereal diseases reached epidemic proportions.

Leadership Characteristics

Just as people of all walks of life marched to war together, many did the same while volunteering in their home towns. Those whose *noblesse oblige* put them in leadership roles with Community Chests, Councils, and War Chests, welcomed the side-by-side participation of the blue-collar workers whose workplace generosity had increased the campaign proceeds of the 1930s. Support of the war effort and civil defense was everybody's job, and nowhere could people be better seen working together for their communities than with United Way organizations. Leaders of organized labor sat with business executives. Women moved from board membership to board leadership. "Negro Divisions" of campaigns, many of which became local Urban League affiliates in the years ahead, became integral parts of War Chest organizations.

> *"We shouldn't confuse the notoriety of Community Chest offices with those who occupy them."*
>
> —C.M. BOOKMAN, *Past Executive Secretary,*
> *Community Chest and Council of Greater Cincinnati, Ohio*

Staff leadership began to shift from a predominance of male social workers to an equal number of women and men. As men were drafted to serve in the military, women were called upon to take Chest and Council leadership positions, particularly in smaller communities.

How Approaches Reflected the Needs and the Times

CAMPAIGNS EXPANDED TO INCLUDE
NATIONAL AGENCIES AND GLOBAL RELIEF

As the decade began, daily newspapers and radio reports cited the number of families who had lost their homes to the wars raging across Europe, Africa, and Asia. Refugees, many of whom were widows and orphans, called out to American families and friends for assistance. Their photos in newspapers and magazines stilled the hearts of everyone who saw them. Increasingly, the donations of clubs and associations that had been going to local welfare agencies were directed to programs of refugee relief. Community Chests and Councils were challenged to do the same while at the same time, local health and welfare needs persisted. Incremental campaign growth wasn't enough to meet needs which were doubling and tripling. Chests and Councils were being confronted with fund-raising challenges and fund distribution choices that tested the mettle of every volunteer and staff member.

Community

BULLETIN OF   COMMUNITY CHESTS AND COUNCILS, INC.

Vol. 18   FEBRUARY 1943   No. 6

From Cincinnati's 1943 "One Plus One" Campaign *(See also page 92)*

WAR CHEST
1+1

FREEDOM IN 43

One Day's Pay for the Home Front
One Day's Pay for the Fighting Front

The February 1942 issue of *The Bulletin of Community Chests and Councils* summarized the choices that were coming into focus in every city: " . . . . today Community Chests and Councils of Social Agencies are making practical decisions inevitably prophetic of their future function and usefulness. Multiplying and mounting appeals for the war emergency—the USO, the Red Cross, British, Russian, and Chinese relief—are forcing communities to immediate and practical decisions affecting Chest responsibilities and relationships. During the next three months, the actions taken in these communities—East and West, North and South—inexorably will determine not only the war, but the postwar role of the Chest and Council movement."[3]

In 1941, Pittsburgh's Community Fund leaders demonstrated a new approach to structuring community fund-raising that they hoped would temporarily position the organization's annual appeal to meet both war-related and ongoing service needs. The campaign was modified to combine appeals for funds to meet the needs of their traditionally affiliated agencies and those of wartime causes. *Community* described Pittsburgh's approach: "A consolidated campaign goes over big with contributors. Through the United Fund, a contributor can *give once for all, enough for all,* with the assurance that he is meeting his responsibilities to the affiliated appeals through a single gift."[4]

Permanent change, however, was not promised in Pittsburgh. "The United Fund differs from the Community Fund in that the latter is a permanent organization. As long as the emergency lasts, the United Fund will likely be in the picture raising funds for the various charitable 'home front' agencies and for the dramatic wartime appeals, but it is an emergency organization and its life is limited to five years."[5]

Volunteers in two states demonstrated creative approaches to reach areas outside of the campaigns in their population centers. Just as their national organization, Community Chests and Councils, Inc., had asked President Roosevelt to enlist volunteer and professional Chest leaders to spearhead a national War Chest, volunteers in Alabama and Rhode Island asked their governors to call upon Chest and Council leaders to head statewide War Chests. According to Harold J. Seymour, author of *Design for Giving, the Story of the National War Fund, Inc. 1943–1947*, both governors charged these new state organizations with responsibility for "correlating local programs of health, welfare, and recreation agencies, and financing them in one annual united appeal."[6]

PAYROLL DEDUCTION GIVING AND
IN-PLANT FEDERATION WERE INITIATED

While levels of voluntary service and charitable giving were growing dramatically, more was needed. Leaders of business, industry, and organized labor took the lead in searching for large-scale approaches to increase involvement of their constituents. Community Chest/War Chest campaigns had shown double-digit increases, but were nearing the limits of their capacity to solicit and collect contributions. In 1943, community fund leaders hit upon an idea that would streamline and enhance workplace giving. They asked several major employers if they would withhold and transmit War Chest contributions from employee paychecks, just as they did tax and Social Security payments.

How Can Chests and Councils Help to Win the War? (See page 135)

Elwood Street, in "The United Way, A History," recounted the actions of Detroit's community fund leadership. "Since the [corporate] machines set up for computing and deducting tax payments had room for additional deductions, it was not too difficult to persuade employers to authorize Chest deductions. Organized labor favored this practice because it became possible to know the numbers as well as the amounts of employee gifts and to give labor credit for its impressive and growing share of support for united health and welfare services."[7] Within one year, over half of the affiliates of Community Chests & Council, Inc. reported that businesses in their communities were making use of payroll deduction giving, and by the end of 1945, payroll giving had become the mainstay of nearly every War Chest campaign.

THE MOVIE INDUSTRY DISPLAYED PATRIOTISM IN GIVING

The war years were a time when business advertising related products and services to defense and victory. This was particularly true in the motion picture industry in which the moviegoer's attention was focused on the drama of war and its impact on the lives of people. Heads of the movie studios continuously searched for more ways in which to involve their industry in supporting local and national efforts related to the war. One of the ways they found inadvertently created competition for the Los Angeles War Chest. It became known as "PCC," the Motion Pictures Permanent Charities Committee. Its genesis made sense.

In 1943, representatives of the major studios came together under the aegis of the Community Chest to search for ways to do more for "community and country." They determined that increased giving among their employees would make an important statement of "the concerns and patriotism" of motion picture personnel. Francis X. McNamara Jr. wrote in *Community* that "Studio executives felt that their employees would give more to their campaign if they had a hand in deciding how their combined contributions would be spent. The result was the creation of an approach to allocating contributions that was based on company-level donor perceptions of need, as opposed to that of the community-level Chest/Council committee volunteers. They formed their own Permanent Charities Committee, 'PCC,' as a move toward coordinated campaigning."[8] Motion picture employees, with representatives of their management, had made "in-plant" decisions on how their personal and company contributions should be allocated. Instead of entrusting their contributions to Chest and Council volunteers, the proceeds of the motion picture industry's employee campaigns arrived at the War Chest office with instructions for their use. This practice drew the attention of several national corporations that emulated the movie industry's approach. The practice became known as an "in-plant federation," because criteria for the allocation of employee contributions were made within company "plants," rather than at Community Chest offices. This approach, however, did not meet with the favor of those business and agency leaders whose participation in Chests and Councils had led them to value community-based federation decisions over the company-by-company decisions of "in-plant federations."

IN-PLANT FEDERATIONS WERE IDENTIFIED AS COMPETITORS

In-plant federations were discussed in national *Bulletin* articles as "competitors." Plans were laid to use business strategies to limit the growth of in-plant federations and within a few years, a "United Fund Chapter Plan" was introduced. It offered an alternative to the in-plant federation by designating employers and their employees as "chapters" of the community campaign and invited them to send representatives to serve as members of Chest and Council allocation committees. "The 'Chapter Plan' seems to have stemmed the tide of 'in-plant federation' by offering to company/employee group representatives the chance to participate in community-level decision-making. This approach offers increased responsibility to those who allocate Chest contributions compared to those who only allocate the funds raised within one company."[9] Even communities that did not adopt the Chapter Plan approach found value in inviting employers to suggest candidates for volunteer service on budget/allocation committees.

ORGANIZED LABOR AGREED TO SUPPORT
UNITED WORKPLACE CAMPAIGNS

Until this time, the leaders of trade unions had remained distant from Community Chest workplace campaigns. They had their own fund-raising programs that supported peer counseling programs and did not want to give up their leadership role in a "union service" that allowed members to help other members. They were also concerned that, by participating in combined union/nonunion workplace campaigns, union members and unions would not be recognized for their contributions because union members' gifts would be submerged within a grand total of corporate and employee giving. But in 1941, when the national leaders of the labor movement were asked to give direction to the Chest/Council movement, teamwork and cooperation between labor unions and the local affiliates of Community Chests and Councils, Inc. took a giant step forward. Progress began when representatives of the Committee for Industrial Organization (CIO) and American Federation of Labor (AFL) were elected to the board of Community Chests & Councils, Inc.[10] CCC and the national labor organizations could now jointly encourage their local affiliates to include labor representatives on Chest boards and to "organize employee solicitation with employers and unions working jointly."[11]

"In 1942," as reported in *Design for Giving*, "at the request of Community Chests, and later at the request of the American Red Cross, both the AFL and the CIO abandoned their plans for independent campaigns, and made common cause with the two annual major appeals—the Red Cross in the spring, and the Chest campaigns in the fall."[12] Later that year, a number of Chests and Councils offered support to local labor organizations for their programs to counsel members of labor unions on how to make effective use of public and private health and social service organizations. In Cincinnati, a "labor community service" program was instituted at the War Chest office. It was staffed by an individual employed from the ranks of organized labor.

Within a year, "labor staff" had also been employed in Kansas City, Pittsburgh, Chicago, Detroit, and Buffalo.[13] "Pete" Culver, in *An Angel with a Union Label: A History of the AFL-CIO Community Service Program*, characterized these new hires as indicative of the "broader federation of fund-raising and expansion of service. For organized labor," he wrote, "it means a unified and dynamic movement. . . . Through our partnership in service, we can do more for people."[14]

In 1944, a study of union members who were providing counseling to their "brothers and sisters" was conducted jointly by Councils in Detroit and Philadelphia. "Professional assistance is needed in planning and conducting training to familiarize the counselors with communities' facilities and teach them the elementary principles of interviewing and making referrals," the study concluded.[15] Within months, classroom training programs to teach union stewards how and when to make referrals to agencies were offered jointly by local union leaders and Chests in those cities. Representatives of agencies presented information on their services and how to get access to them. This "union counselor training," combined with targeted donor recognition programs for labor unions and their members, cemented a strong alliance between organized labor and the Chest/Council movement.

CAMPAIGNS ROSE TO MEET UNUSUAL NEEDS

Record contributions poured into local War Chest campaigns during this period. But for every new dollar that was made available for volunteers to allocate to local, national, and global needs, two more dollars were needed. CCC regularly reported stories of communities whose War Chest campaigns had doubled, even tripled prior year results. But no community had ever achieved the result that Madison, Wisconsin, reported in early 1942:

"The 1941 Madison fund-raising campaign met its goal of $100,000— a tiny 3 percent increase over the previous year," according to its executive secretary Carl Warmington. "The country hadn't recovered from the Great Depression of the 1930s; money was scarce and many people were still unemployed.

"At one of the early War Chest meetings, prominent community leaders discussed the campaign goal. Joseph C. Ford, chair of the first War Chest campaign, told them,

> *'I'm convinced the goal should be four times last year's because we have four times the needs. The goal must be $400,000.'*

I remember thinking how difficult it had been to raise 3,000 new dollars—and now the proposed goal would require raising 100 times that amount.

> *'Our country is at war,' Joe told the dozen men at the meeting. 'We are asking everyone to give to the War Chest four times the amount they gave last year.'*
>
> *[To union leaders, he said,] 'Your firm is getting war contracts and you'll be working plenty of overtime. . . . I'm prepared to go to your management and get you a five-cent-an-hour increase with two cents to be pledged to the War Chest.'*

"The campaign raised $412,000, a 312 percent increase over the 1941 campaign. National attention focused on Madison for this amazing fund-raising achievement. If the *Guinness Books of World Records* had been in existence then, the Madison War Chest would have been listed for its 312 percent increase, the highest federated fund-raising increase in one year."[16] Madison's 312 percent campaign increase stood as a beacon of leadership in 1942 when War Chest campaigns throughout the country averaged an 86 percent increase.

EXAMPLES OF NEW ROLES FOR CHESTS AND COUNCILS

The fund-raising and community planning success demonstrated by Chests and Councils brought invitations to them to apply their organizational skills in new fields of endeavor. Here are three examples for which documentation has been preserved.

FEDERATED CAPITAL CAMPAIGNS

Madison's success with War Chest fund-raising gave rise to the inclusion of agency capital (bricks and mortar) needs within their campaign goal. "I believe the adding of 17 percent to the goal for agency postwar building needs was the first of such a campaign," Carl Warmington wrote in his career recollections. He added, "Incidentally, we went well over the campaign goal that year, as well."[17] While the inclusion of capital needs in annual campaign goals did not become universal, Madison's approach spread to over a dozen communities.

URBAN-RURAL AND REGIONAL PLANNING

The expansion of manufacturing to vacant land outside of cities, coupled with the mass production of nearby tract housing, brought major challenges to the heretofore rural public agencies that were responsible for services such as roads, sanitation, and education. When newcomers asked if they could work together with long-time residents to deal with the problems brought about by the influx of "city folks," the people whose lives had been spent outside of cities resisted. After a number of failed attempts at working together to find ways to deal with increased youth vandalism in the communities surrounding Syracuse, New York, the Syracuse Council of Social Agencies was asked to help.

"On a humid July evening, a group of 50 men and women gathered at picnic tables in a local state park. . . . They represented nine different communities. . . . This picnic had been the culmination of three years of effort to achieve throughout our county community planning both for the individual village and for the whole county, city, and rural area," wrote Walter Driscoll, Council Secretary of the Syracuse Council of Social Agencies, in 1945.[18] He compared urban-rural relationships to those of the newly formed United Nations: ". . . the villages and towns fear the urban colossus in the same manner that small nations look suspiciously upon the aims of the 'Big 5.' And yet no clairvoyance is needed to foresee that growing anxiety over such problems as youthful delinquency and the needs of veterans might result in expensive duplication, poorly planned programs, and misdirected effort. Failure to achieve unity within the towns and cooperation among them might well result in chaos."[19] Building on the experience in Syracuse, other Chests and Councils were asked to assume roles as "community conveners." Their historical roles as conveners of agencies and their benefactors served as a strong foundation for this new role. Chests and Councils offered a cadre of professionals with skills in "community organization" and organizational structures whose concern for "community" was held in esteem by most citizens. People needed the skills these professionals brought to bear on increasingly complex community issues.

INTERRACIAL COMMUNICATION

As African Americans moved north to get war related jobs, racial tensions increased. This could be seen in workplaces, neighborhoods, and schools. People's lack of familiarity with fellow employees, neighbors, and classmates of different races and backgrounds manifested itself in fear, racism, and conflict. Neutral parties were needed to bring people together to resolve race relations issues, but it was hard to identify people and organizations who would be acceptable to both sides. The Council of Social Agencies in Kansas City, Missouri, was asked to help resolve mounting race relationship problems in its city. Recalling what he believes to be the first Council involvement in "diversity," United Way veteran Owen Davison wrote, "It took one hothead with red hair to stir white neighborhoods to stop the movement of African Americans into Kansas City. Our Council of Social Agencies assigned me to staff an effort to cool things down. With the help of a prominent manufacturing executive who desperately needed workers and a much respected African American school principal, we secured permission to bring representatives of black and white leadership together in KC's skyscraper City Council chambers. Using his position and experience as a Chest and Council volunteer, our school principal initiated a series of dialogues aimed at increasing mutual understanding of white and black people of one another's needs and values."[20]

"Do what you feel in your heart to be right—for you'll be criticized anyway. You'll be damned if you do, and damned if you don't."
—ELEANOR ROOSEVELT, *First Lady of the United States of America*

CODES OF ETHICS

In 1943, Detroit's Council of Social Agencies convened representatives of a variety of racial groups in their community to "give leadership and take a progressive step toward meeting serious [race relations] problems."[21] The result of their work defined a step toward improved race relations and served as a model for other communities. They developed a series of "codes of ethics" related to agency clientele (e.g., 'People in need of service should be served without regard to race.'), agency staff (e.g., 'In the selection of all staff members, an emotional, acceptable and an intellectual understanding of minority groups should be considered essential.'), and agency boards (e.g., 'Board members should be selected on the basis of their ability and interest, and the board should secure qualified representation in their membership for any racial group which is consistently represented in its community.').[22] Detroit's "codes" provided benchmarks for the Chest/Council movement and served as model statements of ethics and standards of behavior in hundreds of communities for Chests and Councils, their affiliates, and other nongovernmental organizations.

"RED FEATHER" BRAND BECOMES AGENCY DESCRIPTOR

By 1945, so many local Chest/Council organizations had adopted the "Red Feather" as their symbol that it was adopted by CCC as the national symbol of the Community Chest movement in the United States.[23] The next year, the Community Chests Division of the Canadian Welfare Council adopted the Red Feather with a circlet of twelve maple leaves as the national campaign symbol for Canadian Community Chests.[24] In 1945, the Red Feather had become the hallmark of local and national Community Chest public service advertising. Red-dyed feathers appeared in the hatbands of contributors and in storefront window displays that promoted local campaigns. The Red Feather became the recognized "brand identifier" of Community Chest campaigns in nearly every city. Member agencies, however, shared a problem. They were not so easily recognized. The leaders of Boston's United Fund found a solution.

Taking advantage of local radio and newspapers for their Red Feather campaign, representatives of Boston's United War Fund invited radio personalities George Burns and Gracie Allen to come to their community for a "major announcement." With the fanfare of a special radio broadcast and attendant newspaper coverage, George and Gracie announced that Fund agencies would, henceforth, be known as "Red Feather agencies."[25] The Red Feather became a hallmark of the value Chests and Councils placed on member agencies and was widely used on agency signage, stationery, and publications. Boston volunteers took a step that was to be followed by nearly every U.S. and Canadian Community Chest within the following year.

VOLUNTEER RECRUITMENT REFLECTED NATIONAL DEFENSE
The question, "How can I help?" was on the lips of every man and woman who was not in military service or an occupation designated as "critical" by the federal government. Voluntary efforts to help were visible everywhere. Most obvious were the USO shows and canteens. Motion picture stars volunteered as tour entertainers wherever military people were based.

Local USO Service Centers provided aid to service personnel in train and bus stations or city center locations. These were staffed by volunteer adults and teenagers. Youth organizations, scouts, and YMCAs mounted neighborhood drives for scrap paper and metal that could be used in manufacturing war materials. Children's household chores were expanded to include the collection of tin cans and cigarette and chewing gum foil wrappers for recycling. Added to their games were hunts for bits of string and cloth to be donated for use in manufacturing ammunition wadding.

Many communities' Chests and Councils followed Pittsburgh's 1941 lead in organizing volunteer service at the community level. Responding to the call of the Allegheny County Defense Council, the Pittsburgh Federation of Social Agencies had created the first Defense Volunteer Office. The Federation's written history records that in Pittsburgh, "The Civilian Defense Volunteer Office registered and directed 130,000 volunteers to civilian defense activities during the four years of war [1941–1945]."[26] The idea of centrally assembling an inventory of needs for volunteers, publicizing the needs, and advertising for people to fill the needs made use of the Federation's own volunteers and staff in a way that added value to each Chest and Council that copied the Pittsburgh approach. For the many communities that copied Pittsburgh's design, the Defense Volunteer Office became the forerunner of postwar "volunteer bureaus," which, with the help of local affiliates of the Junior League and National Council of Jewish Women, became centers for recruiting and placing volunteers in all manner of nonprofit and government organizations.

THE ADVENT OF THE ATOMIC AGE DIMMED
MEMORIES OF THE DEPRESSION

Not since the Revolutionary War victory had a western nation so quickly moved its vision from the past to the future. During one-half of a decade, preoccupation with past tribulations—world war, economic depression, massive unemployment, and natural disasters—were replaced with views of the future. Hopes for peace rested with a new organization, the United Nations. Dreams of prosperity were based on peacetime applications of the inventions and technology of war and the new jobs that increased manufacturing capacity. As nations and people recovered from years of war, pledges were made that caring nations would never again stand by while others carried out atrocities against humanity.

Drawings by Gluyas Williams, reproduced by permission of the S. D. Warren Co. and the Albany, N. Y. Community Chest.

Local community social planners and fund raisers were proud of their wartime achievements. None could guess at the profound social and urban changes that would follow the years of world war. Everyone knew that visions of the future would depend on agencies focusing more on preventing problems for the future, than solving problems of the past. The years of recovery from economic depression had required empathy. The years of war had required action. The dawning of the Atomic Age invited discovery.

Key Innovations in the United Way of Serving Communities Between 1941 and 1945

1941	Community and War Funds unite	Pittsburgh, PA
1941	First WWII War Chest introduced	Pasadena, CA
1941	Civilian Defense volunteers recruited	Pittsburgh, PA
1941	First industry-wide in-plant federation formed	Hollywood, CA
1942	Racial tensions addressed	Kansas City, MO
1942	First statewide War Chest campaigns begun	Rhode Island and Alabama
1942	Labor community services staff hired	Cincinnati, OH
1942	Quadrupled campaign results achieved	Madison, WI
1943	Workplace payroll deduction giving introduced	Detroit, MI
1944	Union counselor training established	Detroit, MI and Philadelphia, PA
1944	Interracial code adopted	Detroit, MI
1945	Agencies identified as "Red Feather" services	Boston, MA
1945	Capital funds for agency building included in campaign goal	Madison, WI
1945	Rural-urban planning initiated	Syracuse, NY

---

[1] Blanchard, Ralph H. "Federation Looks Ahead, Three Cs Chief Remembers the Past and Eyes the Future." *Community*, Community Chests & Councils of America, June 1955, p. 183.

[2] Blanchard, p. 183.

[3] "Community Leadership, the Larger Issue." *The Bulletin of Community Chests and Councils*, February 1942, p. 1.

[4] ibid, p. 24.

[5] ibid.

[6] Seymour, Harold J. *Design for Giving, the Story of the National War Fund, Inc., 1943–1947.* New York: Harper & Brothers, 1947, p. viii.

[7] Street, Elwood. "The United Way, A History." Unpublished memoirs on file at the University of Minnesota Social Welfare History Archives, 1958, p. 412.

[8] McNamara, Francis X., Jr. "Centralization, the Los Angeles Story." *Community*, September-October 1971.

[9] ibid.

[10] *People & Events, A History of the United Way*. United Way of America, 1977, p. 91.

[11] "AFL and CIO Cooperate with Appeals." *Bulletin*, Community Chests & Councils, Inc., August 17, 1941.

[12] Seymour, p. 97.

[13] "A Silver Anniversary: Labor Marks 25 Years of Participation in the United Way." *Community*, United Community Funds & Councils of America, May-June 1967, p. 12.

[14] Culver, B.G. *Leo Perlis, An Angel with a Union Label, A History of the AFL-CIO Community Service Program*. New York: Jewett, 1996, p. 177.

[15] Krughoff, Merrill. "New Retail Outlet for Social Work, Union Counseling's an Aid in Getting People and Services Together." *Bulletin*, April 1946, p. 144.

[16] Warmington, Carl. "A Legacy of Leadership." *Community*, February 1987, pp. 17-18.

[17] Warmington. Personal correspondence with the author, January 2000.

[18] Driscoll, C. Walter. "It Started with a Picnic and Developed into a Program of Rural-Urban Community Planning." *Community*, November 1945, p. 52.

[19] ibid, p. 53.

[20] Davison, Owen R. Personal correspondence with the author, January 2002.

[21] "Inter-Racial Code." *Community*, March 1944, p. 111.

[22] ibid.

[23] *People & Events*, p. 60.

[24] *Community*, February 1946, cover story.

[25] Meyer, T. Spencer. "You Can Knock 'Em Over With a Feather." *Community*, May 1946, p. 90.

[26] "Then Came War." *Impact, A History of the Health and Welfare Planning Association 1922–1991*. 1992, p. 10.

CHAPTER FIVE

Responding to Demographic Phenomena

1946—1959

Stretching to Meet Postwar Social and Urban Challenges

S prawl. "By most accounts, nothing moved the suburbs so efficiently toward sprawl as a certain stroke of President Dwight Eisenhower's pen, signing into law the Federal-Aid Highway Act of 1956, which launched a 41,000-mile interstate highway system."[1] *National Geographic* senior editor John Mitchell identified this signal of postwar change in the U.S. as the one most significant factors that led millions of young families to dream of an idyllic life outside of crowded cities, a life without traffic jams, high taxes, or pollution. Between 1946 and 1959, one-sixth of America's population, 25 million people, moved from cities to suburbs in "one of the most astounding voluntary migrations in history."[2]

As children of the postwar "baby boom" entered school, they carried with them their parents' dreams that they would reach higher levels of educational and career achievement than their forebears had. For many of those parents, the hours tied up in commuting to and from their postwar jobs limited the time they could spend watching their dreams come true. As breadwinners spent after-school hours at work and in their cars, agencies were needed to fill the voids their absences left for their children. Boy and Girl Scouts, YMCAs and YWCAs, and Boys and Girls Clubs were among the agencies which, in effect, were asked to serve as surrogate parents.

Millions of jobs that were relocated to the suburbs also took more young families with them.[3] As urban-dwelling older people waved goodbye to their young relatives, they also said farewell to the local income and sales taxes that had supported public services. As the families left city housing, their homes and apartments were subdivided and rented to the lower income people who remained in the city. As a result, urban service needs increased as quickly as those in the suburbs. Elderly people who hadn't left their old neighborhoods no longer had families close enough to provide meals, socialization, and trips to the doctor. Services were needed to help them remain independent. Many of those who had come to the cities for jobs during World War II did not leave. They filled vacant jobs and dwelling places as quickly as they became available. They needed job training and family support services, and their children needed after-school services.

Planning councils studied and articulated the service needs of the cities as well as suburbs. Agencies were convened to plan and design services for two distinctly different population groups: urban and suburban. Community Chests scrambled to find the money to help agencies cover the costs of new and expanded services in old and new locations, but couldn't raise enough. Hundreds of new suburban Chests were created by suburbanites out of their frustration with the inability of city-based fund-raising organizations to produce enough money to meet the needs of their growing communities. Competition for contributions between urban and suburban Chests began, initiating fund-raising rivalries that would continue for decades.

The challenges of suburbanization, along with population growth, stretched America's social fabric in ways that made its flaws increasingly visible. In *The Fifties*, David Halberstam explained why the population grew. "Young men who had spent three or four years fighting overseas were eager to get on with their lives; so, too, were the young women who had waited for them at home. Everything else in the United States seemed to be booming, so why not the production of children as well?"[4]

Newspaper headlines pointed to society's increasing flaws: "Mental Illness is Greatest Single Health Problem," "Courts Consider Racial Discrimination in Schools," "Jim Crow Rules the South," "Suburban Schools Add Second Shifts," "Subdividing City's Apartments Yields Health Problems."

Mitchell's *National Geographic* article offered an honest look at the major cause of the changes during the years that followed World War II: "It was thought at the time that the interstates would facilitate the evacuation of central cities in the event that our Cold War nemesis might post an intercontinental ballistic missile into city hall. Voilà! A warhead did explode, but it wasn't nuclear.

"It was sprawl."[5]

For Community Chests and Councils, "sprawl" meant more than reaching ever-increasing campaign goals. For them, "sprawl" would lead to fundamental changes in the ways in which they carried out their missions. Unlike their predecessors, they were challenged to do more *and* to do things differently than they had done them throughout their history.

Signs of the Times

GLOBAL/NATIONAL EVENTS

1950s	The equal rights movements gained momentum among African Americans, other minorities, and women.
1950–1953	The Korean War was fought.
1955	Rosa Park's "civil disobedience" gained national attention.
1957	Little Rock, Arkansas, Central High School was integrated.
1957	The U.S. entered the Vietnam War.

IN THE NEWS

1946	ENIAC, the world's first computer was introduced.
1948	Israel achieved statehood.
1949	The North Atlantic Treaty Organization (NATO) was established.
1953	The structure of DNA was discovered.

1954	The U.S. Supreme Court's *Brown v. Board of Education* decision ended the public education doctrine of "separate but equal."
1956	Congress authorized the building of a U.S. interstate highway system.
1959	The computer chip was patented.

STATE/LOCAL COMMUNITIES & NEIGHBORHOODS

| 1946 | Housing, transportation, and manufacturing booms generated urban sprawl, unplanned growth of cities, and the rapid growth of suburbs. |

SOCIAL MOVEMENTS/GOVERNMENTAL POLICIES & PROGRAMS

1946	Congress passed the GI Bill, guaranteeing home and education loans for returning war veterans.
1946	Rent controls were enacted by Congress.
1946	Congress approved the Hill-Burton Act to match local funds for hospital construction.
1948	President Truman banned racial discrimination in federal employment.
1953	The U.S. Department of Health, Education, and Welfare was created.
1955	Congress created the Civil Rights Commission and a civil rights division in the U.S. Attorney General's office.

ECONOMY/BUSINESS CYCLES AND THE WORKPLACE

1948 & 1954	Postwar economic recessions.
1948	Price controls were implemented to curb inflation.
1951	The minimum wage was raised from 40 to 75 cents per hour.
1955	Unemployment reached a record 65 million; the minimum wage was raised to $1 per hour.

SCIENCE AND TECHNOLOGY

1949	The American Cancer Society took a stand against cigarette smoking.
1950	Fluoridated water was shown to reduce tooth decay.
1952	A polio epidemic struck over 50,000 victims.

1954	Virologist Jonas Salk tested a polio vaccine.
1954	The Canadian Broadcasting Company experimented with in-school telecasts.
1955	Albert Sabin developed an oral polio vaccine.
1955	Russia launched Sputnik, spurring Congress to fund increased scientific education and research.

DEMOGRAPHY

| 1945–1959 | The dramatic postwar birth rate was labeled a "baby boom." |
| 1951 | The total population of Canada passed 14 million. U.S. population reached 150 million. |

FAMILY/HOUSEHOLD STRUCTURE

| - | Prewar "extended family" housing gave way to "nuclear" family homes. |
| - | Women in the wartime workforce were required to relinquish jobs to returning GIs. |

HUMAN NEEDS

| - | Racial discrimination and the lack of equal educational opportunities accented a growing racial disparity in economic and employment opportunities. |

How Approaches Reflected the Needs and the Times

Most people were anxious to be part of the bright future they were sure would follow two world wars and a devastating depression. In his retrospective of the 1950s, Halberstam said, " . . . the American Dream was to exercise personal freedom, not in social or political terms, but rather in economic ones."[6] Parents wanted their children to do better than the parents had. That desire was translated into expectations that local agencies and institutions would provide the education and personal skills that would allow children to compete successfully in a job market that was quickly becoming more white collar than blue.

"The history of United Way is the story of the American spirit of volunteerism, caring and community. It is our nation at its best and it is a privilege and a joy to help write new chapters."
—JOE TOLAN, *President and CEO, Metro United Way, Louisville, Kentucky*

Councils, Chests, and agencies all wanted to do what they could to be sure that services for the current and future generations were better than they had been for the generations that preceded them. This led Councils to develop community-wide "comprehensive community surveys and plans" that painted health, recreation, and social services on a community-wide canvas. Concepts of "integrated service planning" challenged representatives of agencies to look more at "community needs" than "agency needs." Campaign goals rose as fund-raising volunteers and staff stretched to meet the newly identified needs.

Leadership Characteristics

Thanks to the GI Bill, hundreds of professionally trained veterans, mostly male, were pouring out of schools of social work. Demands for increased campaigns produced more than enough jobs to absorb these Chest/Council career seekers. Before too long, staff professionals in larger city Community Chests and Planning Councils were required to have Master of Social Work (MSW) degrees.

Volunteer profiles changed, as well. The proliferation of agencies after the war led businessmen to question the ability of agency representatives on Chest and Council boards to remain impartial in their decision-making. Could agency representatives maintain perspective on the needs of all agencies when they had originally been recruited to represent individual agencies? Could they focus on the needs of "community" as opposed to "agencies?" The answers to these questions led to the replacement of volunteers who had been assigned to their Chest and Council roles by agencies with volunteers who were asked to serve as representatives of the community.

In 1956, the Community Chests and Councils of Columbus, Ohio; Pittsburgh, Pennsylvania; and New York City restructured their boards and committees. Most agency representatives were replaced by community representatives from large companies; government, religious, and educational groups; and organized labor. During the years following World War II, Councils stepped out of their historical roles as conveners of representatives of agencies and redefined themselves as "impartial conveners of both community/donor and agency representatives." At the same time, Community Chests began to reconstitute their boards and committees with people who would place donors' concerns about meeting community needs ahead of agencies' concerns for meeting budgetary needs.

"The history of our United Way movement is reflective of a quilt of many people caring and striving to "together" improve the human condition in their local communities. I am indeed honored and feel privileged to have the opportunity to be part of this integral quilt of caring."

—MARIA CHAVEZ WILCOX, *President & CEO,*
United Way of Orange County, California

YOUTH AND WOMEN WERE INVITED TO TAKE LEADERSHIP ROLES

In 1957, young people were invited to take part in what traditionally had been an "adults only" community service when the Kansas City Planning Council created a public school-based youth planning council. *Community* magazine described the Kansas City "Junior Officer" program as "giving young people an opportunity to participate as citizens in civic activities."[7] Through this program, high school students served as board members and officers of school-based "Councils of Services for Youth." Young people reviewed their own needs for after-school and other services such as recreation, counseling, and employment. The content of the Youth Council reports was shared with appropriate standing committees of the main Council. Periodically, officers of the Youth Councils were given opportunities to present their groups' reports personally to the Planning Council board of directors.

The first female campaign chair was claimed by Durham, North Carolina's Community Chest in a 1952 issue of *Community*: "Mary Duke Trent will direct the Chest campaign in Durham in the fall—the first woman ever selected for the job."[8] Even though women had been instrumental in creating the first community-wide campaign federation (Denver, 1887) and the first Council of Social Agencies (Cincinnati, 1913), they had not been called upon to lead the groups. This was consistent with historical definitions of their roles, not their creativity or industriousness, since much of the day-to-day work of these organizations was performed by women.

LOANED EXECUTIVES AND STUDENT
INTERNS SUPPLEMENTED STAFF

The Community Chest and Council in Utica, New York, in cooperation with Utica College, employed student interns in 1952. Writing for *Community* magazine, Raymond Simon, an instructor in public relations for Utica College of Syracuse University, described the program as "an experiment in public relations [training] which may have far-reaching importance for a great many other Chests and Councils." He described the program as "an 'internship' in which students write releases for local newspapers, radio, and TV stations; speak before boards and committees . . . and in general, take care of all the daily public relations and publicity chores which the average agency executive is too busy to handle."[9]

LOANED EXECUTIVES SUPPLEMENTED CAMPAIGN STAFF

Chuck Devine, retired president of the Seattle United Way, told of his predecessor's creative request of local manufacturers to "loan some of their senior executives to the campaign to supplement the efforts of full-time campaign staff members. While they didn't call them 'loaned executives,' they did the very things that became the hallmarks of loaned executive programs in nearly every major city."[10] Jack Dillencourt, Seattle's executive director at that time, added, "San Francisco had tried borrowing junior executive staff for several weeks with some success, so I suggested that we get a group of senior executives for nine weeks. My campaign chairman asked if I was crazy, but we ended up recruiting nine senior executives for nine weeks. The program was so successful that we got two dozen the next year."[11]

"Throughout our history United Way has been revered as the local champion for those most in need. I'm proud to be part of this rich heritage, with experience as both a volunteer and professional leader."

—MARK L. WALKER, *President & CEO, United Way Silicon Valley, California*

LEADERS DEBATED: SHOULD COMMUNITY FEDERATIONS BE AGENCY-DRIVEN OR DONOR-DRIVEN?

"Two Roads to Federation" were debated at national and regional meetings convened by Community Chests & Councils of America. Proceedings of the 1955 Midwest Conference captured two divergent perspectives on the "right" role for community-based planning, fund-raising, and fund distribution. Adherence to the traditional Community Chest organizational structure was defended by the board president of the Cleveland Welfare Federation. A newly emerging "United Fund" approach was represented by the Detroit United Fund's chief volunteer. In 1949, he and his fellow board members had agreed to abandon the Detroit Chest's traditional structure in favor of a shape that was designed to unify all fund-raising drives by nonprofit health, recreation, and welfare agencies in their community.[12] This was the first such organizational experiment, according to John Seeley in *Community Chest*.[13]

The "Community Chest Way," the traditional organizational structure based on agency representation, was presented by John A. Greene, president of the Ohio Bell Telephone Company and chairman of the Cleveland Welfare Federation. "We are not forgetting that the Community Chest idea started in Cleveland, and we're not going to pull down the Chest flag yet. But we have always tried to keep it up to date. We have an open door policy that will take in any organization that can meet our requirements."[14]

In contrast, "The United Fund Way," an organizational structure based on donor representation, was outlined by Ray Eppert, an officer of The Burroughs Corporation and president of Detroit's United Fund board. His comments described Detroit's new organizational approach, the goal of which was to consolidate appeals for contributions, as opposed to meeting the needs of a set group of agencies.

"Giving is no longer developing in an evolutionary pattern," he said. "It has become literally a revolution and must be recognized as such." He reminded the audience that "United Funds, like our businesses, depend on good planning to maintain the interest and enthusiasm of donors, educational and promotional efforts, and a periodic study to see if results are being accomplished." He concluded by asking the audience if they, in their communities, were reducing the "increasing annoyance of many appeals" and cautioned them to "beware of obsolescence."[15]

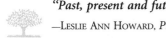

"Past, present and future—we have always been about impact."
—LESLIE ANN HOWARD, *President United Way of Dane County, Wisconsin*

Cleveland's advocate of the Community Chest model retorted, "There is no doubt but that the united campaign would reduce the number of drives somewhat in Cleveland, but it would by no means end them. We're not going to bribe anybody to come in, and we don't want any shotgun weddings, nor will we give up a proper budgetary control." He concluded, with concurrence of his adversary, "We both believe in progress, but we are certain that every town has to decide for itself what form progress should take in light of its own local history, local traditions, local people, and their knowledge of local problems and sense of local responsibility."[16]

CAMPAIGN STRUCTURES BEGAN TO DEAL
WITH MULTIPLE CAMPAIGNS

In most communities, managing the conflicting issues on which the Midwest Conference debate had been based was becoming the daily business of federated campaign leaders. They found themselves juggling conflicting demands of agencies and donors. Both wanted to control the list of agencies participating in the campaign and the membership of committees that were responsible for allocating contributions at the end of the campaign. Agencies claimed that they best knew the needs of clients and community, and they wanted to restrict the list of agencies participating in the campaign to those that met their community's needs as federation members saw them. Donors wanted to use the organization to limit the number of appeals for their contributions by combining all of the separate charitable campaigns into one united effort.

Chest and Council board members in most communities concluded that both sides of the debate had merit. They reconstituted their organizations in ways that might best be described as *donor-driven campaigns* that were conducted *for* federations of agencies and *collaborative planning and allocation programs* in which decisions were made by representatives of donors *and* agencies. In some communities, those functions were combined into one organization. In others, fund-raising was organizationally separated from planning. The responsibility for allocating campaign proceeds went with as many United Funds as it did with Social Planning Councils.

"The greatest challenge has three parts. You have to do all three if you are going to be effective. The challenge is to be mission-focused, values-based, and demographics-driven."

—FRANCES HESSELBEIN, *Past President, Girl Scouts of America*

Between 1950 and 1959, the leaders of Funds designed a variety of organizational models to reduce the number of fund-raising campaigns.

Detroit is credited with creating the "first modern United Fund."[17] Volunteers there attacked the problem of a growing number of separate charitable campaigns in two steps. First, they reconstituted their board with "donor" or "citizen" representatives. Then, the new board, with the full support of corporate executives, invited the agencies that were conducting separate campaigns to join a single, community-wide effort. The invitation made it clear that the agencies' continued support depended on their acceptance of the invitation to join the "United Foundation's Torch Drive."

Most cities followed Detroit's lead, while corporate leaders in several cities tried other approaches to reduce the number of separate campaigns in their communities.

ASSOCIATED IN-GROUP DONORS (AID)
WAS TRIED IN LOS ANGELES

In 1951, leaders of the Los Angeles Community Chest took what Frank McNamara, who would become its general manager years later, termed a "dramatic step in an attempt to systemize and coordinate fund-raising. They had no idea that donors would care as much about the needs for which their money was used as they did for convenience of giving once for all through AID [Associated In-Group Donors]."[18] He described their discovery in a *Community* magazine article.

"Realizing their failure to raise the vast dollars needed for social services on their own and beginning to feel the real impact of in-plant federation [campaigns for groups of agencies selected within individual companies] monies going to non-Chest agencies, the Chest leaders joined with a concerned group of business executives and labor leaders to form AID, the single drive that would eliminate multiple appeals for employees. All Chest accounts with payroll deduction were transferred to AID, with the Chest receiving a formulated percentage of all AID contributions. AID permitted employee designation for any and all social service agencies and charitable organizations anywhere in the world.

"As AID grew," McNamara continued, "Chest leaders encountered a problem they had not foreseen . . . once corporate chief executives had enrolled their companies and employees in the AID program, they felt their fund-raising problems (multiple campaign solicitations) were solved. Unknowingly, they were considering fund-raising as the end, rather than the *means* to an end. The emphasis on raising dollars with little consideration for allocating based on need was to eventually lead to the downfall of the

AID program. Leaders lost interest as they became less and less involved in the action—*the decisions* [about how contributions would be allocated]."[19]

LOCAL HEALTH FEDERATIONS WERE TRIED

In 1952, the corporate leaders who represented the majority of the directors of the Champaign-Urbana Community Fund in Illinois brought representatives of their local and national health agencies together. According to Dan MacDonald, former executive secretary of the organization, the corporate executives advised the health agency leaders that corporations would support their campaigns only if they took part in a spring campaign to be conducted on their behalf by the Community Fund. Most agreed to do so.[20]

"What lies behind us and what lies before us are tiny matters compared to what lies within us."
—RALPH WALDO EMERSON

A less arbitrary approach to multiple health campaigns was taken by members of the Lorain, Ohio, Community Chest soon thereafter. Medical, hospital, and university community leaders were invited to join the leaders of national health agencies' local affiliates to develop a solution to the problem of multiple campaigns in Lorain. The Community Chest-directed result was known as the "United Health Foundation." According to Amos Burrows, former Community Chest executive secretary, the resulting organization served as a "classic Community Chest fund-raising organization whose campaign results were divided on a predetermined formula by representatives of each participating agency."[21]

People & Events describes the steps that leaders in Durham, North Carolina, took: "Concurrent to the formation of a statewide United Medical Research Foundation, the Durham United Fund founded the Durham Dread Disease Society." According to Burrows, "It did not include any chapters of national health or disease agencies. It provided a locally managed alternative for contributors frustrated by so many disease agencies' campaigns. It funded medical research, patient services, and health education under the supervision of local health professionals."[22]

In 1958, the board members of the newly reorganized United Fund of

Metropolitan Boston determined that the components of medical research and health education were missing from the "package" of agencies they had presented to the community during their first campaign under its new structure. An article in *Community* described their action to form a "medical foundation" and incorporate it into the following year's campaign: "The abstention of certain [health agencies] from the United Fund created a somewhat anomalous situation. In a sense it severely restricted the area of medicine to which the United Fund giver might contribute."[23]

BALTIMORE'S COMMERCE AND INDUSTRY COMBINED HEALTH APPEAL (CICHA) FELL SHORT OF ITS OBJECTIVES

Driven by the Mayor's Fund-Raising Campaign Coordinating Council position that it would not approve solicitations by individual health agencies after 1960, CICHA was formed to mount a 1959 combined health agency campaign. The drive, however, lost the city's endorsement when the March of Dimes refused to cooperate with the joint effort. Leaders of that agency refused to place their program funding decisions in the hands of people less involved with their clientele.[24] Other health agencies following the March of Dimes lead and withdrew from the combined campaign.

Even though a number of large and popular health agencies dropped out of Baltimore's CICHA, leaders of the appeal attempted to nationalize their approach. The Baltimore plan was replicated in a number of east coast cities, but the program floundered because of its inability to combine all health appeals and the CICHA movement died out.

NATIONAL AGENCIES OPPOSED CHANGES IN FEDERATION

As campaigns increased their efforts to "Put All Begs In One Askit"[25] [put all requests for funds into a single request]most national health agencies mandated that their local chapters could no longer continue to participate in federated campaigns. They based this requirement on their view that their affiliates could raise more money by conducting separate campaigns and the use of contributions to find cures for cancer, tuberculosis, heart disease, etc. would be better determined nationally, instead of locally by volunteer allocation committees.

Heated arguments, locally and nationally, ensued between health agency and federated campaign leaders. Contributing to the difficulty was the fact that Funds and Councils were locally autonomous and the health agencies were not. Local citizens couldn't make all of the decisions. For this reason, most cities found it impossible to pull their national health agency affiliates into a United Fund as Detroit had prior to the health agencies' prohibition of local federation participation.

"Ultimately, United Ways and service providers must report results to the total community—a confluence of contributors, service providers, community institutions, public and private partners—and tangibly demonstrate how together, rather than apart, United Way builds strong and healthy communities."

—José Peña, *Past President & CPO United Way of Eastern Fairfield County, Connecticut*

DETROIT'S UNITED FUND MODEL BECAME THE INDUSTRY STANDARD

Over the years, most of the models that had been aimed at developing cooperation among health agency leaders and reducing the number of fund-raising campaigns fell short of expectations. Perhaps they could not bring the affiliates of large national health agencies to campaign in harmony with the local health, recreation, and welfare agencies. Or perhaps, as the AID program had demonstrated, campaign donors would not continue to support a *convenient means without supportable end.* Detroit's model prevailed, however. Corporate leaders had joined together in a position that if health agencies were to qualify for any contributions from their companies, they would have to subject themselves to the same independent scrutiny that has characterized Community Chest budget committee reviews of social services. In addition, Detroit's business leaders insisted that the health agencies in their community present themselves in the context of a community-wide pattern of services. Whether the health agencies finally came to share the business leaders' point of view or simply followed their edicts to survive is not known. What *is* known, however, is that Detroit's "united fund" model became the predominant campaign approach. Throughout the U.S. and Canada during the remainder of the 1950s and into the next decade, many donors insisted that to qualify for their contributions, health, recreation, and welfare agencies had to join together to present a common picture of community needs and justify their roles in meeting those needs.

Ralph Blanchard articulated the prevailing value that supported the proliferation of Detroit's model in his comments at the 1955 Midwest Conference of Community Chests & Councils of America. "The most important task of the United Funds today," he said, "is the synthesizing and harmonizing of national and local health and welfare needs and services. The elimination of appeals is important, of course, with its attendant saving of leadership and manpower, but the goal that transcends all others is the development of a well-rounded program of national and local health and welfare services."[26]

NEW GIVING AND GEOGRAPHIC DIMENSIONS
FOR ANNUAL CAMPAIGNS

Annual campaigns continued growing without disruption in most communities as organizational structures underwent changes. Innovation in techniques also continued, but not at the prewar rate. Fortunately, the operational creations of past decades met the needs of Chests and Councils as they dealt with increasing numbers of employers and larger geographic areas.

In Washington, DC, five independent fund-raising organizations serving nearby Virginia and Maryland communities were brought together into a single, regional campaign organization. At the same time, the agencies' social planning councils were restructured to serve the same geographic area under the name Health and Welfare Council for the National Capital Area.[27]

A different geographic challenge faced the Community Funds of Kansas City, Kansas, and Kansas City, Missouri, during the early 1950s. The wide-open farm land that had surrounded their cities was filling with businesses, factories, and residential neighborhoods. Volunteers from both organizations met together to find a way to see that the river that separated the two cities didn't keep them from consolidating the campaigns of 88 communities within five counties into the Heart of America United Campaign. Their teamwork demonstrated that local initiatives could consolidate the needs of more than one state into one *local* campaign organization.[28]

Finally, when asked by volunteers from Community Chest organizations from a number of small South Carolina communities, Charlotte, NC executive director Gorman Mattison hired three young staff professionals from the Michigan United Way. He asked them to apply their Michigan experience to create Carolinas United, the first two-state organization known to Community Chests and Councils of America. Dave Atwood, "Shorty" Meador, and Tony Williamson crafted the organization so that it could provide campaign and social planning assistance to three sizes of cities within the two states.[29]

GIVING GUIDES WERE INTRODUCED

Suggested levels of giving for hourly employees and corporations were seen for the first time during this period. The 1949 Detroit campaign featured a "Fair Share Guide" for employees who gave at work. The recommended standard was "Only one hour of pay during each month you are employed."[30] Cleveland made use of "Yardsticks for Corporate Giving" during the 1951 campaign. At the biennial Community Chests & Councils of America Conference in 1952, Kenneth Sturges, retired senior executive with the Cleveland Community Chest, noted that, "The yardstick plan should aim to win the confidence and cooperation of corporation donors by proving that it is equitable and practicable."[31] Yardsticks combined factors such as number of employees, net profits, and giving levels in comparable industries to produce recommended levels of corporate giving.

Fair Share on the Hoof

"Chester" was the name of the 1,120 pound Hereford steer that was presented to the chairman of the 1946 Yonkers, New York, Community Chest campaign. While in-kind giving wasn't new to agencies, such a gift was new to community-wide campaigns. This in-kind gift needed President Truman's action to lift postwar meat controls before it could be auctioned for $500. According to a cover story in the November 1946 *Community* magazine, Chester "pastured contentedly in the center of the business district" while awaiting dispensation.

COMMUNITY CHEST AND RED CROSS CAMPAIGNS WERE CONSOLIDATED

The consolidation of independent Community Chest and Red Cross campaigns during the 1950s led to further changes in the structure, name, and look of local federated campaign organizations.

Following World War II, most local affiliates of the American National Red Cross had followed a directive of their national office to leave the local War Chest and conduct separate annual campaigns.[32] Donor sensitivity to multiple campaigns was magnified by the existence of separate campaigns by the two organizations to whom most gave their largest contributions: the fall Community Chest campaign and the spring Red Cross drive.

Following the development of a 1955 national agreement between Community Chests & Councils of America and the American National Red Cross that supported local development of a joint campaign, corporate donors in many communities pressed for consolidation of their fundraising programs. Their efforts gave rise to a reconstitution of the relationship these organizations had enjoyed as part of the War Chest. Symbolic of their joint campaigns with Red Cross, most Community Chests adopted names such as United Appeal, United Fund, United Crusade, and United Good Neighbors. Some only changed the names of their campaigns; others changed the names of their organizations.

In addition to new names, new logos were adopted. Some modified their "Red Feather" logos to include the Red Cross. Others adopted a nationally developed "U" and used the common slogan, "You put the 'U' in the United Fund [or Appeal, Crusade, etc.]."

 "If one is lucky, a solitary fantasy can totally transform one million realities."

—MAYA ANGELOU, *Poet*

PLANNING COORDINATION AND TEAMWORK
INCREASED AS CAMPAIGNS WERE REFOCUSED

As campaign organizations were changing from being agency-driven to being driven by donors, social planning volunteers and professionals began to take a hard look at local Council structures. They questioned whether similar changes could be made in social planning and allocations functions without losing agencies' knowledge of needs for services. They wanted answers to these questions:

- Were the best intentions of the agency representatives who populated committees and boards as community oriented and impartial as they hoped to be?
- Why did problem identification lead to studies, instead of action?
- Why were so many of their plans gathering dust on the shelf instead of being implemented?

Council leaders from all over the U.S. and Canada watched with great interest as the members of the Health and Welfare Federation in Pittsburgh explored these questions. When the exploration was over, Pittsburgh's leaders produced the most significant change in community planning since Cleveland's agency leaders formed the first Council of Social Agencies in 1909.

In answering their questions, the Pittsburgh volunteers raised fundamental issues about the ways in which their community's social planning institution was/was not working. Readers of the July 1949 issue of *The Assembly Letter* (a monthly publication of the National Social Welfare Assembly) read a no-holds-barred description of the volunteers' findings. Many realized that Pittsburgh's findings described the state of social planning in general.

1. There has been a lack of adequate structure through which to plan. Without an adequate planning structure, the process of interrelationships becomes extremely difficult . . .

2. Real planning has been at a minimum. Much of what we have called planning has actually been coordination, teamwork, or united action . . .

3. Local communities have not always recognized their responsibilities for teamwork with state and national groups. It was only natural under such circumstances for state and national organizations to build their relationships with their local affiliate or constituency rather than with the local community . . .[33]

The "Assembly" reported the recommendations that came to reshape voluntary social planning in Pittsburgh and most other cities in Canada and the U.S.

1. Development of an adequate planning structure. Such a structure must be broadly representative of the community, so that it can speak for the community and not just for the established agencies.

2. Adherence to community organization principles. This approach calls for more planning and less promotion, for more community organization and less community pressure on behalf of a particular program.[34]

Change did not come easily to the representatives of Pittsburgh's health, recreation, and welfare agencies. They didn't want to let go. But, with the help of a 1957 Pennsylvania Economy League study, the "Federation" was restructured as the Health and Welfare Association of Allegheny County, an association of citizens.[35]

Other communities quickly adopted Pittsburgh's model with hopes that it would, as recommended in Pittsburgh, "solve community problems by enabling the planning organization to respond more quickly to the varied demands of the day, putting more emphasis on comprehensive planning, as well as program development, and bringing a greater variety of citizens into its activities and policy-making areas."[36]

ENVIRONMENTAL SCANNING SERVED AS THE
BASIS OF A MULTIYEAR PRIORITY PLAN

Multiyear forecasts of human needs and strategies to meet them were described by the Pittsburgh volunteers who cochaired the development of the first "environmental scan." All available social, economic, demographic, service financing, service beneficiary, and service delivery data was assembled as a reference to priority planning committees. Relative priorities for the financing of *all* public and private health, recreation, and welfare services in their city were organized into a "Priority Determination Plan." In their plan, they grouped agencies into categories they called "fields of service"[37] and looked at programs and services without regard to the sources of funds that agencies used to provide them.

PLANNERS LED AN ARRAY OF SOCIAL CHANGES

Social planning achievements of this period ranged from the specific to the sublime. Thanks to "Project Unshackle" undertaken by the Council of Spartanburg, highly focused attention saw to it that the use of chain gangs in South Carolina was ended.[38]

With a far broader perspective, Louisville's Social Planning Council teamed up with the Junior League to formulate a *community-wide* plan for the coordination and development of the fine arts and the creation of the Louisville Community Fine Arts Council. Simultaneously, in Canada, the Community Chest of Hamilton, Ontario, created a city Arts Council, and the Vancouver Council led the creation of the province-wide British Columbia Council of Fine Arts.[39]

In New York state, Councils got the help of the State Charities Aid Association to create and staff a State Association of Councils of Social Agencies, "in order to channel information to local health and welfare planning groups on specific matters of legislation being considered in Albany that would effect the services of agencies."[40] In 1956, Councils assigned representatives to their state legislatures and registered them as lobbyists to "influence, through education, the facts of human conditions."[41] Subsequently, statewide reforms of public welfare and employment services involved representatives from Councils throughout the state.

"It is an extraordinary privilege for me to be associated with United Way of King County. We are the leading human services provider, improving our community and changing lives for the better every single day."

—JON FINE, *CEO, United Way of King County, Washington*

COMPREHENSIVE COMMUNITY SURVEY CONDUCTED

In 1952, Merrill Krughoff, a member of the United Community Funds & Councils of America staff who was highly regarded for his strategic planning skills, was called to Hershey, Pennsylvania, by the chairman of the Hershey Chocolate Company. He was asked to provide staff support to the "city fathers" as they conducted an examination of "every agency and institution that touches the lives of our citizens."[42] Their study took them beyond the traditional limits of social planning to include land use studies made by physical planners, new business development plans of the Chamber of Commerce, and the Board of Education's designs for curriculum and facilities. Krughoff termed the results a "comprehensive survey of the community that served as the basis for integrated physical, social, and financing recommendations to all of the city's institutions."

Community planning changed the shape and substance of services. From the mid to the late 1950s, volunteers and professional staff members' contributions to community planning technology in conferences, national newsletters, and *Community* magazine exceeded those of their colleagues responsible for fund-raising. Bob Walther, United Community Funds and Councils of America's research director, termed the changes he observed during these years as "a quiet revolution in the shape and substance of our community health and welfare services."[43] His reference captured the variety and depth of changes reported by local Councils as they made use of Pittsburgh's model of a *citizen-driven community planning* organization. The volunteers who served without the responsibility to represent specific agency points of view challenged traditions of year-to-year priority-setting. They looked at community needs beyond the boundaries of health, recreation, and welfare agencies, and they considered changes in service delivery systems that would prevent problems, instead of treating them.

RED FEATHER SERVICES OF THE COMMUNITY CHEST
SERVED 1 OUT OF 4 FAMILIES IN 1946
7,657 FAMILIES FROM EVERY WARD AND METROPOLITAN DISTRICT
BENEFITED DIRECTLY FROM ONE OR MORE RED FEATHER SERVICES*

LOOK at your ward or suburb and you will see that you have a self-interest in keeping the quality of these services at a high level. So have your check—and a smile—ready when a volunteer worker calls on you.

Give Now   TO YOUR METROPOLITAN   *Give Now*
                        MADISON COMMUNITY CHEST

STRESS WAS PLACED ON PROBLEM PREVENTION, AS OPPOSED TO TREATMENT

One of the most significant social planning achievements during these years was the call to "Invest our precious voluntary contributions in the prevention of social problems, rather than their amelioration." The concept was first articulated in the report of Bradley Buell's 1950s "Study of Dependency in St. Paul."[44]

Buell shared observations drawn from experiences with several community studies conducted by his firm, Community Research Associates, from the platform of the Community Chests & Councils National Conference in 1956. They all pointed to his conclusion, "Services should be organized to prevent or curtail the processes of deterioration which sap capacity for self-maintenance . . ."[45] The phrase "prevention and alleviation of human suffering" soon took its place with the hallmarks of "efficiency in fund-raising" and "effective allocation of community resources" within the mission statements of hundreds of local Fund and Council organizations.

Buell's presentation stimulated a *Look* magazine article about approaches to meeting human needs that prevented problems. Soon thereafter, the federal government initiated funding for state and local "preventative service" programs that provided funds to nonprofit organizations in local communities. Examples included a federal initiative to establish networks of centers for senior citizens modeled after San Francisco's "Golden Gate Club for Golden Agers," a program that had been created by the Group Work and Recreation Council of the Community Chest.[46]

Programming aimed at preventing problems that limited the independence of older people led Congress to approve the Older Americans Act during the next decade. Similarly, the Community Mobilization for Youth was developed by the Welfare Council of Metropolitan Chicago using the principles and practices learned in St. Paul. The success of Chicago's program led to Congressional enactment of predecessors to the Juvenile Justice & Delinquency Prevention Act.[47]

EFFORTS WERE MADE TO DIFFERENTIATE
PUBLIC/PRIVATE RESPONSIBILITIES

Before World War II, nonprofit agencies had implored cities, counties, and states/provinces to take more active roles in financing and operating health, recreation, and welfare services. The nonprofits always had more clients than they could possibly serve. In the years following the war, old waiting lists got longer and with agency expansions to suburban communities, unmet needs became increasingly apparent.

In response to their own perceptions of the needs, a number of political subdivisions of government opened recreational facilities and curtailed public welfare programs and maternal and child public health programs without consultation and without reviewing their intentions with others. The result was an unanticipated shift in patterns of service that increased the availability of services for some people and eliminated services for others. Leaders asked, "Who is responsible for what services?"

"The United Way offered me the opportunity to work for 36 years as a professional with volunteers who represented the very best that a community, indeed our society, had to offer. Together we, volunteers and staff, through the United Way, made major contributions to improvement of the human condition in our communities."
—Cy Cochran, *Executive Director United Way of San Joaquin County, California*

Chicago's Council of Social Agencies came up with a reasonable answer in a white paper that explored the "Principle of Division of Responsibility between Voluntary and Tax-Supported Welfare Agencies." It served as a model for many other cities. The purpose of the statement was conveyed in its preface.

"A strong and complete welfare system requires the presence of both voluntary and tax-supported services, coordinated in functions and responsibilities, supplementing and supporting each other in an integrated and orderly fashion. Adjustments in the total system must be approached as a cooperative venture."[48]

"MEMBER AGENCY" AGREEMENT AND SUPPLEMENTAL FUND-RAISING POLICIES DEVELOPED

With a standard for the relationships between public and nonprofit agencies in place, volunteer leaders of the Council of Social Agencies of Franklin County, Ohio, came up with the idea of differentiating the responsibilities and obligations of community federations and their affiliated agencies. The statement they developed obligated signing parties—i.e., the individual agencies and the Fund or Council—to abide by minimum standards for participation in meetings, accept responsibilities on committees, and provide statistical information to one another.[49] A large number of communities used the Franklin County statement as the basis of locally worded "agency agreements."

Within a few years, limitations on agencies' "fund-raising for self-support" were added to the agency agreements. This language, coined by the Los Angeles Community Chest in 1953, became a universal Chest standard. In many cities, it formed the basis of ordinances that regulated fund-raising and established community campaign calendars. From the Community Chest point of view, local legal requirements would reduce fund-raising by agencies, particularly by those that were not affiliated with the federation. It would also create a schedule of agency supplemental appeals that would minimize calendar conflicts among them. From the point of view of local governments, the regulations would minimize fraudulent practices. Permit applications generally asked for information on the amount to be raised, the ways in which money would be raised, the campaign schedule, the planned use of funds raised, and the names of board members who would assure that each agency would abide by "fair and honest practices."[50]

"Very few CEOs in North America today can say their businesses embody the souls and the values of the communities they serve. When you consider that United Way has done so through times of great social, political and economic change this past century, it is a rare privilege indeed to be an inheritor of this legacy and a contributor to its endurance."

—RUTH RAMSDEN-WOOD, *President, United Way of Calgary and Area, Alberta*

ONE VOLUNTEER'S "AFFIRMATION OF FAITH" PLANTS THE SEED FOR LOCAL, THEN NATIONAL CODES OF ETHICS

"I believe in the work of the Madison [WI] Community Union [Community Chest and Council]." These are the opening words of a "Credo" written in 1946 by Lowell Frautschi, Madison's volunteer board president. He articulated his personal values for:

- welfare work and social progress

- private and public agencies
- the Community Union, itself.

He asked every member of the board to sign a personal statement of principles similar to his. Little did he know that his statement would form the basis of generations of Codes of Ethics.

Among 16 standards, Frautschi expressed his belief that the "movement" he served "should be based on broad representation" and "should be an integrating force in the community." His belief that the Community Chest and Council in his community "should be concerned with the welfare of every individual and the total community" became the basis of credos adopted in other communities and by Community Chests and Councils of America.[51]

CENTRAL SERVICE EXPERIMENTATION CONTINUED: PROPERTY MANAGEMENT AND POOLED ALLOCATIONS

Some things never change. Chests and Councils, since their birth as a centralized Social Service Exchange in 1876, represented communities' efforts to increase the quality and quantity of their services through collaborative effort. Two first-time ventures that began during the late 1940s/ early 1950s demonstrated continued commitment to this goal: centralized agency property management and pooled, statewide allocations to state and national agencies.

The Community Chest of Philadelphia was the first to offer property management services to agencies, according to Owen Davison, former executive director. "In 1950, a staff man was hired to help agency members identify what to do about repair and maintenance problems and assist in getting skilled repairs and replacements from local companies. He also made recommendations to the Chest budget committees on whether to allocate funds for these purposes."[52] The practice was adopted by a number of cities, especially those whose central office facilities included agency offices. One of the greatest cost savings developed through Philadelphia's efforts came through their joint purchasing of heating oil and gasoline for agency-operated vehicles.

Combined allocation efforts to provide a "fair share" of funds to state and national agencies by all Community Chests began in 1946. The Massachusetts Community Organization Service conceived of an orderly way to handle the multiplicity of state and national appeals now confusing the contributing public, according to an article in *Community*. First, local staff members forwarded state and national agency requests to the state office, rather than their local budget committees. Then, volunteers representing local Fund/Council budget committees developed a recommended *package of state and national agencies* to be included in every local community campaign in Massachusetts. They also proposed a "yardstick to determine each city's fair share level of support of each agency." The recommended "packages" of agencies were included in local campaigns. Following campaigns, local budget committees allocated the prescribed "fair share" to each of the state and national agencies with the statewide package to the best of their ability.

"In 1947, $345,688 was distributed to 33 state and national agencies through the Massachusetts approach. . . . 25 percent more than the year before," according to Ray Jones, general secretary of the Boston YMCA and a member of the statewide committee. He summarized the Committee's philosophy in *Community* magazine. "If community leaders want to reduce the number of campaigns, they must assume more responsibility for financing needed services."[53] This statewide approach served as a model for the development of similar programs in more than a dozen states.

MARKET RESEARCH USED TO STRENGTHEN
COMMUNITY CHEST CAMPAIGNS

When the Community Chest of Worcester, Massachusetts, asked a market research agency to find out what others thought of their work, they were surprised to learn that volunteers and donors alike wanted the campaign to be more fun. They learned a lot more, too.

The Econometric Institute of New York began a market analysis with an opinion poll. "People were asked how much they knew about the Chest's purpose and function; what they thought of the Chest; how many of the Chest services they could identify; what they considered wrong with the Chest,"[54] according to *Community* magazine.

"The details revealed by the study," according to Executive Secretary

Lyscom Bruce, "were astonishing in the extreme." A high proportion of citizens didn't know that the 25-year-old Community Chest existed, and few people knew the purposes or location of the Chest. People considered the Chest's annual "Golden Rule campaign" to be a good thing, but could not describe it.

The Econometric Institute did analyses of respondents' answers by places of residence, age, and income. The Institute pinpointed "10-year targets for information in each category of analysis" and projected dramatic growth in Chest income for the decade ahead. They assured Chest leaders of sustained campaign growth, "if your message is aggressively and positively communicated to the targets that have been scientifically identified." They also reminded leaders that the people who worked most closely with the organization wanted to get more joy out of their involvement.

Market research made sense to many readers of the article that described Worcester's innovation in *Community*. Dozens of communities followed Worcester's lead and, in 1949, Community Chests and Councils of America initiated a national program of market research. In the decades ahead, national market research would continue to provide data with which local researchers could compare their own communities. Worcester's inventive use of market research for their Community Chest provided a model approach that hundreds of local communities used to develop their own public relations strategies in the decades ahead.

What about fun? No record remains of Worcester's use of that important bit of research data, but clear evidence can be seen of generally lighter and happier messages and themes in the years that followed. Photos and movie trailers showed the smiles brought to the faces of agency service recipients "Because You Cared."[55] Slogans such as "Give 'til It Hurts" were replaced with "Give 'til It Helps." The call heard in Worcester was heard throughout North America.

VALUE OF BRANDING WAS RECOGNIZED

Pittsburgh's Community Chest leaders approached their public relations duties with the advice of one of America's most prominent ad agencies, BBD&O (Batten, Barton, Durstine, and Osborn). Their work together developed the movement's early appreciation of the importance of their trademark and *brand*.

In a presentation to the Pittsburgh Community Chest Board, later described in *Community* magazine, BBD&O's executive vice president J. Davis Danforth made the case for careful attention to the "Chest brand": "Manufacturers and advertisers spend millions designing trademarks and burning them into the public mind." He illustrated his point by displaying well-known trademarks of the day, including the Cream of Wheat *chef*, the Prudential Insurance Company *rock*, and the Heinz *57 Varieties* logo. "None of these was made dominant by feeble or spasmodic effort," he observed. "Their owners have never lost an opportunity to stamp them on your mind . . . Go then and do likewise. See that every Red Feather service uses that Red Feather symbol everywhere it can be used."[56]

Chicago's "Oscar"

Chicago has created this Red Feather "Oscar" as an award to outstanding campaign leaders. He's 8 inches tall, made of wood fibre plastic in full color. A plate at the base allows for an inscription. Oscar is now available to other Chests, through CCC.

The *Red Feather* trademark was well known at the time, but it was far more associated with fund-raising than services and the agencies that provided them. But agencies' use of the trademark could best be described by Danforth's word "spasmodic." "Spasmodic" would have been a generous description of agencies' use of the wide variety of "marks" that accompanied the changes from "Chest" to "Fund." "We should have kept the Red Feather" was not an uncommon reflection after name and logo changes made "brand" more a memory than a reality.

MUSICAL JINGLES AND TELEVISION BROADCASTS
BECAME ADVERTISING VEHICLES

From 1946 through 1959, community campaigns used every possible medium to tell their stories.

Musical jingles first appeared during a 1946 New York City broadcast of President Harry Truman's "Feather message to the people," according to Elwood Street's memoirs. "The 30-minute program included a series of recorded musical 'spots' featuring the voice of Lanny Ross with the accompaniment of the Jon Gart trio. 'It's a feather in your cap when you fill the needed gap, so try, try, try.' "[57] In 1947, six ballet students of New York's Ballet Arts School entertained New York campaign volunteers with their interpretation of the jingle with "amusing dances, shown in shadow silhouette," Street said.

The "First Campaign Television Show" was the title of the *Community* magazine article that described Chicago's Community Fund 1947 campaign kickoff: "Held in the window of the Fair Store on State Street, the show attracted thousands." Public Relations Director Bernie Roloff reported that police were called out to manage the crowd that formed in front of the Fair Store's windows. "Publicity-wise, television is a wow," he said. "Program-wise, we're all going to have to learn how to use it because it will be here soon, a powerful medium of communication, education, and entertainment."[58]

In Hollywood, Johnny Carson welcomed the staff of the Los Angeles campaign's neighborhood division to his daily TV show, "Johnny's Cellar." They presented their "campaign training package" during the broadcast. Subsequently, 2,500 women were invited to the Pasadena Auditorium for 30 minutes of campaign training hosted by composer/TV personality Hoagy Carmichael, after which the women served as the audience for "Queen for a Day," according to Frank McNamara.[59] No medium was overlooked as campaigners and public relations leaders throughout the United States and Canada explored every way they could find to support their annual fund-raising programs.

"Oscar" left Hollywood in 1948 as Chicago presented namesake statuettes—"Red Feather Oscars"—to outstanding campaign leaders.[60]

STRONG CURRENTS SWIRLED BENEATH THE
QUIET WATERS OF THESE POSTWAR YEARS

On the surface, the late 1940s and 1950s were placid years in which families worked to get ahead. They were the years in which people who had been denied equal opportunities to enjoy the quality of life they saw in magazines, movies, and on television began to openly express their concerns. They were also years in which scientists, researchers, and engineers developed technologies that redefined North Americans' concept of community.

The late 1940s and 1950s were reasonably comfortable years for local United Way organizations. They served as social planning and federated fund-raising hubs as the pace of technological and social change increased. Their relationships with the agencies who had founded them changed from predominantly agency-driven to predominantly donor-driven. They made differences in the lives of people day by day, but the problems of individuals that added up into problems for communities didn't go away. Most of them got worse.

Beneath the surface, fundamental questions were forming about the true impact that increasing numbers of health, recreation, and welfare agencies were having and the multiplicity of campaigns to support them.

- To what degree did agencies' services overlap and duplicate one another?
- To what extent were voluntary dollars being spent to prevent problems, rather than treat people who suffered?
- With the consolidation of Community Chest and Red Cross campaigns, where was the "one campaign" for the agencies who were lining up at donors' doors?

Halberstam described the passing of *The Fifties*: "They were years captured in black and white, most often by still photographers; by contrast, the decade that was to follow would, more often than not, be caught in living color on tape or film. Not surprisingly, in retrospect, the pace of the fifties seemed slower, almost languid. Social ferment, however, was beginning just beneath this placid surface."[61]

He added, "Some social critics, irritated by the generally quiescent attitude and boundless appetite for consumerism, described a 'silent' generation. Others were made uneasy by the degree of conformity around them, as if the middle-class living standard had been delivered in an obvious tradeoff for blind acceptance of the status quo."[62]

Acceptance of the status quo was about to end as the calendar heralded the 1960s, years that beatnik poets termed the "age of disillusionment."

Hold onto your values—the Sixties are next.

Key Innovations in the United Way of Serving Communities Between 1946 and 1959

1946	In-kind gift of a prize steer	Yonkers, NY
1946	Planning for the arts was instituted	Louisville, KY; Hamilton, ON; and Vancouver, BC
1946	Musical radio jingle promotes campaign	New York, NY
1946	Campaign event broadcast on TV	Chicago, IL
1946	State/national agency allocations done statewide	MA
1947	Market research conducted	Worcester, MA
1947	Public/private responsibilities differentiated	Chicago, IL
1947	Organizational "branding" considered	Pittsburgh, PA
1947	Youth planning council established	Kansas City, MO
1947	Signed agency agreements required	Columbus, OH
1947	"Oscar" statuette award initiated	Chicago, IL
1948	First senior center funded	San Francisco, CA
1949	First United Fund, donor-driven campaign	Detroit, MI
1949	Fair share guide offered to donors	Detroit, MI
1949	Council-driven state planning begun	NY
1949	Payment made to student interns	Utica, NY
1950	Centralized agency board training conducted	Chicago, IL
1950	Regional staff conference created	Greensboro, NC

1950	Agency property service management offered	Philadelphia, PA
1951	Multistate United Way created for North and South Carolinas	Charlotte, NC
1951	Loaned junior executives help out	San Francisco, CA
1951	TV stars promote campaign training	Los Angeles, CA
1952	Campaign loaned executives recruited	Seattle, WA
1952	Claim of first female campaign chair	Durham, NC
1952	Combined health agency drive introduced	Champaign-Urbana, IL
1952	Comprehensive community survey completed	Hershey, PA
1952	Corporate giving yardstick introduced	Cleveland, OH
1952	UW conducts spring United Health Fund campaign	Champaign-Urbana, IL
1953	Code of ethics adopted	Boston, MA and Chicago, IL
1953	Study results in end of chain gangs	Spartanburg, NC
1953	Agency fund-raising regulations set	Los Angeles, CA
1954	Campaign crosses state lines	Kansas, MO/KS and Cincinnati, OH/KY
1955	Priorities differentiate fields of service	Pittsburgh, PA
1955	Agency capital needs included in annual United Way campaign	Omaha, NE
1955	Dread disease federation launched	Durham, NC
1956	Call for services to prevent problems	St. Paul, MN
1956	Relative priorities set for financing health, welfare, and recreation services	Philadelphia, PA
1956	United Health Foundation created to support patient services & research	Lorain, OH
1956	Lobbyists registered	Omaha, NE and Indianapolis, IN
1957	Area-wide campaign introduced	Washington, DC
1957	Medical foundation consolidates health agency campaigns	Boston, MA

| 1958 | Auspices of planning moves from agencies to citizens | Pittsburgh, PA |
| 1958 | Mobilization for youth focuses on juvenile delinquency | Chicago, IL |

---

[1] Mitchell, John G. "The American Dream." *National Geographic*, July 2001, p. 62.

[2] Chafe, William H. *The Unfinished Journey, America Since World War II*. New York: Oxford University Press, 1986, p. 117.

[3] According to John Naisbitt in *Megatrends*, "In 1950, we created 93,000 industries." New York: Warner Books, 1982, p. 52.

[4] Halberstam, David. *The Fifties*. New York: Fawcett Columbine, 1993, p. x.

[5] Mitchell, p. 63.

[6] Halberstam, p. x.

[7] "Junior Officers." *Community*, June 1947, p. 205.

[8] "A Hundred Percent with Mary Trent." *Community*, October 1952, p. 31.

[9] Simon, Raymond. "Internships in PR." *Community*, November 1952, p. 49.

[10] Devine, Chuck. Reflections shared with author during 2002 personal interview.

[11] Dillencourt, John B. Correspondence with the author, April 2001.

[12] *People & Events*, p. 113.

[13] Seeley, John R., et al. *Community Chest, A Case Study in Philanthropy*. Toronto: University of Toronto Press, 1957, p. 27.

[14] Greene, John A. "The Community Chest Way." Proceedings of the 1955 Midwest Conference of Community Chests & Councils of America, *Community*, March 1955, p. 127.

[15] Eppert, Ray. "The United Fund Way." Proceedings, p. 127

[16] Proceedings, p. 138.

[17] *People & Events*, p. 113.

[18] McNamara, Francis X., Jr. "Decentralization, the Los Angeles Story." *Community*, September-October 1971, unnumbered page.

[19] McNamara.

[20] MacDonald, Dan. Correspondence with the author, January 2002.

[21] Burrows, Amos. Correspondence with the author, January 2002.

[22] Burrows.

[23] "Boston's New Medical Foundation, Providing Medical Research and Health Education Through the United Fund." *Community*, January 1958, p. 67.

[24] *People & Events*, p. 146.

[25] Lexington, Kentucky's 1954 campaign slogan.

[26] Blanchard, Ralph H. "Federation Looks Ahead." Presentation at the 1955 Midwest Conference of Community Chests & Councils of America as reported in "Three C's Chief Remembers the Past and Eyes the Future." *Community*, June 1955, p. 184.

[27] "Planning Takes a Giant Step." *Community*, March 1957, p. 30.

[28] *People & Events*, p. 130.

[29] Orrell, David. Correspondence with the author, August 2002.

[30] Street, Elwood. "The United Way, A History." Unpublished memoirs on file at the University of Minnesota Social Welfare History Archives, 1958, p. 714.

[31] *Community*, April 1952, p. 153.

[32] "Policy Regarding American Red Cross Fund Raising and Joint Fund Raising." American National Red Cross, Board of Governors meeting minutes, December 8, 1947, pp. 1-2.

[33] *The Assembly Letter*. National Social Welfare Assembly's monthly newsletter, July 1949.

[34] *The Assembly Letter*.

35 Bower, Mary A., with John G. McCormick and Elmer J. Tropman. "Impact, A History of the Health and Welfare Planning Association 1922–1991." Health and Welfare Planning Association of Allegheny County. February 1992, p. 12.

36 Bower, pp. 12-15.

37 Church, Mrs. Walter S. and Dr. L.B. Moseley. "Priorities in Pittsburgh, the Federation Tries a New Approach to an Old Problem." *Community*, November 1955, pp. 44-45.

38 "Planners' Progress." *Community*, June 1953, p. 206.

39 Comer, Virginia Lee. "The Arts and Your Town." *Community*, November 1946, p. 44.

40 Street, p. 1061.

41 MacDonald.

42 Krughoff, Merrill. Recollections shared with the author, 1964.

43 Walther, Robert J. "Long Range Planning." *Community*, January-February 1963, p. 9.

44 Buell, Bradley. *Community Planning for Human Service* (based on a project conducted by Community Research Associates). New York: Columbia University Press, 1952.

45 Clark, Irving. "Retooling for Prevention." *Community*, March 1956, pp. 130-131.

46 Hance, Eva. "San Francisco Senior Center." *Community*, October 1953, p. 26.

47 Shireman, Charles H. "Community Mobilization for Youth, Chicago Takes a Long Step Forward in Delinquency Control." *Community*, February 1958, pp. 83-87.

48 "Public-Private Relations." *The Council Hopper (Passing Along News and Views to Local Community Planners)*. Community Chests & Councils of America, September 1947, pp. 15-16.

49 "Council-Agency Agreement." *Community*, September 1947, p. 17.

50 Spaulding, Evelyn. "City Ordinance 77,000." *Community*, October 1953, pp. 23-24.

51 Frautschi, Lowell. "A President's Credo." *Community*, November 1946, p. 46. *(Author's note: The April 1953 issue of Community reported that, in 1951, CCC charged a committee of professionals to "formally express the ethics of practitioners in the Chest-Council field." It included all of Mr. Frautchi's points, and more. In 1953, CCC's Board of Directors accepted the code and "made it available to the entire country." The code was updated periodically by the national association; in 1962 by the Board of United Community Funds & Councils of America under the name "Guidelines for Action"; in 1973 by the Board and National Professional Advisory Committee of United Way of America under the name "United Way Credo." Along with the Credo, the National Professional Advisory Committee adopted the "Code of Conduct for United Way Professionals." Both were published as part of the 1988 Standards of Excellence, a United Way dedication to "Our Second Century of Service." A national "Ethics Committee" of United Way's Board of Governor's, under the leadership of Ira A. Lipman, brought an expanded Code to every local United Way in the United States. Most recently, standards for volunteer and professional practice, written by William Aramony during his presidency of United Way of America, formed the basis of a 1990 publication titled Mobilizing A Caring America, Principles for the 1990s.)*

52 Davison, Owen R. Correspondence with the author, January 2002.

53 "The Massachusetts Plan." *Community*, February 1948, pp. 105 and 112.

54 Bruce, Lyscom. "A Chest Uses Market Research, Worcester, Mass., Applies Businesslike Methods to Chest Business." *Community*, February 1947, pp. 105-106.

55 1951 Campaign "Thank You Program," Greensboro, North Carolina.

56 Heinz, H. J. "The Power of a Symbol." *Community*, March 1947, p. 123.

57 Street, pp. 1193-1194.

58 "The First Campaign Television Show." *Community*, November 1946, p. 47.

59 McNamara.

60 "Chicago's Oscar." *Community*, October 1947, p. 29.

61 Halberstam, p. i.

62 Halberstam, p. xi.

CHAPTER SIX

Local Initiatives Wane

1960—1969

Federal Dollars Flow Directly to Agencies

"Come gather 'round people \ Wherever you roam
And admit that the waters \ Around you have grown
And accept it that soon \ You'll be drenched to the bone
If your time to you \ Is worth savin'
Then you better start swimmin' \ Or you'll sink like a stone
For the times they are a-changin'."[1]

W hen Bob Dylan sang those words in 1964, his words described the sweeping changes that were touching every person and institution.

Bruce Schulman observed in the Introduction to his book *The Seventies*, that the "phenomenal economic growth—the nation's vaulting advances in productivity, output, and wages—had allowed Americans to accomplish unprecedented achievements. The U.S. fought the cold war and rebuilt Europe and Japan. It incorporated millions of working Americans into a home-owning, college-educated middle class. And it still had enough left over to lift millions of Americans out of desperate poverty and to establish the social safety net for all citizens."[2]

Dylan and Schulman were both right. As the decade of the '60s began, it was clear that things would be "a-changin'" and the nation was on the precipice of significant achievements.

Whitney Young, National Urban League president, saw change riding on the wings of the "resistance movement."[3] The acquiescence of minority people who had lived with racial discrimination was being replaced by protest. The patriotism of the war years was being replaced by demonstrations opposing America's involvement in the war in Vietnam. The assassinations of President John F. Kennedy, Rev. Martin Luther King Jr., and U.S. Attorney General Robert Kennedy shook the nation. While many rode the wave of prosperity, the number of families and individuals living in poverty was increasing. Riots were disrupting cities. Alternative lifestyles tore at the institutions of family and religion. Flower children, runaways, and hippies did "their own things."

Presidents Kennedy and Lyndon Johnson recognized opportunities for achievement and called for Congressional legislation that would deal with impediments to needed social and economic changes. For the first time in American history, programs were established through which the federal government reached around state governments and funded health, recreation, employment, and education programs within cities and towns. Not only did they finance the creation of new direct service agencies, but they provided money for program planning independent of Community Councils, most communities' established human service planning organizations.

To fight the "War on Poverty," the Office of Economic Opportunity (OEO) called for the creation of "community action agencies." The new federal Office of Housing and Urban Development (HUD) required the establishment of "neighborhood or community councils." Advisory groups for local agencies administering the new Medicare program and numerous federal urban crime initiatives were established with policies and procedures designed in Washington, DC, breaking with the community-by-community right to "local determination" that had been outlined by the authors of the U.S. Constitution.

The number and variety of federally "guided" programs appeared to grow without restraint. *The Conquest of Poverty*, written by conservative Henry Hazlitt, reported that, "In 1968, Congressman William V. Roth Jr. and his staff were able to identify 1,571 programs, including 478 in the Department of Health, Education, and Welfare alone."[4] Officials at all levels of government were confused about where to refer people who came to them for help. Leaders of established agencies were confused about the names and numbers of agencies who were providing services similar to theirs. People in need of service were confused because they couldn't determine which agency to go to. Things became more difficult to understand with each passing year.

Signs of the Times

GLOBAL/NATIONAL EVENTS

1960	A Canadian Bill of Rights was approved giving native people the right to vote in federal elections.
1960	Lunch counter sit-ins began in Greensboro, North Carolina, to protest the local practice of not serving African Americans.
1961	President Kennedy proposed a 10-year space program to "land a man on the Moon."
1965	Congress appropriated $1.1 billion for Appalachian development.
1965	President Johnson created the Department of Housing and Urban Development (HUD).

IN THE NEWS

1962	*Silent Spring* warned of ecological dangers.
1963	Betty Friedan brought women's rights issues to a national dialogue.
1963	November 22: President Kennedy was assassinated in Dallas; Vice President Johnson assumed the presidency.
1964	Military aid to Vietnam was increased; student antiwar rallies on college campuses began.
1967	Race riots erupted in Detroit.
1967	Anti-Vietnam War protests grew; 75,000 protestors marched on the Pentagon.
1968	Martin Luther King Jr. was assassinated; riots broke out in over 100 cities.
1968	U.S. Attorney General Robert Kennedy was assassinated.
1968	Riots broke out at the National Democratic convention in Chicago.
1969	Men walked on the moon.

STATE/LOCAL COMMUNITIES & NEIGHBORHOODS

1960	Responding to an Ohio Attorney General's ruling, counties assumed operation of public school classes for developmentally disabled children.

SOCIAL MOVEMENTS/GOVERNMENTAL POLICIES & PROGRAMS

1964	The Civil Rights and Economic Opportunity Acts approved by Congress heralded direct federal funding of local nonprofit organizations.
1964	Canadians received social insurance cards.
1965	The Older Americans Act approved funding for research, planning, and programming for older people.
1965	Congress created Medicaid, supplemental health care insurance for poor people.
1968	Picketers at Chicago's Democratic National Convention demanded "equal rights for women."

ECONOMY/BUSINESS CYCLES AND THE WORKPLACE

1960	A year-long recession preceded a decade of moderate economic growth.

SCIENCE AND TECHNOLOGY

1960s	Room-sized computers become commonplace in large companies and governmental agencies.
1960	Oral contraceptives became available by prescription.
1964	The U.S. Surgeon General identified the health hazards of cigarette smoking; the Federal Trade Commission called for health warnings on cigarette packages.
1965	A measles vaccine became available.
1967	Cholesterol was named a factor in heart disease.

How Approaches Reflected the Needs and the Times

In most communities, long-established agencies were called upon to do more and then criticized because they had not done enough to eliminate the problems they had been created to treat. Funds and Councils tried to weather this criticism by clinging to their established practices and doing their best to raise the funds or apply for funding from emerging federal initiatives to help agencies eliminate growing operating deficits while serving their clients. Funds and Councils also searched for answers to questions that had never been on their agendas before.

- How do local community organizations relate to the offspring of marriages between federal and local agencies?
- How do local Funds and Councils influence the programs and budgets of the local offspring of the Offices of Economic Opportunity, Housing and Urban Development, and Model Cities when their budgets, policies, and guidelines were being written in Washington, DC?

The answers were not to be found until late in the decade.[5] In the meantime, local Funds' agendas increasingly were called upon to differentiate the values of the voluntary agencies supported by the campaign from those supported with governmental funding. Contributors and prospective contributors wanted assurance that their donations were receiving far more intense oversight than they perceived was the case with their tax dollars.

Councils continuously struggled to bring order to the prioritization of needs and the funding of services in a community planning environment that was closer to "do your own thing" than collaboration. Their work fostered increasing impetus to find ways to transcend the loss of local cooperation and led to experimentation with regional and national initiatives.

The agendas of national conferences echoed the words of President Dwight Eisenhower's 1960 "State of the Union" message: "The 1960s promise to be the most prosperous years in our history. Yet we continue to be afflicted by nagging disorders."[6]

Leadership Characteristics

The people who led local campaign and planning organizations during the 1960s were characterized by Art Kruse, executive director of Chicago's Community Fund, as sharing "a preoccupation with the duality of cause and function . . . saving the world and saving the individual." While lecturing graduate students at The Ohio State University in 1967, Kruse suggested that Fund and Council leaders, both paid and volunteer, behaved far more like social workers than business managers. He mused that "even senior businessmen's hearts bleed when they hear the stories told by agencies appealing for the contributions for which we are stewards."[7]

"Try to remember the people who wrote great words as well as those who delivered them."

—LYMAN FORD, *Past Executive Director, United Community Funds & Councils of America*

Professionals during the 1960s considered a master of social work (MSW) degree to be required for senior positions in Fund and Council organizations in cities of all sizes. Exceptions to the requirement were most often made in fund-raising positions in order to attract people with sales experience to campaign positions. Planning Council specialists often held postgraduate degrees in areas of their specializations, such as health or recreation. This, too, began to change as shown by this statement from a 1966 article in *Community* magazine titled "The Endless Demand for 'Social Statesmen' in the United Way."

> *"Looking ahead over the next 20 years, we need to think of the qualifications of individuals who occupy key Fund and Council positions in terms other than our current standards. As Funds and Councils emphasize the efficiency and effectiveness of those operating services on whose behalf they are raising funds and planning services, it becomes even more important to evaluate the efficiency and effectiveness of our central services. As more demands are placed upon the voluntary field to justify its existence in competition with governmental welfare services and to maintain its leadership role, it becomes increasingly necessary that better educated people fill key positions in budgeting, planning, and fund-raising."*[8]

Without question, the challenges that lay ahead for the United Way movement required states*men* and states*women* who understood national, as well as local, needs, services, economies and politics. The rate of change in all of these areas was increasing so quickly that the people leading Funds and Councils needed more capacity and training to do their daily jobs. They also would come to realize and discuss openly their need to better reflect the diversity of their communities, but would not generally do so during this decade.

SOCIAL PLANNERS EXPLORED NEW PATHS OF SERVICE

The traditional Council was at what Elmer Tropman called a "crossroad" when he addressed a 1966 meeting of the 35 largest planning councils in the country. "It has three choices: It can move in the direction of becoming more *service-oriented*. It can move in the direction of a nonpartisan, problem-centered voluntary planning body. It can continue to remain as it is."[9] The demands of the 1960s gave local planning groups little choice but to follow the paths of his first two choices.

COMMUNITY PROBLEM SOLVING AVERTED AN ECONOMIC CRISIS

"Twenty-two years and two days after Pearl Harbor, an economic bombshell rocked the economy of South Bend, Indiana, and tore at the roots of nearly 8,000 of the city's families. The Studebaker Corporation announced that the company planned to shift its primary base of automobile manufacturing to Hamilton, Ontario."[10] Those words opened a 1964 *Community* magazine article written by Stanley Ladd, president of the St. Joseph Council AFL-CIO and past-president of the St. Joseph County United Fund.

> *"Philanthropy is commendable, but it must not cause the philanthropist to overlook the circumstances of economic injustice which makes philanthropy necessary."*
> —MARTIN LUTHER KING JR.

"The United Community Services," he continued, "worked out a detailed plan (Project ABLE—Ability Based on Long Experience) and entered into a contract with the federal government to cope with the problems of the large majority of Studebaker workers over 50 years of age and those others at a potential disadvantage in seeking employment or retraining." United Community Services Executive Director Bill Aramony brought people together who hadn't sat around a common table in the past. They spanned all levels of business management and labor leadership and included leaders of the South Bend community and the nation. The teamwork of organized labor, local and national leaders, and United Community Services solved a critical community problem by attracting new business to a community with an "overabundance" of skilled and highly experienced workers. "Eight months after a local problem put thousands out of work, the city was bustling."[11]

UNITED WAY ORGANIZATIONS HELPED
SHAPE THE WAR ON POVERTY

Two years before Congress passed the Economic Opportunity Act of 1964 (the "War on Poverty"), New Haven, Connecticut's United Fund pulled together a cross section of business, civic, university, and agency leaders to engage in what United Way President Daniel Kops called, "a comprehensive fight against poverty and deprivation."[12] It was a prototype for the Community Action Agencies designed by the Office of Economic Opportunity.

"To mount the attack [on poverty] in New Haven," Kops continued, "a comprehensive planning and action organization called Community Progress, Inc. (CPI) was established with a sizeable grant from the Ford Foundation, subsequently augmented by even heavier federal financing, with the result that CPI's current annual expenditures are approximately $3 million in this city of 152,000. Thus, if the fight to overcome urban poverty is going to pay off anywhere, it ought to pay off in New Haven."

 "We are very human people doing super-human jobs that can only be done together."
—GORDON BERG, *Past President, United Way of Central Carolinas, North Carolina*

Small city programming in the "War on Poverty" was first tackled by the Aurora (IL) United Community Services (UCS) organization. Then Executive Director Don Wingard remembered that "As the experts in Washington were trying to figure out how to help people fight poverty in communities of our size, volunteers from both sides of the Burlington Railroad tracks came together at the UCS office to talk about what was best for everyone."[13] Aurora was the first small city United Way organization funded as one of OEO's Community Action Program agencies. In order to implement poverty-fighting programs, the volunteer UCS board was expanded to include representatives of local government and poor people. Federal grant funds and campaign contributions were pooled and allocated by the board based on recommendations of the UCS budget committee. Margaret Smith, volunteer chair of the committee, was asked by the OEO's Chicago Regional Office to help write federal "guidelines" for the distribution of OEO funds to small cities.

Newark, Ohio, became the first small city whose Head Start preschool children's services were funded by OEO. Like Aurora, leaders of the Licking Council United Appeal restructured its board of directors to include heretofore uninvolved leaders of poor people. When the Head Start program began its second full year of operation under United Appeal's "LEAP-Licking Economic Action Program," the Head Start staff numbered 170 and reported to the United Appeal executive director along with the two other employees who managed all other United Appeal business.

"I never wish I could do things over again because I would have to relearn why I did them in the first place."
—WILLIAM A. SOHL, *Past Executive Director, Community Chest of Louisville, Kentucky*

A 1965 SUMMER YOUTH EMPLOYMENT PROGRAM
PROVIDED A MODEL TO COOL HOT CITY STREETS

Creativity was a hallmark of community approaches to problem solving, as the following *Community* article shows:

> *(Detroit) Instead of an aimless summer like so many previous ones, some 3,500 disadvantaged teenagers found personal guidance, cultural benefits, employment opportunities, and education. SWEEP (Summer Week-End Emergency Program) was conceived by United Community Services of Metropolitan Detroit after the findings of the local Citizens Committee for Equal Opportunity confirmed UCS research that a summer crash program was needed for troubled, idle youth.*[14]

A long, hot summer became hopeful, fun-filled weeks for 14-to-19-year-old youth—runaways, juvenile offenders, school drop-outs, and members of gangs in Detroit's 10 neighborhoods of greatest need and racial tension, thanks to a $50,000 staffing grant made to six member agencies. The Detroit model served as a benchmark for hundreds of summer youth employment programs in cities of all sizes.

GRANTS WERE USED TO DEVELOP AND DEMONSTRATE
NEW APPROACHES TO SOLVING OLD PROBLEMS

In 1967, the United Fund in Seattle departed from years of funding agency operating deficits by placing $25,000 in a fund to encourage experimentation in the field of social services. The Fund's allocation attracted grants from the Boeing Employees Good Neighbor Fund, the Washington State Department of Public Assistance, and a local foundation. In total, nearly $60,000 was made available for member agencies to try new approaches to solving old problems.

The United Fund's "Development and Demonstration" program made several experimental programs possible. The YWCA's "Unwed Mother's Project" accepted 58 previously unserved pregnant teens. A nonprofit adoption agency added a caseworker to concentrate on the placement of minority children. The local Urban League used their grant to attract Ford Foundation funding for a three-year program to "prepare Negro families to move out of the central city and encourage white families to move into the urban core."[15]

DADE COUNTY'S UNITED FUND CONVENED
THE GREATER MIAMI COALITION

In 1968, following the national lead of John Gardner's Urban Coalition,[16] the Dade County (FL) United Fund brought employers, agencies, schools, and municipal and county governments together to coordinate "immediate, urgent community efforts such as employment, housing, and education. Leading this effort was Bill Aramony, then the executive vice president of the Dade County United Fund. Aramony, who had led a similarly successful program in South Bend several years earlier, described this local United Way *coalition planning* effort as "comprehensiveness in community planning" in a *Community* magazine article titled "Out of Turmoil, Opportunity for the United Way."

"Our United Way movement for some time has recognized the 'whole man' concept in the health field," he wrote. "We now must recognize the 'whole community' in the planning field. We must deal with the totality, however complex, and not the pieces. We must develop the techniques of problem definition and problem solving."[17] His words described the direction in which he would lead the United Way movement as the next president of the national Fund/Council organization.

COMMUNITY PLANNING BEGAN TO SHIFT
FOCUS FROM PROGRAMS TO RESULTS

Rudy Evjen, UCFCA's associate executive director for community planning, spoke of a direction that was beginning to take shape within the United Way movement—"outcomes-driven allocations." Although the practice would be known by other names as it was refined over the ensuing 30 years, Evjen saw the roots of this approach sprout in programs like the ones begun in South Bend, New Haven, Aurora, Miami, and countless other cities.

"The pressures of the 1960s," he wrote in *Community* magazine, "may require United Funds to . . . develop a more problem-oriented budgeting process which places greater emphasis on agency responsiveness to changing community problems and less weight on allocations in previous years."[18]

JUST WHAT UNITED FUND LEADERS WANTED
TO HEAR: "I GAVE AT THE OFFICE"

Campaigns during the 1960s rode the crest of increased employment in large companies by concentrating on employee giving and corporate pledges based on total numbers of employees.

> *"Campaign leaders need to remember that when all the risks are gone, all the fun will be gone."*
>
> —CHARLES H. BROWER, *Past Chairman of the Board, Batten, Barton, Durstine & Osborn, Inc.*

Armed with campaign materials that featured new names and logos, Fund volunteers visited corporate head offices to make presentations that laid out bold goals, based on calculations that most often presented the sizeable contributions that could be recorded if companies and their employees gave at the levels of the best performers with their Standard Industrial Classifications (SIC). Volunteers were trained to make the "CEO visit" and cover lists of requests that varied little from community to community. They often looked like this:

CEO Visits
Study the Firm Data Form
- Number of employees
- Last year's corporate gift
- SIC leadership corporate gifts per employee
- Last year's employee gifts
  - Average
  - Per capita
- Be ready to help calculate:
  - Corporate gift based on SIC group
  - Leaders' gifts per employee
  - Xs (times)
  - Number of employees
  - Employee gift based on .6 percent of wage
  - SIC leaders' gifts per employee
  - Xs (times)
  - Number of employees

Review the list of United Fund agencies and think about how difficult your job would be if you had to ask for a gift for each agency.

Make a personal CEO visit at which you should
- Update the firm data form
- Number of employees
- Name of "Keyman"
- Help the CEO calculate corporate and employee gifts at SIC group leadership levels
- Ask the CEO for
  - *his* corporate gift
  - *his* employee goal
  - a date when he will personally address an employee group rally

Be sure to say THANK YOU!

SUBMIT one copy of the FIRM DATA FORM to Campaign Headquarters and FOLLOWUP with the Keyman.[19]

Chief executives called upon their fellow CEOs and often brought the kind of competition they enjoyed on the golf course into campaign report meetings. They often personally "worked" the campaign from training sessions through the delivery of corporate and employee report envelopes to campaign report meetings.

Public report meetings often were followed by detailed newspaper stories that listed each volunteer's percent achievement on the way toward his division or personal campaign goal. With the knowledge that their results would be public, CEOs took the subject of reaching their goals seriously and the sum of their efforts attained annual campaign increases in most communities.

 "Ever since its founding convention in 1955, the AFL-CIO has enjoyed an excellent working relationship with the United Way at national, state and local levels. Now, more than ever, the partnership between organized labor and United Way plays an important role in achieving the Community Impact that both organizations work for."
—JORDAN L. "BUD" BISCARDO, *AFL-CIO Community Services Liaison Vice President, Department of Labor Participation*

The campaign approach that had been developed over the years since the Second World War continued to wear well. Company campaigns were almost universally accepted by employees with more pride in achievement than resentment that "fair share" gifts were expected. Residential campaigns went smoothly as solicitors went to every door in search of donations, except those that bore a sticker with a Fund logo and words that said, "I gave at the office." Some stickers even said, "I gave *proudly* at the office."

PAYROLL DEDUCTION GIVING CAME
SLOWLY FOR FEDERAL EMPLOYEES

Until the early 1960s, the federal government prohibited employee solicitation on its premises. Late in President Eisenhower's administration, Congressional leaders were able to persuade John W. Macy, chairman of the U.S. Civil Service Commission, to allow campaigns in the federal workplace. Macy, who had opposed extension of local community campaigns to a national level, took three years to design a test campaign for federal employees in the Los Angeles area.

Frank McNamara, retired general manager of the Los Angeles United Way, recalled his experience with the first year of federal campaigns. "There could be a maximum of three concurrent campaigns: United Fund, Red Cross, and health agencies. As what appeared to be an incentive to become part of United Fund campaigns, separate Red Cross and health agencies were only allowed to solicit cash gifts, while United Funds could have pledges.

"Initial plans called for individual privacy—United Funds used *gold* colored envelopes; Red Cross used *red*, and health agencies used *green*. Not until 1962 was payroll deduction giving made available. Then, a number of other cities wanted to become part of the experiment."[20]

"It is no tragedy to miss goals; it is a tragedy to have none."
—DR. BENJAMIN MAYS, *Educator*

As other cities' Funds jockeyed to become part of a 1964 test of payroll deduction giving in federal employee campaigns, members of Congress began to ask the Civil Service Commission to allow agencies that were not affiliated with United Funds to take part. Just before the fall campaign was to begin, Macy announced that federal employees would be allowed to designate their payroll deduction gifts to a list of agencies to be determined by an employee committee within each local federal agency. Some Funds that had been given permission to take part in the trial program withdrew.

People & Events reported that, "Objections to the plan stemmed from feelings that, even though payroll deduction was now permitted, campaigning was being taken out of United Fund hands . . . contributor designations were substituted for community-wide budgeting and allocations and United Fund agencies were being discriminated against in favor of go-it-alone agencies by making the United Fund 'just another drive.' Further, a charge was instituted for payroll deduction, and the plan provided no immunity to contributors from separate house-to-house drives by national health agencies."[21] Six cities agreed to participate in the first "Combined Federal Campaign" (CFC) in 1964 in hopes that a more satisfactory approach could be developed with local administrators of federal offices. Despite the efforts to make local adaptations, none were allowed in CFC campaigns as they were "demonstrated" in Washington, DC; Chicago; San Antonio; Bremerton, Washington; Macon, Georgia; and Morristown, New Jersey. By the end of the decade, most cities with federal employers had acquiesced to continually modified Civil Service Commission rules for the solicitation of payroll deduction gifts from federal employees.

INCONSISTENT BRANDING CONFUSED AN
INCREASINGLY MOBILE WORKFORCE

One element of the freedom that autonomy provided to the over 2,000 Fund and Council members of United Community Funds and Councils of America was the right to identify their organizations however they wished. People who weren't directly involved with them, however, could never have guessed that they were part of the same movement from the variety of their names and logos. This became a problem for many UCFCA members as employee relocations within national corporations increased.

When contributors to the Rochester Community Chest moved to Birmingham, they were asked to give to the local United Appeal. (The variety of organizational names is illustrated in the endnotes of the Introduction.) They were confused. As a result, local campaigns placed the gifts of newcomers at risk, and planning and allocating organizations sometimes lost the experience that workers who had been transferred from other cities could have brought to them.

Steve Nelson, executive director of Shelby (County) United Neighbors in Memphis, developed an approach that he thought would help end the confusion: a universal contributor recognition pin. Recognition pins were commonly used, but since the Community Chest name and "red feather" had been abandoned by most cities, there was no uniformity. Nelson believed that use of his community's "check pin" (derived from a "check the fair share square" slogan used in many cities) could serve as a common identification for all united community campaigns.[22] He and several colleagues personally invested in product development and a novelty sales company that marketed "check pin" merchandise at conferences and in direct mail. The "check pin" never quite replaced the "red feather" as a universal symbol of local campaigns, but something else did.

"UNITED WAY" NAME WAS ADOPTED
BY 33 LOS ANGELES AREA FUNDS

In 1963, 33 of Los Angeles County's 39 community funds consolidated to form the "United Way" of Greater Los Angeles. Frank McNamara described this unprecedented action in a *Community* magazine article: "Although it is probable that their reasons for merging were mainly financial, they optimistically envisioned this new organization as one which could have an impact on the total industrial force and thereby provide increased leadership as well as dollars for the agencies back home in the suburbs."[23]

The merger didn't achieve all of the objectives for which its participants had hoped, but the use of a common name and logo (though not the logo that became commonly used in the years ahead) demonstrated the value of a common identification to the entire movement. When a 1968 United Community Funds and Councils study recommended that all members adopt the "United Way" name and a common look, the Los Angeles experience was held up as an example of such success.

> *"You should never take more than you give."*
> —From Elton John's *The Lion King*

NATIONAL CORPORATE CAMPAIGNS UNIFIED

The number of national corporations began to grow during these years. Local businesses with long histories of supporting their local Funds and Councils became divisions or branch offices of larger companies. The patience that these consolidated corporations showed for working with multiple community campaigns came to an end in Canada in 1966. A study of campaign giving by the 1,500 national corporate home offices conducted by Toronto's campaign volunteers provided warnings of problems if campaigns didn't adapt to corporations' needs.

"[The study] indicated that 70 percent approved of the United Appeal concept. They liked 'its oneness, lower cost, greater efficiency . . . the overall coverage in canvassing.' But the picture is not all rosy," reported John Yerger, then executive director of the United Community Fund of Greater Toronto.[24] In a *Community* magazine article subtitled "An Alert from Toronto," Yerger shared corporate leaders' expectations that the United Fund in their home office city would work with its counterpart organizations in their "branch office" cities to present a *united* appeal. Corporate leaders thus gave impetus to the development of campaign materials and a giving standard called the "Gift of Good Measure" that Canadian national corporations could use company-wide. The result, according to Yerger, "preserved a partnership in which business and the United Way both have a stake in preserving and enhancing voluntarism in our society."

Toronto's contribution to United Way technology crossed the border during the next decade as United Way of America promulgated under the names "National Corporate Development," and later, "National Corporate Leadership."

ACCOUNTABILITY AND TEAMWORK WERE STRESSED AS FUNDS AND COUNCILS TRIED TO REESTABLISH ORDER

If only communities' successful Fund campaigns were indicators of the general health of the nation's health, recreation, and welfare services. But they weren't. Instead, with a few exceptions, the services that had appeared to be so well organized and coordinated prior to the '60s could be better described as duplicative, competitive, and uncoordinated. Early efforts in "coalition planning" were demonstrating a return to orderliness, but in most communities, the availability of government funds for independent service planning continued to support disorganization.

Creative thinking on the part of several cities identified new approaches to the organization and use of information by Funds and Councils:

- *Standards of Accounting and Financial Reporting* were tested by the Philadelphia United Fund in cooperation with the National Social Welfare Assembly and National Health Council. The work in Philadelphia led to the development of the *Standards of Accounting and Financial Reporting for Voluntary Health and Welfare Organizations.*[25] The "Standards" were adopted by the American Institute of Certified

Public Accountants, the accounting industry's national standard-setting body, and became the basis of financial accounting and reporting throughout the nonprofit field.

- *Functional budgeting* grew out of the Rochester Council of Social Agencies' efforts to relate the planning and financing of health and welfare services. A *Community* article titled "Program Management Through Costing of Services" described the community's approach: "In addition to keeping the usual account of total income and total expenditures, Rochester agencies now keep a separate account for each service so that the agency knows what income and expenditures are directly attributable to each."[26] This allocation tool was developed as a standard within the nonprofit field and served as the basis of future "purchase of service" relationships between United Ways and agencies.

- *Electronic information management* that had been in use for campaign records became available to Philadelphia's Health and Welfare Council in 1968. With the help of a full-time technician, programs were written that would allow clerks to manually transfer agency budget information from typewritten budget forms to electronic spread sheets. Owen Davison, the Council's executive director at that time, recalls that the early use of electronic data processing allowed interagency comparisons of budget factors. By the end of the decade, the Council identified ways in which electronically manipulated information could be used to help agencies learn cost-cutting techniques from one another.[27]

- *Systems planning* was introduced to San Bernardino, California's "Priorities Project" in 1968 by representatives of a local aerospace contractor named TRW Systems. With the loan of a systems engineer, a sociologist, and an economist from the TRW staff, a cross-section of community volunteers applied resource management tools to: (1) define goals and objectives, (2) identify constraints and required resources, (3) construct a work plan, and (4) outline evaluation procedures for each community need that the committee and agencies had identified. After going through each step, Priorities Project volunteers had sufficient information and familiarity with the human service needs to confidently rank need in an order of priority that could lead to immediate action. Larry Merrill, associate director of United Community Services in San Bernardino, presented a step-by-step outline of his community's experience with systems planning in *Community* magazine.[28] Some communities were then able to apply the systems approach to priority plans, while most found San Bernardino's experience of greatest value in strategic planning activities during the next decade.

As the decade neared its end, the community teamwork often fostered by Funds and Councils began to help human service providers understand their complex interrelationships. But even though factual material helped organizational leaders understand one another, the bowl of spaghetti-like relationships among local, state, regional, and national funding organizations defied local understanding. Something larger than local collaboration was needed.

"You can't do the Lord's work if you're broke."

—Daniel J. Ransohoff, *Late Special Projects Director, United Way & Community Chest, Cincinnati, Ohio*

FUNDS AND COUNCILS DECIDED TO NATIONALIZE INITIATIVES AS THE TUMULTUOUS DECADE ENDED

In his final State of the Union speech in 1969, President Lyndon Johnson tried to give perspective to the sweeping changes that citizens and their various levels of government had brought about during the 1960s. Much had been done well, but the tears in the fabric of society remained. "Urban unrest, poverty, pressures on welfare, education of our people, law enforcement, and law and order," he said, "have this much in common: They and their causes—the causes that gave rise to them—all of these have existed with us for many years. Several Presidents have already sought to try to deal with them. One or more Presidents will try to resolve them or try to contain them in the years that are ahead of us."[29]

Albeit on a different level, local Fund/Council presidents had worked to solve and ameliorate these problems, as well. They, too, had done much, but needs persisted. Local leaders would continue to try to resolve and contain them—but *differently*.

The 1960s had taught them an important lesson: too many of the factors that caused the problems that individuals and families suffered were beyond the understanding or control of individual leaders and individual cities. United Way leaders searched for a way in which their organizations individually and collectively could be more effective.

Following the only avenue left open to them by the federal government's assertion of its direction over the health, recreation, and welfare services of local communities, Fund and Council leaders decided to work together to lead their movement nationally, instead of locally, as they had done since they formed the American Association for Community Organizations decades ago.

 "I fear that our corporate budgets have more to say about the proliferation of health, welfare, and recreation agencies than Chest and Council studies of need."
—C. VIRGIL MARTIN, *Past Chairman & CEO, Carson, Pirie, Scott & Co.*
Past Board Member, United Community Funds & Councils of America

They began in 1968 with a study of the objectives and role of their national association, United Community Funds and Councils of America. Peat, Marwick, Mitchell and Company (PMM) was retained to help UCFCA and member community organizations look at "Voluntarism and Urban Life." It began with plans to review the United Way movement just as local budget committees reviewed agencies. "The United Way, along with all other community institutions, was being challenged as to its relevancy and its ability to adjust to rapidly changing conditions. It was most timely to have this searching inquiry in process—the United Way could truthfully say that it was examining itself even as local budget committees and boards were insisting that participating agencies do likewise."[30]

The study of UCFCA didn't focus on the needs of the national association, however. It looked at the needs of its member community organizations and sought to reshape the national organization to meet local needs. When the study was released, it said this about the United Way movement:

"The Study Committee recommends that the movement reaffirm its belief in the united voluntary way; in its future role as a viable partner and sometimes critic of government; as a spokesman stressing local responsibility and local decision-making as a counterweight to pressures for national centralization; and as the voice of citizens' concern for human beings who are victims of developments keyed to the masses rather than individuals. In short, to give national leadership and strength to local operations by formulating policies and procedures in areas where a common thrust is wise and practicable. Within the framework of local autonomy, more unity of thought and action can and must be developed nationally."[31]

UCFCA's approval of the recommendations of the "PMM Study" signaled the reassignment of the responsibility for the development of new programs and techniques from their own communities to their national association. Local creative lamps would dim over the years ahead as the "United Way of America," successor to United Community Funds and Councils of America, replaced the national *association* with a national *organization*. United Way of America, like the 1960s federal government, would come to give leadership to its constituents, as well as respond to the leadership of its constituents.

"The '60s appeared as a historical divide, a decade of turmoil with the future hanging in the balance," Schulman observed. "But the era, and its climactic 12 months [the year 1968], have also been regaled as 'the Year the Dream Died'—the year, to quote one journalist 'when for so many, the dream of a nobler, optimistic America died, and the reality of a skeptical conservative America began to fill the void.'[32]"[33]

It was time to rebuild the dream. On to the '70s.

Key Innovations in the United Way of Serving Communities Between 1960 and 1969

| 1960 | Standards of Accounting & Financial Reporting tested | Philadelphia, PA |
| 1960 | Functional budgeting applied | Philadelphia, PA and Rochester, NY |

1962	Combined Federal Campaign tested	Los Angeles, CA
1963	Common United Way name adopted by 33 area organizations	Los Angeles, CA
1964	United Way served as "War on Poverty" Community Action Agency	New Haven, CT and Aurora, IL
1964	Community problem solving averted economic crisis	South Bend, IN
1964	Payroll deduction tried with federal employees	Washington, DC; Chicago, IL; San Antonio, TX; Bremerton, WA; Macon, GA; and Morristown, NJ
1965	Summer youth employment coordinated	Detroit, MI
1965	Head Start administered by United Appeal	Newark, OH
1967	"Check" pins for fair share donors	Memphis, TN
1967	National corporate campaigns centralized	Toronto, ON
1967	Demonstration fund established	Seattle, WA
1968	"Systems" approach applied to social planning	San Bernardino, CA
1968	Collaborative planning demonstrated "comprehensiveness"	Miami, FL
1968	Financial accounting computerized	Philadelphia, PA

---

[1] Dylan, Bob. "The Times They Are A Changin." Columbia Records, February 1964.

[2] Schulman, Bruce J. *The Seventies, The Great Shift in American Culture, Society, and Politics*. New York: DaCapo Press, 2001, p. 7.

[3] Young, Whitney M. Jr. *To Be Equal*. New York: McGraw-Hill, 1964, p. 105.

[4] Hazlitt, Henry. *The Conquest of Poverty*. New York: Arlington House, 1973, Chapter 9.

[5] In 1968, at the request of member Funds and Councils, the national association employed the accountants and consultants of Peat, Marwick, Mitchell, and Company to lead a national staff and volunteer exploration of the ways in which their movement could best serve their changing communities. The "PMM Study," which came to be known as the "Voluntarism and Urban Life Project," concluded that the increased role of the federal government in social policy, social action, and social services could best be met by Funds and Councils together on a national, rather than local, basis. The study observed that "the entire history of the Fund/Council movement had been built upon the creativity and cooperation of autonomous community organizations that were 'united in spirit' and depended on local communities to develop and share tools and practices that met every local community's needs." In its recommendations, the study called for the restruc-

turing of member-service oriented United Community Funds and Councils of America into a prominent national organization that could both serve and lead the Fund/Council movement. The organization would be charged with the responsibility of supporting local "community members" with *national initiatives* which could be localized as desired by each community's Fund/Council leadership.

6   Eisenhower, President Dwight D. 1960 "State of the Union" message.

7   Kruse, Arthur H. "The Management Function in Planning Human Care Services." A lecture delivered at the School of Social Work of The Ohio State University, March 1967.

8   Kruse. "The Endless Demand for 'Social Statesmen' in the United Way." *Community*, September/October 1965.

9   Tropman, Elmer J. "Future Role of the Council." Speech delivered on September 29, 1966, New York City.

10 Ladd, Stanley J. "Ready and Willing for South Bend's Project ABLE." *Community*, September/October 1964, pp. 7-10.

11 *People & Events, A History of the United Way*. United Way of America, 1977, p. 170.

12 Kops, Daniel W. "New Haven's Community Progress, Inc., Ivy League Prototype for the Attack on Poverty." *Community*, September/October 1964, pp. 3-5.

13 Wingard, Donald E. Conversation with the author, 2001.

14 "SWEEP: Detroit's Summer Program for Idle Urban Youth." *Community*, November/December 1965, pp. 12-13.

15 Thibaudeau, Roger. "United Good Neighbor's Development and Demonstration Fund." *Community*, March/April 1968, pp. 3-5.

16 Just weeks after leaving government service, John Gardner became chairman and CEO of the Urban Coalition, a group of leaders who came together to tackle the problems of race and poverty that underlay the nationwide riots of 1968. Two years later, Gardner left the Urban Coalition. In the words of the *New Yorker*, he realized that "he couldn't put all the kings' horses together again."

17 Aramony, William. "Out of Turmoil, Opportunity for United Way." *Community*, September/October 1968, pp. 3-5.

18 Evjen, Rudolph N. Editorial comments. *Community*, March/April 1968, p. 3.

19 Content taken from "C.E.O. Visits" brochure developed by the Evanston United Fund, 1962.

20 McNamara, Francis X. Jr. Correspondence with the author, April 1962.

21 *People & Events*, p. 167.

22 Caldwell, Jim. Correspondence with the author, March 2001.

23 McNamara. "Decentralization, the Los Angeles Story." *Community*, September/October 1971, p. 21.

24 Yerger, John H. "An Alert from Toronto. The Corporation 'Home Office'—A Challenge to United Fund Leadership." *Community*, January/February 1967, pp. 12-14.

25 Davison, Owen R. Correspondence with the author, January 27, 2001.

26 Hill, Dr. John G. "The Rochester Experience: Program Management Through Costing of Services." *Community*, September/October 1963, pp. 7-9.

27 Davison.

28 Merrill, Larry D. "A 'Systems Approach' to Social Problems." *Community*, July/August 1968, pp. 5-7.

29 Johnson, President Lyndon B. 1969 "State of the Union" message.

30 *People & Events*, pp. 195-201.

31 Report of the "Voluntarism and Urban Life" Study of the Role of United Community Funds and Councils of America, 1970, p. 3.

32 Pompidou, Georges, quoting Jules Witcover in *The Year the Dream Died*. New York: Warner Books, 1997, p. 215.

33 Schulman, p. 2.

CHAPTER SEVEN

Proliferation and Competition Increase

1970—1979

Applying Business Management Practices to Community Service

J ournalist Christopher Booker wrote, "The sober, gloomy '70s, . . . a time of radical protest and flower power, polarization, experimentation, and upheaval . . . the source of everything good or everything evil in contemporary life."[1]

As the 1970s began, leaders in every community sought to return their institutions to the orderliness of the postwar years. Business leaders called on their local United Ways (the name adopted by all but a handful of Funds and dual-purpose Fund/Councils) to make sense out of what seemed to be a "crazy quilt" pattern of fund-raising campaigns, agencies, and services. They made it clear that they would increase their contributions only if United Ways acted more like the managers of social work than social workers. Management guru Peter Drucker characterized their attitudes this way in 1973: "Businessmen will soon realize their fondest wish, that [those who serve others] . . . employ the tools of private enterprise, rather than those of government, to satisfy the country's social and economic needs."[2]

"Trying to get our local service providers to work together these days is like trying to herd ducks." Those were the opening words of Atlanta

United Way executive Dick Hicks when he spoke at the 1970 annual meeting of 10 Key Cities (a professional leadership group that had been formed during the 1960s to help its members manage their rapidly changing United Way organizations). His comments told of the difficulties that he and his colleagues had experienced in "sorting out responsibility for coordinating all of the new agencies and services with which our cities have become suddenly blessed."[3] Hicks went on to say, "I'm not one to look back, but we've started this decade by playing with the cards that were dealt to us during the wildest years our movement has ever known."

"As a society, we are uncertain of our advances in the social and political arenas. We question our ability to move forward. Each of us could quickly make a long list of sins of omission. But are we really just standing still—milling around without advance? I believe we are doing ourselves a great injustice by downplaying our remarkable ability to help change society for the better."
—MARY M. GATES, *Past Chair, United Way of America Executive Committee, Past Vice Chair, United Way International Board of Directors, Past Chair, United Way of King County, Washington*

The 1970s began in the shadow of "the '60s." "For a while, we spent too much time complaining about how everyone else was interfering in *our* business," according to Gordon Berg, retired executive director of the Charlotte (NC) United Way. "I guess we had a short lapse of memory. We begged others to get involved with us in saving the world, and we complained about it when they did. Unfortunately, we bit off more than we could handle in just a few years . . . a small dose of the '60s was good for our communities . . . too much wasn't. Local communities tried what seemed to be hundreds of different approaches to coordinate things that were beyond their ability to coordinate. We stopped bragging to one another about how well we were doing. We were ready to add some top-down national leadership to our bottom-up way of running things."[4]

The observations that Hicks and Berg made were predicated on four significant issues that confronted all local United Way organizations in one way or another.

- Corporate support of local campaigns was becoming centralized.
- National media was not giving United Ways much support.
- National public policy was being formed without United Way participation.
- Volunteers did not represent the diversity of their communities.

Under the 1970s leadership of Bill Aramony, United Way of America provided local leaders with a vision of themselves as part of a national movement that was experiencing "Rebirth and Renewal."[5] Aramony mobilized his professional colleagues to support the work of United Way of America's board and staff as a "Program for the Future" was developed. In 1975, the national organization took an unprecedented action by introducing a package of *national* initiatives to constituents whose *local* initiatives had driven the national association since its inception in 1918.

As this and succeeding chapters continue to explore *"Grassroots Initiatives"* that shaped the United Way movement, the wealth of national initiatives developed at or by the United Way of America will not be described herein. Readers can find information on those that were initiated between 1970 and 1977 in *People & Events*. To this date, subsequent United Way of America initiatives have not been collected or summarized in a single publication.

As national strategies were carried out to address the issues that troubled United Way of America's local constituents, local United Way organizations continued to develop and share their "best practices" through conferences and publications.

Perspective on how initiatives, both local and national, fit together to define the typical local United Way organization of the 1970s was offered by Paul Akana, United Way of America's senior planning and allocations staff member, during his presentation at a national staff conference. His sketch of "three concentric rings of organization" stimulated a dialogue that would grow to become a generally accepted view of local United Way organizations who gave "full service" to their communities.[6]

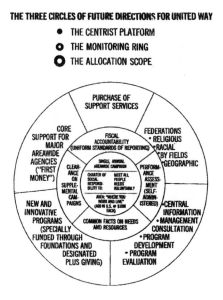

THE THREE CIRCLES OF FUTURE DIRECTIONS FOR UNITED WAY
- THE CENTRIST PLATFORM
- THE MONITORING RING
- THE ALLOCATION SCOPE

Akana saw local United Way organizations as "umbrella organizations that were uniform and consistent in their essence and strong enough to tolerate different methods to be applied to different circumstances." Above all, he saw local organizations as "centrist" or "community tables" at which leaders representing donors, agencies, volunteers, and professionals could sit with representatives of "communities of need" to solve community problems.

"When things go wrong, it's more important to talk about who is going to fix it than who is to blame."
—THE REV. LEON H. SULLIVAN, *Pastor, Zion Baptist Church/Philadelphia, Past Member, United Way of America Board of Governors*

Akana's sketch showed an orderly model to which he urged professionals to subscribe, and his comments provided descriptors that would become commonly used to identify United Way's local community role for several decades. In his closing comments, Akana summarized the challenges that faced all local United Way organizations during the 1970s. "If the United Way movement does not change *somehow*, we will become a venerable vestige of the past—an acceptable survivor of goodness in the present, but not a vital, dynamic force as it has been and it might be."

Signs of the Times

IN THE NEWS

1973	Paris Peace Accord ended U.S. involvement in Vietnam.
1974	President Nixon resigned.
1978	First "test-tube baby" was born.

SOCIAL MOVEMENTS/GOVERNMENTAL POLICIES & PROGRAMS

1970	Environmental Protection Agency (EPA) was created to unify America's efforts to combat pollution.
1972	As part of his "new federalism" program, President Nixon introduced "revenue sharing" as an instrument to return dollars and the decision on how to use them to the states.
1972	Equal Rights Amendment passed by Congress, but not ratified by the states.
1972	Community Mental Health Act broadened access to mental health services; Title IV-A of the Social Security Act financed coordinated community day care programs.
1973	YWCA adopted its "prime imperative," the elimination of racism.
1975	Title XX of the Social Security Act integrated child care into comprehensive social service programs; Aid to Dependent Children programs expanded to Aid to Families of Dependent Children.
1977	Quebec restricted English schooling to children of parents who had been educated in English.

ECONOMY/BUSINESS CYCLES AND THE WORKPLACE

1970	Occupational Safety and Health Administration (OSHA) was established by Congress to promote a safe and healthful working environment.

165

1972	Equal Employment Opportunity Act required equal hiring practices.
1974	Comprehensive Employment and Training Act (CETA) opened agency jobs with 75 percent federal subsidy.
1977–1979	Recession and inflation combined to produce "stagflation."

SCIENCE AND TECHNOLOGY

1977	Brains of schizophrenics were found to have chemical imbalances.
1979	U.S. Surgeon General affirmed that cigarettes cause heart disease, cancer, and other illnesses.

How Approaches Reflected the Needs and the Times

The 1960s had recorded "two strikes" against the continuation of traditional Fund/Council organizations' staffing and structure.

Strike one: The authors of the federal guidelines and regulations that interpreted "War on Poverty" legislation wanted every community they served to have "community organizers." The model they used, however, came from their political organizing experience and not that of the social discipline called "community organization." Temporary confusion between the two was resolved by sheer numbers—it seemed that the federal Office of Economic Opportunity hired more people without professional training as *community organizers* in its first year of operation than graduate schools of social work had trained in all of their years of attention to *community organization.*

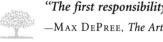

> *"The first responsibility of a leader is to define reality."*
> —MAX DePREE, *The Art of Leadership*

Strike two: By making large sums of money available to each funded agency for service planning, federal grant makers supported the proliferation of human service planning. Until the '60s, social planning divisions of combined Fund/Council organizations or separate Councils served at the hub of most communities' social planning programs.

As Funds and Councils compared their continued strengths in fund-raising and agency service planning to their weakened positions as community social planning and funding organizations, many realigned themselves through mergers of separate Funds and Councils into their United Way organizations. They hoped that this change would not only provide financial economies, but it would bring the variety of their functions into closer alignment and thereby increase their capacity to deal effectively with the multiple community planning centers that recently had been created.

FUND/COUNCIL MERGERS IN MANY CITIES ALTERED
RELATIONSHIPS BETWEEN PLANNING AND FUND-RAISING

From the inception of the twentieth century Chest/Council movement, United Way predecessor organizations had grown from roots of *community need* and had been tended by professionals who identified themselves and were identified by their communities as *social workers* or *community organization social workers*.

> *"The best bargain for a community can only be negotiated when all interested parties are at the table."*
> —GLENN E. WATTS, *Past President, Communications Workers of America,*
> *Past Chair, United Way of America Executive Committee*

In most communities, United Way functions had come to be grouped into several categories:
- Planning, including
  - Assessment of needs and resources
  - Resource and program development
  - Public policy review and development
  - Community education and advocacy
  - Program evaluation
  - Interagency coordination and cooperation
  - Consultation services to agencies
  - Consultation services to the general community[7]
- Fund-raising, including[8]
  - Workplace campaigns

- Door-to-door campaigns
- Special gift programs to promote and sustain large individual gifts
- Budgeting (also known as Allocations or Fund Distribution)[9]
- Central services, including[10]
  - Information on and referral to services for callers or walk-in clients
  - Volunteer recruitment/placement to meet volunteers' and agencies' needs
  - General and special holiday social service exchanges to eliminate duplication of services
- Public relations in support of planning, fund-raising and central services[11]
- Support services, including
  - Accounting for receipts and disbursements
  - Payroll
  - Facility maintenance[12]

The merger of Funds and Councils in cities in which Councils were no longer serving community planning organizations resulted in the consolidation of the planning and budgeting functions. This shifted the focus of planning from *community planning* to the support of the United Way's fund distribution program.

In a smaller number of communities, Councils had the support to continue or reestablish themselves as centers for *community planning* and continued to operate independently from the campaign-driven organizations. Some carried responsibilities for additional functions, including budgeting and central services; some did not.

"One of the reasons I have felt that fund-raising has been more recognized in United Way than planning is that fund-raising is easier to measure and has deadlines. When we finished something in planning, we always have more to do . . . it is never finished."
—ROWLAND TODD, *Past Executive Director, United Way of Wisconsin*

Leadership Characteristics
Business and civic leaders continued to invest their time, as well as their money, in local United Way organizations. But, as the decade saw an

increasing nationalization of companies, the number of corporate executives in many communities decreased. And with the demands of off-site headquarters, the time that business people could devote to non-business activities was beginning to wane.

As the 1970s progressed, the ratio of executive-level volunteers to others began a downward shift that would continue for several decades. The quality of commitment and degree of knowledge of volunteers in most communities did not change, however.

With the increased number of management-level volunteers and the decrease in executive-level volunteers, it was inevitable that the interest of board and committee members in United Way and agency management increased. Given the disorganizational aftershocks of the '60s that volunteers saw in uncoordinated, overlapping, and duplicative services, their interests in management, systems, and controls were welcome. As the tools that volunteers brought to United Way changed, so did their expectations that staff members' skills would change, as well.

"BoardWALK," a series of training modules for board members, expressed local United Ways' priorities for increased volunteer skills in policy-making.

PROFESSIONAL TRAINING AND EXPERIENCE REQUIREMENTS BEGAN TO SHIFT FROM SOCIAL WORK TO BUSINESS

The majority of local United Ways' organizational structures became more focused on the "business of social work" than on social work itself during this period. Experience and educational requirements for staff positions began to drift from social work to business. Job requirements began to include graduate degrees in business administration and business experience, along with the traditional degrees in social work and job experience in the United Way field.

SOCIAL PLANNING SEARCHED FOR ITS NICHE IN THE '70s

The editors of *Community Focus* articulated an all-too-common concern among United Way volunteers and staff who valued the community planning and its social work roots when they wrote, "Voluntary community planning may be declining. . . . " Those words introduced the comments of Elmer Tropman, Pittsburgh's Health and Welfare Planning Council executive. His article was titled "Let's Put Our Planning Act Together: The Future of Voluntary Community Planning," and it called for action.[13]

"The timeliness of the question, 'What is the mission and role of planning within the United Way movement?' is underscored by the current emergence of many new local and regional planning organizations, the trend toward combining the fund-raising-allocating-planning aspects of United Way operations. . . . " Tropman suggested that his United Way planning colleagues move beyond questions of mission and role and end " . . . years of bickering, strife, and contention over structure and functions and get on with the task of making planning the vital, effective, influential element that it should be within the United Way movement."

> *"While we may compromise our positions as United Way leaders, we may not compromise the neutrality, integrity, and professionality that characterizes these vital community organizations."*
> —LEO PERLIS, *Past Director, AFL-CIO Community Services and Past Member, United Way of America Board of Governors*

Responses to Tropman's challenge were demonstrated in a number of new, locally introduced tools whose practices and vocabulary became commonplace in the United Way field.

- *Environmental scan* was the term that defined Westchester, New York's "better guide to planning," as it was described in a 1970 *Community* magazine article titled "A New Tool for Social Planning." The Council of Social Agencies completed the first stage of its community profile with answers to three questions. "Who and where are the poor? Who and where are the troubled? Who and where are those receiving help?"[14]

- *Coalition planning* was described by national staff member Lowell Wright when he described the work being done by people representing a cross-section of the heads of agencies, governments, and companies with civic and indigenous neighborhood leaders in New Brunswick, New Jersey. "Together, they developed a comprehensive manpower program."[15]

- *Private and public sector cooperation* defined Orange County, California's Immigrant and Refugee Planning Center, "not an independent agency, rather it is a three-year project that . . . serves as a vehicle for stimulating and encouraging *all* major sectors of the community— business, voluntary, and governmental—to cooperate in mainstreaming immigrants and refugees into Orange County life."[16]

- *Consortium* in Philadelphia brought together "leaders from all sectors of the community—business, voluntary, and governmental—to form the Consortium for Human Services in an effort to coordinate a community-wide response to a community-wide problem. The Consortium set out to:
  - Serve as a forum for exchanging information on problems in health and social services resulting from budget cuts.
  - Identify needs and suggest which programs should have priority.
  - Clarify the roles of the public and private sectors.
  - Define and advocate realignments in resources for human services.
  - Pursue courses of action that can be implemented on a cooperative basis."[17]

- *Contingency planning* by the United Way of Southeastern New England (Rhode Island) "helped keep a number of Rhode Island agencies afloat despite crippling losses of federal funding."[18]

- *Strategic planning* was introduced to the United Way field by two corporate planners from General Electric (GE) World Headquarters, Lynne Hall and Ian Wilson. Their efforts, along with staff members of the United Way of Eastern Fairfield County in Bridgeport, Connecticut, resulted in a presentation to the 1979 Northeast Regional Staff Conference by George Wilkinson, then associate executive director of the Bridgeport United Way, and Marian Heard, then the agency's director of allocations and membership. Shortly thereafter, Wilkinson joined the United Way of America staff to help other communities learn environmental scanning and long-range planning techniques.[19] Both techniques became universally applied tools by which local United Way organizations could better understand community needs and resources and define ways to achieve their goals and objectives.

Pittsburgh historian Mary Bower described the new directions as "Impact . . . Impact . . . Impact that gave new direction to human service agencies as they restructured their boards and developed their programs in the following years."[20]

LOCAL UNITED WAYS REACHED OUT TO
HELP NEWLY INVOLVED POPULATIONS

When new groups of community leaders were invited to join efforts from which they had been previously omitted, they needed skills so that they could participate on the same level as those who had been previously involved as members of policy-making groups.

"You can holler, protest, march, picket, demonstrate, but somebody must be able to sit in on the strategy conference and plot a course."
—WHITNEY M. YOUNG JR., *National Urban League*

Birmingham, Alabama's United Way leaders designed lesson plans that would expose new minority board members, and people who wanted to serve on nonprofit boards, to the processes of "boardsmanship," according to Dave Orrell, retired Birmingham United Way president.[21] The 1971 program devised in Birmingham served as a prototype for United Way of America's development of a minority skills training program called "Project Blueprint," and board skills "BoardWalk" modules subsequently developed by United Way of America's National Academy of Voluntarism to train United Way and community leaders in the subjects of board roles and responsibilities.

The United Way of King County in Seattle reached out to low-income and handicapped people in a program named Project LIVE (Low-Income Volunteer Experience). When the program was described by Jo-Anne Larsen, United Way staff member, in *Community* magazine, volunteers reported that their "perceptions of themselves changed during the course of the experience. Their survey answers indicated an overwhelming change from 'negative' to 'positive' attitudes (about themselves and their value to the community) during the period of the volunteer experience."[22] The reasons that newly involved low-income volunteers gave for volunteering were no different than those that had been expressed by people from population groups that traditionally had been welcomed as volunteers: 57 percent stated a "desire to help," 46 percent sought "personal growth," 38 percent had an "interest in agency service," and 29 percent wanted to "work with clients."

"People often oppose a thing merely because they had no hand in planning it."

—LAWRENCE D. BOLLING, *Past Chairman, L.D. Bolling & Son Box Dealers, Inc, Past Member, United Way of America Board of Governors*

NEW VOLUNTEERS HELPED DESIGN NEW APPROACHES TO FUND DISTRIBUTION

"Town meetings" weren't new to those who administered city government, but until the United Fund of the Philadelphia area brought people together in an open community forum, town meetings hadn't been used to contribute to fund distribution strategies. They served a purpose that Eleanor Brilliant, when discussing community decision-making in *The United Way, Dilemmas of Organized Charity*, described as an embodiment of the hopes of the Philadelphians who convened the session. Brilliant said, "The model therefore supports the notion of shared values in American society as the basis for community life, and tends to underplay differences that may exist in power and influence, as well as differences in interest, among groups within a community."[23]

Bob Reifsnyder, executive director of the Philadelphia organization, said, "The organization put itself on the line in calling the public meeting. We had no idea what might happen. We knew we wanted to go out to the people and let them know that we were interested in what they had to say."[24] When quoted in the summer issue of *Community*, Reifsnyder continued, " . . . if the Fund—and the agencies—are going to serve this community, they must be responsive to the needs of its people. We saw this meeting as one important way of ferreting out those needs." Speakers at the forum ranged from 10-year-old Michael Candelaria, who asked that more money be allocated to the Big Brother Association to help fatherless boys, to a man identified only as "John" who suffered from alcoholism and asked that more services be made available to provide "realistic drug education" for his son. Town meetings and community forums modeled on Philadelphia's experience were tried in hundreds of communities and served as resources for new United Way volunteers, as well as fountains of information to support the development of new services and increased fund distribution flexibility.

 "My father, the United Way executive in Philadelphia for many years, and I have 'lived' more than 50 years of this history. I can't imagine work that is more important than the work we all do together to serve our communities."

—ROB REIFSNYDER, *President, United Way of Greater Cincinnati*

"VENTURE GRANTS" SPAWNED NEW AND DIFFERENT SERVICES THAT BECAME COMMONPLACE

The term "venture grant" was borrowed and adapted from the business world's term "venture capital" to describe an approach to funding experimental agency programs and was first used by the Madison (WI) United Way, according to Amos Burrows, retired executive director. "In 1970," he reported, "our board decided to put 5 percent of the total raised into this innovative fund. Proposed experimental programs had to deal with local unmet needs and be different from any program ever tried elsewhere in the United States. . . . In a typical year about 10 projects were funded."[25]

Venture grant funds under a variety of names appeared in most cities during the 1970s.

"How well a corporation prospers depends to a large extent on the well-being of society. By helping nonprofit organizations to operate more efficiently, we may be giving something more valuable than outright grants of money."
—A.W. Clausen, *Past Chairman, Bank of America, Past Member, United Way of American Board of Governors*

"Urban self help" was the objective of Baltimore's special fund that was created at the suggestion of newly recruited inner-city volunteers, according to Art Redding, manager of the program that was called PUSH (Project Urban Self Help).[26] Allen Larsen, then United Fund executive director, described the purpose of the special fund in Baltimore's *Evening Sun*. "We want to be more relevant to urban needs," he said. "PUSH [will] be separate from the United Fund, reaching out beyond the established programs to

"I couldn't have finished it without federal matching funds."

help indigenous and newly emerging organizations."[27] PUSH didn't forsake the United Fund, however. In 2003 correspondence, Larsen stated his belief that "Affirmative action, with its director as a ranking staff member, evolved from our experience with PUSH. We felt that our experience in quantifying

175

equal opportunity objectives for the United Fund and its funded agencies and services in Baltimore was probably the first such program in the United Way field. We were sure that it had grown from our involvement of minority people in volunteer and staff positions during the '60s."[28]

Venture grant funds in nearly every city were modeled on the approaches developed in Madison and Baltimore. They commonly fostered experimentation and development of a wide range of services.

- In Houston, $3 million was awarded to newly formed organizations in the Mexican-American community that were aimed at supporting education for children and community centers for the elderly, according to former planning and allocations director Al Henry.[29]

- Boeing employees in Seattle received United Way venture funds for a "one-stop service center" for 12,000 families in need of help, according to Chuck Devine, who served as United Way President at that time. It provided employment counseling, family counseling, training in resume writing, and emergency food in one location.[30]

- Pittsburgh citizens came together to create one of the nation's most comprehensive health education centers, according to John McCormick, then executive director of the Health and Welfare Planning Association. In a *Community Focus* article titled "Enjoy Life, Stay Healthy: A Community Response," he described the citizens' motivation as follows: "They felt that education could make a difference, that it could motivate people to assume greater responsibility for their own health."[31]

- "New Freedom for the Handicapped" described what communication interns at the United Way of Erie County Pennsylvania believed to be the "first residence designed and furnished by and for people with physical handicaps."[32]

- "Medetect" was a health exposition on wheels, according to Jim Cuffaro, staff member of the United Way of Allegheny County, Pennsylvania. "A mobile center that could test for anemia, take blood pressure, and screen for diabetes, hearing disorders, and some heart abnormalities traveled through the neighborhoods of people who didn't have ready access to personal physicians."[33]

- Finally, agency professionals and volunteers in Louisville sought the

help of Council of International Programs executive Henry Ollen-
dorf to design an agency/university experience for foreign youth
workers, educators, and social workers. The program they designed
began during the summer of 1971 and included the first United Way
internship in the United States for a foreign United Way professional. For three months, Yoshiaki Nemoto, national secretary of
the Community Chests of Japan, spent his days in training at the
Health and Welfare Council of Jefferson County.[34]

BUSINESS VOCABULARY AND TOOLS BECAME COMMONPLACE

As local United Way organizations increasingly viewed themselves as *businesses* that supported human services, instead of community organizations
that practiced *social work,* they adopted business vocabularies. For example,
public relations staff became *marketers,* and campaign *prospects* became *accounts.* Changes in function didn't always follow changes to more businesslike
names, but when new tools were introduced, functions changed dramatically.

> *"The most effective way to manage change is to help create it."*
> —LOUIS E. MARTIN, *Publisher, Chicago Daily Defender and Past Member,*
> *United Way of America Board of Governors*

The United Way of America Service Identification System (UWASIS) was
introduced in 1973. Its definition of health, recreation, and welfare services,
with stated methods of measuring each, became for local United Way organizations and affiliated agencies what the Standard Industrial Classification
(SIC) codes had become in the business world. Once in use, UWASIS served
as the "gold standard" by which all United Way and agency services could
be defined and counted. Local budget and allocation committees seized upon
the new tool, and within months most required the submission of agency
financial and service data in UWASIS language. In Bridgeport, the United
Way contracted affiliated agencies to deliver units of service proscribed by
UWASIS, thereby setting the stage for "purchase of service" contracts that
would be developed over the decade ahead.[35]

The board of the Ohio Citizens Council saw the potential for making use of a UWASIS-like tool for *all* human services, public and nonprofit, within their state. They asked Cincinnati's Community Chest & Council to modify the national compendium so that it could be used by state agencies.[36] Cincinnati's research director Madeline Hertzman and then information management consultant Doug Warns adapted UWASIS. In early 1974, the Ohio General Assembly adopted "OSIS," the Ohio Service Identification System. OSIS served as a model for a number of other states, but not enough for a standard service classification system to become standard practice for all government human service agencies.

AGENCY SERVICE DATA AUTOMATED

With standard definitions and measurements in place, and a nationally fashioned *Accounting and Reporting* manual in use, local business leaders sent a number of their information management employees to the United Way of Metropolitan Tarrant County (TX) to create a "computerized statistical data gathering and reporting system." John Stevenson, president of Ft. Worth's Continental National Bank, provided a helpful "how to" guide for other local United Way organizations to do the same in a *Community Focus* article titled "Creating a Computer System for Services Accountability." In a step-by-step narrative, he told readers how Ft. Worth brought agencies together for training on how to complete an "IBM keypunch" card for each client.[37]

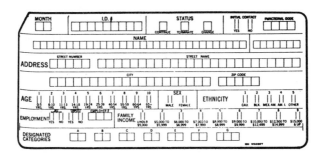

"If we had information in which we had high confidence, information that told us where our users came from, what they used, and how they ultimately benefited, we know we would have a great campaign tool," he concluded.

THE NEXT STEP WAS COMPUTERIZED CENTRAL ACCOUNTING FOR AGENCIES

In an attempt to provide business-like economies to its member agencies, the United Way of Jefferson, Shelby, and Walker Counties in Birmingham instituted an automated central accounting service and "sold" 23 of its 40 affiliates on the idea of using it, according to Dave Orrell in a *Community Focus* article titled "Birmingham, Alabama's Computerized Central Accounting System."[38]

"Leaders need to forget Uncle Remus' song, 'Doin What Comes Naturally.' Leaders often need to do what come unnaturally."
—DON PLAMBECK, *Past Director, National Academy for Voluntarism*

Agency income was deposited with the United Way "to increase interest earning capability." Agencies ordered payroll and other checks with "charge authorizations" and received regular and annual reports and audits. "One [could] see many of the obvious cost savings of centralized accounting for agencies," Orrell wrote. " . . . and United Way has been able to reduce its EDP [electronic data processing] charges from $117,000 to $45,000 per year."

Not all agencies bought the idea, however. After reading Orrell's article, Bill McCurdy, the director of Information Systems and Services for the Family Service Association of America, criticized the Birmingham approach in his agency's newsletter for its local executives. "If you read [Orrell's] article carefully, it's a good bet most of you will conclude something is wrong. Stripped down, the article seems to be saying:

1. Local agencies, by and large, are incompetent . . .
2. The United Way, together with its member agencies, form a single, centrally controlled enterprise analogous to a corporation . . .
3. A centralized accounting system will not only offset agency incompetence but also provide an effective policing tool for improved centralized control.

"While this image is irritating we think it probably results more from high enthusiasm for the system and oversight in writing than from any hidden motives on the part of the authors," McCurdy concluded.[39] His point was not a new one to readers of the United Way of America publication. Local agencies valued their autonomous freedom from local United Way controls every bit as much as local United Way organizations valued their distance from United Way of America.

Did the dialogue stop there? No. United Way of America invited a rejoinder from Orrell. His comment pointed clearly to a business reality that was fast becoming a fact of life for United Way organizations. "We would have to say that we believe it is no longer possible for any public or private social service agency to make decisions in a unilateral way in today's world. If, indeed, we are apart in our thinking concerning accountability, we would be disagreeing only as to 'how much and to whom?' "[40] In the months ahead, several local United Way organizations followed Birmingham's lead, but most did not, choosing to avoid conflict similar to that which had been aired in United Way of America's national publication.

CAMPAIGN GROWTH REQUIRED CREATIVITY

Persistent inflation throughout the 1970s eroded the economic prosperity that continued from the end of World War II until the late 1960s. In 1973, the first of two Arab oil embargos during the decade created shortages and doubled gasoline prices. Even after the embargo ended, gas prices stayed high. Inflation rose and caused rising rates of unemployment, spiraling inflation, federal deficits, and a phenomenon the economists called "stagnant demand."

"Funds will only come from the reputation of those who ask for them."

—CHARLES F. ADAMS, *Past Chairman, Raytheon Co. and Past Member, United Way of America Board of Governors*

Needs for agency services increased dramatically in most communities. Faced with small workforces from which to solicit funds, campaigners searched for a tool that would carry the message that larger gifts were needed from those who had jobs and their employers.

"Campaign to potential" was introduced to Wilkes-Barre, Pennsylvania

CEOs by United Way campaigners to help counter the affects of major layoffs in two of the community's largest firms. Layoffs, however, were not the only reasons that prompted local United Way organizations to make use of this new concept. Shortly after Wilkes-Barre introduced campaign to potential, United Ways in Wichita Falls and El Paso, Texas; Wilmington, North Carolina; and Seattle adopted the approach to deal with their annual campaign challenges to increase contributions. They used Wilkes-Barre's innovative concept to ask corporate and individual donors to give based on their potential, instead of their history.

If you don't do it, it won't get done.

GIVE THE UNITED WAY

COMMUNITY
United Community Funds and Councils of America
March-April 1970

A checklist of "elements critical to campaigning to potential" (CTP) was presented in a *Community Focus* article titled "CTP Works, Five Problems—One Solution."[41] The list included:
- Analyze each company's past performance in relation to potential.
- Help companies develop measurable objectives based on potential.
- Ask companies to develop multiyear goals to sustain growth.
- Help firms build strong employee information programs and cases.

Calculation of "potential" was simple. Each community selected its 10 best campaign performing companies based on corporate gift per employee, per capita employee giving, and percent employee participation. Others were told, "If they can do it, then we'd like you to learn how." Employee giving guides were held up as targets for increased numbers of employees, and representatives of the high-performing companies shared their campaign techniques as part of highly publicized training programs for volunteer solicitors and company representatives. CEOs wanted to see their companies' names on the "top 10" list and welcomed the CTP approach. Besides, they knew that local campaigns were becoming increasingly dependent on workplace campaigns, as residential efforts were waning.

DOOR-TO-DOOR CAMPAIGNS FADED
QUICKLY AS GASOLINE PRICES ROSE

It was lines at the gas pumps in the summer of 1973 that sealed the fate of door-to-door campaigns. The Arab oil embargos that had contributed to dizzying increases in inflation also produced gasoline shortages, lines at pumps, rationing (the last digits of auto license plates dictated which days of the week car owners could purchase gas), and prices that seemed to increase daily.

Once a mainstay in every community campaign, residential efforts disappeared in most communities by the end of the decade. They were largely replaced with three separate approaches: the most generous door-to-door contributors were placed in a special gifts division whose prospects were personally solicited; individuals and families with records of smaller gifts received mailings and telephone follow up; and neighborhood prospects that had never given were simply dropped from the campaign. Increasingly, people who supported the campaign were seen in the same way that stores viewed shoppers.

CONTRIBUTOR RESEARCH TREATS DONORS LIKE "CUSTOMERS"

"Just as businesses do, we wanted to treat the people who spend money with us as 'customers,'" said Don Lifton, assistant director of the United Way of Tompkins County in Ithaca, New York, when the author sought background on a contributor survey that appeared in the form of a tear-off stub on the campaign pledge card. "So many products we buy include customer research response forms in their packaging, we decided to do the same with ours," Lifton concluded.[42]

The Ithaca approach to donor research had been described by Lifton in the July 1978 issue of *Community Focus*. "Each year in communities across the nation, significant numbers of adults use the same procedure to indicate their financial support for local human services—they fill out a United Way pledge card. Such a process seems tailor-made for a survey."[43]

"What others think of our contributions is far less important than what we think of them."

—Mrs. John B. Greene, *Past Board Member, United Community Funds & Councils of America*

Ithaca's 1977 survey found that contributors were most concerned about unemployment, services for the elderly, and drug and alcohol abuse. Thirty-three percent of those returning pledge cards responded to the United Way's "customer survey."

CONTRIBUTIONS DESIGNATED TO AGENCIES
WERE AWARDED AS "LAST DOLLARS"

United Way leaders in Philadelphia found that their "donor-customers" wanted their designations to United Way agencies to make a difference in the amount of money agencies received from the campaign. Speaking at a meeting of the National Professional Advisory Committee, Philadelphia United Way President Ted Moore reported that designations to member agencies would be held back from the funds available for distribution by the United Way Allocation Committee. Following the volunteers' decisions on the amount of money to be distributed to each agency, designated gifts were added to each agency's allocation as "last dollars."

" . . . I would like to challenge a few myths, including the thought that the original United Fund concept was conceived on a myth. The myth was to 'give once for all.' We are all very much aware that this has never happened, and frankly, I hope it never does

> *happen . . . It is the concept that the United Way can meet all*
> *community needs. This is ridiculous."*
>
> —LOUIS A. WERBANETH, *United Way Volunteer, Volunteer Leaders'*
> *Conference 1979*

"DONOR OPTION" CREATED TO PRECLUDE
CHARGES OF A UNITED WAY MONOPOLY

In 1977, after 10 years of mutual cooperation based on a contractual agreement, the Los Angeles United Way sought to merge with Associated In Group Donors, then known as AID-United Givers. (AID had been created by a number of Los Angeles companies during the 1960s as a means of getting their employees to increase their giving. Instead of going to the United Way for distribution by allocation committees, employee contributions from these firms went directly to agencies determined by donors or committees of donor-representatives.)

Heated debate and litigation ensued as the organizations battled over the ways in which funds would be counted and allocated. "On March 13, 1978, AID-United Givers filed a lawsuit against the United Way for attempting 'to create a charity monopoly.' "[44]

The court battle ended when both parties accepted a settlement agreement that required the United Way of Greater Los Angeles to establish a "donor option plan," later described by United Way of America as "a program that allows the contributor to designate all or a portion of the contribution to any tax-exempt, volunteer-run, health and social services agency, in addition to agencies funded by the United Way campaign; and which is in some way publicly communicated to the potential donors."[45] United Way leaders begrudgingly agreed to do so to avoid future charges that the organization's operation of workplace campaigns for a given list of member agencies was a monopolistic practice.

> *"They drew a circle and shut me out,*
> *Heretic, rebel, a thing to flout;*
> *But love and I had the wit to win,*
> *We drew a circle and brought them in."*
>
> —EDWIN MARKHAM

Several other local United Way organizations in California followed Los Angeles' lead, but it would not be until the 1980s that "donor option" or "donor choice" would be more commonly made available to local United Way donors.

THE 1970s ADDED "SIZZLE" AND BEGAN A SEARCH FOR "SOUL"

When Bruce Schulman described "the great shift in American culture, society, and politics" in his retrospective of *The Seventies*, he observed that "The long, gaudy, depressing Seventies *reinvented* America."[46] For the United Way movement, the 1970s may have been long and gaudy, but they were anything but depressing. United Way of America produced programs and tools that brought back what Bill Aramony called "sizzle." The environment in hundreds of communities lived up to the marketers' claims that "United Way brings out the best in all of us."

Technology provided an ideal platform on which local United Way leaders could change and reconstruct their organizations. Inspired by a new national mission statement "to increase the organized capacity of people to care for one another," leaders refreshed their goals, objectives, and strategies to achieve them in cooperation with donors, agencies, and civic leaders at a "community table." They increased their capacity to serve their communities by making increased use of business management practices, high-speed communication, and electronic information management tools.

As the decade came to a close, The Ramones, a 1970s band, recorded an album titled "The End of the Century." Kurt Loder's *Rolling Stone* review said, "Its songs paid homage to a musical past—'Do You Remember Rock'n'Roll Radio?' one asked—but made it clear that the time had come for something new. 'It's the end, the end of the Seventies,' The Ramones sang. Of course, this ultimate garage band hardly meant to weigh that chorus with philosophical pretensions. They were just looking for a line than sounded good."[47]

Local United Way organizations, as well, were looking for something that did more than sound good as the 1970s ended. It couldn't be as simple as a line in a song. The rate of social and technological change was spiraling far more quickly than they were, even with the technologies that they had begun to use. United Ways were looking for a fundamental change in the ways they approached their work. Aramony articulated the challenge when he spoke, "We need to put the *soul* back into our business," as he presented a "Program for the Future" to a 1977 meeting of United Way professional staff members.[48]

"Soul" sounded good, but the "line" wasn't defined. It didn't fill the need that Paul Akana had identified when, earlier in the decade, he tried to describe a local United Way organization of the future. "If the United Way movement does not change somehow," he said, "we will become a venerable vestige of the past—an acceptable survivor of goodness in the present, but not a vital, dynamic force as it has been and as it might be."[49] The United Way movement's search for "soul" would take it down new and different paths during the decade ahead.

Key Innovations in the United Way of Serving
Communities Between 1970 and 1979

1970	Coalition planning demonstrated	New Brunswick, NJ
1970	"Environmental scan" introduced	Westchester, NY
1971	Venture grant fund begun with 5 percent of campaign	Madison, WI
1971	United Way "town meeting" convened	Philadelphia, PA
1971	Board skills training targeted minority populations	Birmingham, AL
1971	One-stop service center opened	Seattle, WA
1971	International internship established	Louisville, KY
1972	Youth involved throughout campaign	Kansas City, MO
1972	Strategic planning initiated	Bridgeport, CT
1972	"Urban self help" fostered	Baltimore, MD
1973	Statewide service classification adopted	Ohio
1974	Low-income volunteers recruited	Seattle, WA
1974	Allocations focused on needs of Mexican Americans	Houston, TX
1974	Automated central accounting service offered to agencies	Birmingham, AL
1974	Agency service statistic data automated	Ft. Worth, TX
1976	"Campaigning to potential" introduced	Wilkes-Barre, PA

1977	AID and United Way merged	Los Angeles, CA
1977	"Last dollar" donor designation offered	Philadelphia, PA
1977	"Contingency planning" developed	Rhode Island
1977	Donor identified as "customer"	Ithaca, NY
1977	Mobile medical screening funded	Pittsburgh, PA
1978	"Long-range planning" introduced	Bridgeport, CT
1978	Planning "consortium" demonstrated	Philadelphia, PA
1979	Independent living for disabled people developed	Erie, PA
1979	"Donor option" emerged to offset potential allegation of a United Way monopoly	Los Angeles, CA
1979	"Private and public sector cooperation" defined	Orange County, CA

1   Booker, Christopher. *The Seventies*. New York: Stein and Day, 1980, p. 3.
2   Drucker, Peter, and Edward K. Hamilton. "Can the Businessman Meet Our Social Needs?" *Saturday Review*, March 17, 1973, p. 41.
3   Hicks, Richard C. "Making Sense of the Sixties." Discussion notes given to author in 1970.
4   Berg, Gordon. Interviewed by the author, June 2001.
5   Aramony, William. "Rebirth and Renewal" was the title of the published proceedings of the December 3, 1970, annual meeting of the United Way of America Board of Trustees.
6   Akana, Paul. "United Way—1966." Address at the 1976 United Way Staff Conference, March 9, 1976, Boston.
7   Tropman, Elmer J. Unpublished National Academy for Voluntarism "Planning Self-Study Course," reprinted in John E. Tropman's *Grandma Called It Charity: The Collected Writings of Elmer J. Tropman on Community Development and Organization*. Pittsburgh: The Pittsburgh Foundation, 2001, p. 284.
8   United Community Funds & Councils of America Field Services and Personnel Division. *New Executives' Handbook*, revised 1968.
9   *New Executives' Handbook*.
10 *New Executives' Handbook*.
11 *New Executives' Handbook*.
12 *New Executives' Handbook*.
13 Tropman. "Let's Put Our Planning Act Together: The Future of Voluntary Community Planning." *Community Focus*, United Way of America, April 1978, pp. 10-13.
14 Duda, John E., Lawrence E. Fine, and Mary Holt. "A New Tool for Social Planning." *Community*, January/February 1971, p. 5 and p. 15.
15 Wright, Lowell E. "Project ACTION (A Coalition for Training and Industrial Opportunities Now)." *Community*, March/April 1970, pp. 13-15.
16 Nordin, Leslie. "United Ways Lead the Way." *Community*, July/August 1982, p. 9.
17 Nordin, p. 11.
18 Nordin, p. 13.
19 Wilkinson, George W., Ph.D. Correspondence with the author, May 2001.
20 Bower, Mary A. *Impact: A History of the Health and Welfare Planning Association, 1922–1991*. February 1992, p. 18.

21   Orrell, David G. Correspondence with the author, June 2002.

22   Larsen, Jo-Anne. "Project LIVE Expands." *Community*, Fall 1974, pp. 16-17.

23   Brilliant, Eleanor L. *The United Way, Dilemmas of Organized Charity*. New York City: Columbia University Press, 1990, p. 8.

24   *Community*, Summer 1971, pp. 17-19.

25   Burrows, Amos. Correspondence with the author, January 2002.

26   Redding, Arthur. Correspondence with the author, January 2002.

27   "Special UF Fund Air is Urban Relevancy." *The Evening Sun*, January 11, 1972. Baltimore Neighborhoods Section, p. 1.

28   Larsen, H. Allen. Correspondence with the author, October 6, 2003.

29   Henry, Al. Interview comments at the 2000 Minority Roundtable.

30   Devine, Charles. Interviewed by the author, 2002.

31   McCormick, John G. "Enjoy Life, Stay Healthy: A Community Response." *Community Focus*, April 1979, pp. 15-16.

32   Pater, Lisa and Arlene Piskor. "New Freedom for the Handicapped." *Community Focus*, June 1979, p. 24.

33   Cuffaro, Jim. "United Way Helps Medetect Shift Gears." *Community Focus*, January 1980, pp. 24-26.

34   Even though the first Community Chest formed outside North America was founded as early as 1928 (in Cape Town, South Africa) training opportunities in the U.S. and Canada did not occur until 1971. Subsequent to the first International Conference on United Fund Raising for Social Work Services hosted in Tokyo by the Community Chests of Japan, internships for foreign United Way professional staff members became routine. Programming for these professional staff often occurred under the auspices of the International Council, a predecessor of United Way International that was founded in 1974.

35   Wilkinson, George. Correspondence with the author, October 6, 2003.

36   Aft, Richard N., Ph.D. *Painful Decisions, Positive Results*. Cincinnati: Symphony Communications, 2000, p. 117.

37   Stevenson, John M. "Creating a Computer System for Services Accountability." *Community Focus*, September 1977, pp. 21-22.

38   Orrell and Charles H. Attaway. "Birmingham, Alabama's Computerized Central Accounting System." *Community Focus*, June 1977. pp. 22-24.

39   McCurdy, William B. "Planning and Accountability." Family Service Association of America's June 1977 newsletter for local executives as reprinted in *Community Focus*, September 1977, pp. 24-25.

40   Orrell and Attaway. "Rejoinder." *Community Focus*, September 1977, p. 25.

41   Editors, *Community Focus*. "CTP Works, Five Problems—One Solution." March 1980, pp. 2-8.

42   Lifton, Donald E., in conversation with the author in November or December 1978, during preparation of a paper presented at the 1979 meeting of 10 Key Cities. The paper came to be called "The Donor as Customer, an Exploration of the Application of Business Attitudes Toward Customers to Our Contributors."

43   Lifton. "Contributor Survey of Services, Issues, and Use of Services." *Community Focus*, July 1978, pp. 27-28.

44   Brilliant, citing comments of the editors of *Charity Wars*, p. 93.

45   Brilliant, citing an internal "Donor Option Resource Packet" circulated among United Way of America staff members on June 25, 1982, p. 95.

46   Schulman, Bruce J. *The Seventies*. New York: DaCapo Press, 2001, p. 257.

47   Loder, Kurt. "Review of the End of the Century." *Rolling Stone*, March 20, 1980, pp. 54-55.

48   Aramony, William. Comments on the "Program for the Future" (approved by the United Way of America Board of Governors, December 8, 1976), March 1977.

49   Akana.

CHAPTER EIGHT

Priorities for Programs and Teamwork

1980—1989

Purchasing Agency Services to Achieve Common Goals

$\boxed{J}$ ohn Gardner challenged the local United Way leaders who had given him the prestigious national Alexis deTocqueville Award at the 1981 Volunteer Leaders' Conference: "Is this what America has come to?"[1] Gardner had served as President Johnson's secretary of Health, Education and Welfare, had founded Common Cause[2] and had cofounded Independent Sector.[3]

"The fragmentation of [our society] has been growing for decades through both Republican and Democratic Administrations. I saw it in the late '60s when I was working on the problems of the cities. I saw it in the '70s when I was dealing with the Congress of the United States," he continued. His audience understood every word because the United Ways they represented confronted "fragmentation" every day. They had entered the 1980s on the heels of a decade in which the number of nonprofit agencies had increased several-fold, and efforts to bring their leaders together to plan and coordinate efforts had only begun.

Although government deficits reached all-time highs, federal dollars continued to pour into neighborhood and special-interest nonprofit organizations whose funding, unlike that of United Way affiliates, didn't obligate them to practice teamwork with others. They operated without realizing the major government funding cutbacks that would be a hallmark of the decade.

The new and expanded services of United Way member agencies for whom United Way allocations were serving as "matching dollars" for government funds continued to expand as the decade began. They, too, would suffer funding reductions that would punish clients whose employment training, child care, and preventive health care services had given hope for their futures.

Those who listened to Gardner's words also had dealt with the multiplicity of fund-raising appeals that had come to their communities with the chaotic proliferation of health, recreation, and welfare agencies. Donors often asked, as they had since the mid 1960s, why local United Way campaigns didn't fulfill their 1950s role of eliminating appeals for contributions. New federations of agencies approached employers seeking access to corporate gifts and workplace campaigns as *alternatives* to United Way.[4] While private employers, for the most part, turned away the alternative funds, government employers found that they could not, and increasingly they placed decisions for which organizations to support in their employees' hands.

"The best part of this work has been helping people see how their talents, skills and energy can have an impact on problems in their community. It is very rewarding and it never gets old."
—JIM COLVILLE, *CEO, Greater Twin Cities United Way, Minnesota*

Speaking as the 1985–86 "Gus Shea Memorial Fellowship Lecturer," Alan Cooper, executive director of the United Way of Central Maryland and United Community Services of Baltimore, identified "the changing structure and character of the American work force" as another subject of concern. Even though he had been assigned the topic of "United Way in a Competitive Fund-Raising Environment," he stated, "It is my belief that the relevant issue is *not* competition from the so-called 'alternative funds.' The more crucial issue is that we regain and win donors' allegiance, understanding, and even affection for United Way."[5]

Gardner had offered a challenge to the local United Way leaders who were in his 1981 audience. His words served as a compass bearing toward which local constituents of the United Way movement could point their organizations. "Functioning at their best," he said, "the local United Way *builds* community. It has a responsibility not just to its member agencies, but to the total community, and to its partners in social service, government and private, whether or not they are related to the United Way.

"Thirty-plus years in the United Way movement flew by with great memories of those mentors, including staff, who helped me to be more successful. The greatest rewards were observing the successes of agencies, recipients of services, and hard working volunteers impacted by United Way presence and direction."

—MACK D. HIXON, *Past President, United Way of Greenville County, South Carolina*

"And that responsibility is an inseparable part of the role the organization must play. . . . There are a lot of specialized organizations that would like the money-raising privileges without the arduous community responsibilities. But the two go together."[6] Gardner's words could not have better framed the agenda that would command the attention of every local United Way for the balance of the 1980s.

"The two go together"—United Way community building and United Way fund-raising.

Signs of the Times

GLOBAL/NATIONAL EVENTS

1986	National Committee for Responsive Philanthropy identified 79 non-United Way "alternative funds" raising money in workplace campaigns.
1986	Hands Across America campaign raised $100 million for the homeless and poor.
1989	The Berlin Wall, symbol of totalitarianism in the western world, fell.

IN THE NEWS

1981	Deadly AIDS virus identified.
1989	World Wide Web invented.

SOCIAL MOVEMENTS/GOVERNMENTAL POLICIES & PROGRAMS

1981	"Reaganomics" cut 25 percent of federal human service funds and lumped residual into four block grants.
1982	The proposed Equal Rights Amendment (ERA) ran out of time, ratified by just 35 of the required 38 states.
1983	Continued movement of federal health/human service funds into block grants to states included the largest reductions in the history of government for: Social Services (-18 percent) Child Welfare (-23 percent) Women, Infants, and Children (-22 percent) Job Training (-54 percent) Education for the Disadvantaged (-33 percent) Legal Services (-100 percent) Home Delivered Meals (-16 percent)
1983	Congress appropriated $1.75 billion for emergency food and shelter to be deployed under local United Way aegis.
1986	President Reagan's "Reaganomics" instituted deeper cuts in federal budgets and agency grant income.

ECONOMY/BUSINESS CYCLES AND THE WORKPLACE

1981	15 month recession began in June.
1982	The worst Canadian recession since the 1929 depression began.
1982	Unemployment rose to 10 percent.
1987	Dramatic drop in Dow Jones average signaled coming business down-cycle.
1988	Corporate restructuring/downsizing began.

SCIENCE AND TECHNOLOGY

1989	The personal computer was introduced.

FAMILY/HOUSEHOLD STRUCTURE

1980s	One in 11 adults is divorced; 30 percent of children live with a single parent.

HUMAN NEEDS

1980s	The downturn in economic cycles was reflected in increased substance abuse, crime, and family breakdown.

How Approaches Reflected the Needs and the Times

Local United Way volunteers and staff sought ways to encourage cooperation and collaboration among the still growing numbers of local government and nonprofit organizations that were crowding into most cities'
poorest neighborhoods. They echoed the plea that John Gardner voiced
at the 1980 Aspen Institute, when he called for collaborative movement
Toward a Pluralistic but Coherent Society.[7]

As many of the agencies created in the '60s and '70s asked, "What's in it
for me?" Community consensus builders in United Way organizations
spread their limited financial resources beyond their traditional affiliates and
began to purchase services from nonprofit organizations and governmental
units that would not have passed the stringent "admissions requirements"
of years gone by. Gardner observed of that period, "Our capacity to frustrate
one another through noncooperation has increased dramatically."[8]

*"Enthusiasm and commitment rarely leave United Way staffers.
They are dedicated and ready to work with volunteers at all times."*
—BOB GARRISON, *Past President, United Way of the Quad Cities, Illinois*

Local United Way leaders had no choice but to refine the 1970's nu-
ances of venture grants, consortia, public/private partnerships, and coalition planning into techniques that could move their communities from
noncooperation to teamwork. A national task force was convened to ex-
amine "Community Planning in the United Way System" and identify
ways in which local United Way organizations could be of the most help
in reestablishing cooperation and collaboration among the many organizations that either assumed responsibility or were charged with authority
to plan for client populations or programmatic goals such as community
health. In June of 1984, the task force issued a document titled "Revitalizing Community Problem Solving Within the United Way System," in
which it identified "community problem solving" as "United Way's role
in helping resolve problems, issues, and concerns in the human services
arena beyond the immediate scope of United Way fund-raising and member services."[9]

"Within a month of joining a United Fund, I was stunned by the commitment of volunteers who took on tremendous responsibility. They took on the staff, too. United Way pros, each and every one of us, matured and learned to lead thanks to those hard working volunteers."

—RAY UNK, *Past Vice President, Field Services, United Way of America*

The time was right for local leaders to work locally to reestablish relationships that would build community capacity to solve problems. At the same time, local leaders continued to search nationally for approaches that would energize cooperation among their communities and with the government agencies whose funding guidelines had encouraged piecemeal approaches to service planning and funding.

"Implementation is the ultimate test of what we at HWPA call our PLANNING/ACTION CYCLE:

• FINDING OUT WHAT NEEDS TO BE DONE through careful research and community pulse-taking.

• DECIDING HOW TO DO IT by designing workable blueprints, utilizing professional expertise, consumer participation, and incorporating measurement techniques.

• GETTING IT DONE or making the blueprints come alive by developing the necessary resources to strengthen existing or initiating new programs that will derive the maximum return in human dignity for every dollar spent.

• FINDING OUT IF IT'S WORKING by evaluating results."

—JOHN G. MCCORMICK, *Past Executive Director, Health and Welfare Planning Association of Allegheny County, Pennsylvania*

FREQUENT NATIONAL UNITED WAY INITIATIVES SATISFIED MOST LOCAL NEEDS FOR INNOVATION

There was no end to the stream of issues and ideas that local United Way organizations directed to and discussed under the aegis of their national association. Local communities' confidence in the fund-raising, promotion, community planning, and professional skill-development programs and tools that had been generated by United Way of America, under the 1970s leadership of Bill Aramony, prompted them to ask for more.

As the 1980s began, representatives of what United Way of America publications began to refer to as "LUWOs" (local United Way organizations) continued to work under the leadership of national staff and consultants. They shared their needs and designed national tools and initiatives to meet them.

At the same time, national corporate leaders were refocusing their fields of vision from local to national ways of doing business. They began to expect that local United Way organizations would do the same. As the decade wore on, the United Way of America's agenda showed increasing responsiveness to the widely varying needs and interests of national corporations. The number of nationally conceived and driven initiatives grew to the point that communities could only pick and choose from among them. It would be more than a decade until local innovation would again drive the initiative-agenda of the United Way of America and again reflect Peter Drucker's observation that "executives in front offices should not forget that business tools are best designed and sharpened by the people who use them every day."[10]

DIVERSITY BEGAN TO CHARACTERIZE
UNITED WAY VOLUNTEERS AND STAFF

The convergence of several independent facts of life in the 1980s contributed to an increasing diversification of the *education, experience, training, gender,* and *ethnicity* of local United Way volunteers and staff during the 1980s. Unlike the Funds and Councils of the 1950s and 1960s, United Way organizations during the 1980s were often responsible for operating a variety of community services in addition to the core businesses of planning, fund-raising, and allocating resources. It wasn't unusual for what became known as "full service United Ways" to operate as volunteer recruitment and placement programs, management assistance programs for nonprofit agencies, information and referral services, and more.

- Masters degrees in social work and business management still represented the *education* preferred for many senior staff positions, but college degrees with experiences equivalent to advanced degrees became increasingly acceptable.

- With local United Ways involved in so many kinds of businesses, management *experience* in any professional discipline became highly valued. In addition, corporate downsizing created an available pool of talented individuals who welcomed opportunities to take jobs in a profession that was driven by idealistic values.

The diversity of the people who were required to do the work of local United Way organizations was becoming increasingly understood.

- Increased *training* choices at conferences and in seminars and courses provided skills and conceptual frameworks for volunteers, as well as staff. Local United Ways continued to openly share their "best practices" without proprietary concerns, thus allowing open access to information about their knowledge and technologies.
- In keeping with America's increasing sensitivity to civil rights and women's issues, the *gender* and *ethnicity* of volunteers and staff changed measurably, if not proportionally to the population. Increasingly, women were recruited for senior positions and better paying professional positions. Minority staff recruitment programs attempted to compete with similar business programs, but produced fewer candidates because nonprofit budgetary restraints limited their competitiveness.

UNPRECEDENTED INFLATION AND FEDERAL BUDGET
CUTS DROVE LOCAL CAMPAIGN GOALS HIGHER

The double-digit inflation of the late 1970s continued into the 1980s. Hindsight helped the Federal Reserve Board understand that the increases they approved in the money supply were responsible for what the pundits termed "stagflation," a stagnant economic growth and high inflation. Cuts in the money supply returned economic health, but meant dramatic cuts in federally funded health care, child care, and job training programs, particularly in inner cities.[11]

"I am so happy and proud that my United Way family always made me feel a welcome part of the movement. Thankfully, Community Chests and Councils were among the first social welfare organizations to hire women and minorities."

—HENRY SMITH, *Past Managing Director, Archivist, Historian, United Way of America Information Center*

Local United Way campaigners didn't relish the assignment of finding ways to replace lost government dollars, but they couldn't say "no" to the agencies that fought to keep lower budgets from forcing borderline clients back into poverty. More than one volunteer muttered, "What Uncle Sam giveth, he taketh away," but in city after city, United Ways searched for creative ways to fill the gaps in agency budgets.

OBJECTIVES, NOT PROBLEMS, INSPIRED
UNHERALDED CAMPAIGN INCREASES

Volunteers, agency representatives, and staff looked at the bleak picture drawn by the economic challenges facing the United Way of Metropolitan Atlanta in 1980. Its historical campaign growth of 5 to 7 percent a year had been on a par with most cities of its size, but the amount of money that the federal and state government had invested in health and human services was far less. Inflation was taking big bites out of agencies' capacities to serve the people who came to them for help, and rumors of impending reductions in government programs for the poor were commonplace. United Way business as usual wasn't going to provide the money that the organization's stakeholders knew it could produce, unless it had a "game-plan."

"One of our jobs is making it as much fun to do the right thing as it is to do something else."

—DICK GRAY, *Late Executive Director, Heart of America United Way, Kansas City, Missouri*

Corporate leaders asked Deloitte and Touche executive Jim Copeland if he would lead the development of an approach that the United Way could take to boost campaign results well beyond ordinary levels. "You mean you'd like to do something like double campaign results in the next five years?" he asked. Without realizing it, Copeland had framed a goal that the Atlanta planning committee would articulate at the end of its intensive two-month study. As the decade wore on, double-digit economic inflation and government budget reductions motivated hundreds of other cities to adopt the Atlanta approach. Most followed Copeland's advice, "If you are serious about achieving excellence, you will drive your planning with your objectives, not your problems."[12]

"A significant number of people define maintaining clean air and clean water as a community need. Others think that the development of art in all of its forms is a community need. These interests are not peripheral; they are as fundamental to the quality of community life as are social services."

—JOE VALENTINE, *Past President, United Way of the Bay Area, California*

SOME CORPORATIONS FOLLOWED THE
J.L. HUDSON COMPANY'S 5 PERCENT SOLUTION

"For 40 years," Joseph L. Hudson Jr. told a group of retail merchants that had come together at Wayne State University in Detroit, "our company has associated our community gifts with the sales, profits, and number of employees at each of our stores." He challenged the members of his audience to follow the same practice.[13]

"There has never been a more important time to show the leadership of the nongovernmental providers of services to the needy. It is enlightened self-interest," he continued. "Business must serve society, because society holds the franchise on the free enterprise system. As long as society believes business serves it well, the franchise remains secure." Hudson shared the text of his speech with readers of *Community Focus* magazine, and by the mid 1980s, hundreds of United Way campaign volunteers had delivered reprints to their corporate prospects. In 1987, Independent Sector, the national advocate for the nonprofit sector, built on the Hudson model with its "Give Five" campaign, a program for workers to "give five hours a week and 5 percent of their income to the causes and charities of their choice, through nonprofit organizations, religious institutions, or simply by helping a neighbor or friend in need."[14]

"The underlying philosophy of corporate philanthropy is that it is good business to be an enlightened corporate citizen. It doesn't make sense to talk about successful corporations in a society whose schools, hospitals, churches, symphonies, or libraries are deteriorating or closing."

—CLIFTON C. GARVIN JR. *Past Chairman, Exxon Corporation and Past Chair, United Way of America Board of Governors*

NEW LEADERSHIP GIVING PROGRAMS EMERGED

The *Alexis deTocqueville Society* and *minority leadership giving* represented local campaigners' creative efforts to maintain local United Ways' abilities to meet service needs as the decade continued.

In 1981, with the permission of United Way of America to use Alexis deTocqueville's name for an individual leadership-giving program,[15] Nashville physician Thomas Frist Jr. founded the first local Alexis deTocqueville Society.[16] A 1984 article in *Community* described one of the most lucrative innovations of the decade:[17]

This new program was a $10,000-plus leadership-giving program that targeted high-income individuals, families, and private foundations within the Nashville community. Although members of this group *had historically supported the arts, higher education, the symphony, and other worthwhile charities, they had not become significantly involved with United Way.*

In the first year, Nashville's Alexis deTocqueville Society attracted 25 givers in the $10,000-plus range; collectively they increased their giving from a prior-year card value of $65,000 to $650,000.

By the third year, membership in the Society had grown to 50, with total contributions of approximately $850,000, or 10 percent of the total campaign.

Dr. Frist said, "Once this previously untapped resource was identified, the key was to develop an effective marketing program to promote the United Way concept. The Society was our answer."

Interest in the Nashville approach was so high that hundreds of local United Way organizations wanted to create identical programs. In 1984, with the encouragement of the United Way of America Board of Governors, Dr. Frist invited 11 other cities to serve as "test sites" to see if local Alexis deTocqueville Societies could be replicated. All of the test cities shared Nashville's positive results. By the end of the decade, with the help of dozens of personal appearances by Dr. Frist, over 300 cities had incorporated Alexis deTocqueville Societies into their annual campaigns.

"These Americans are peculiar people. If, in a local community, a citizen becomes aware of a human need which is not being met, he thereupon discusses the situation with his neighbors. Suddenly, a committee comes into existence. The committee thereupon begins to operate on behalf of the need and a new community function is established. It is like watching a miracle, because these citizens perform this act without a single reference to any bureaucracy, or any official agency."
—ALEXIS DE TOCQUEVILLE

Minority leaders associated with the United Way of Central Indiana made history when they organized the first minority leadership giving club.[18] Beginning with a membership of 12, African-American leaders in

Indianapolis created the "Minority Key Club." Each member was asked to make a leadership gift of $1,000 or more annually. In its first year (1985), the 12 founders contributed a total of $13,000. By the end of the decade, the gifts of 50 members totaled $141,200.[19]

MATCHING-GIFT INCENTIVES BEGAN AS A PERSONAL CHALLENGE TO LOW-PERFORMING PHYSICIANS

Abe Plough wanted every citizen of his community to give to the United Way of Greater Memphis in proportion to his or her capacity. As founder of the Plough Pharmaceutical Company, later Schering-Plough, giving to United Way had been Plough's passion for decades when he decided to use his personal giving as an incentive to groups of contributors whom he felt were giving below their ability.

"This is not an idle threat," he told the president of the United Way in 1984. "I'm going to increase my Foundation's gift from $250,000 to $300,000 this year, and if you want one nickel of it you'll get one-third as much from the doctors in Memphis. They can afford to give more [in 1983 they had given a total of less than $50,000], but I want to challenge them without making your job impossible."[20] A banner headline in the local medical society bulletin communicated Plough's challenge two weeks later. Memphis physicians pledged $90,000 prior to the scheduled conclusion of the campaign. Plough stood firm on the condition of his gift and suggested that the campaign be extended until the doctors "make it clear that they will not be publicly responsible for the campaign missing its goal by $310,000 [Plough's gift plus the uncommitted $10,000 balance of his challenge to the doctors]."[21]

In 1985, Plough increased his matching grant and softened his matching requirement of the previous year. Less than two weeks before the United Way kicked off its campaign, trustees of Memphis' Plough Foundation announced that they would contribute an unconditional gift of $250,000 and, in addition, the Foundation would contribute $100,000 more if attorneys, dentists, and accountants would collectively pledge $500,000 by the last day of the campaign. These four professional groups had made combined contributions of $200,000 the previous year.

"Determined 'not to leave $100,000 lying around that could be used to help people,' General Campaign Chairman Ira A. Lipman, chairman and president of Guardsmark, Inc., and Vice Chairman Robert M. Bird, managing partner of Coopers & Lybrand, accepted the challenge. Within a week's time, they had corresponded with the city's 4,400 professionals, hosted a luncheon for leaders of the four professional groups and societies, and developed strategies to pursue during the campaign."[22]

When the campaign ended, chairman Lipman announced a nation-leading 22 percent total campaign increase. It included $531,667 from the groups that had been challenged to increase their combined gifts from $200,000 to $500,000.

Plough's idea of using his gift to challenge others to give caught on quickly. Within a few years, dozens of communities had identified donors and groups of donors who wanted their gifts to serve as incentives to others. Few communities, however, suggested that donors of "matching gifts" include the conditions that Plough had put on his contributions.

EFFORTS TO IDENTIFY AREAS FOR MAJOR
INCREASES IN GIVING SPAWNED "CAN-DO"

CAN-DO, Campaign Analysis Now Developing Objectives, was created to help local United Way organizations "learn to invest their time and resources in the areas that provide the 'biggest bang for their buck,' maximizing strengths and overcoming weaknesses," according to United Way of America's *Guide for On-Site Assessment*.[23] The process was created in Vancouver in the early 1980s by Bob Myers and used in a number of

Canadian, then U.S. cities before it was packaged and made available as a consultation service of the United Way of America.

The campaign analysis program was built on a three-phase approach to create a continuous learning and improvement environment with the local United Way, according to Myers and his colleagues Peter Ufford and Mary-Scot Magill.[24]

1. *Pre-On-Site Planning*, during which campaign, financial, service, and human resource statistics were collected from all divisions within the local United Way organization.

2. *On-Site Assessment*, during which statistics were presented, analyzed, and categorized according to their accuracy and relevance to reaching fund-raising potential.

3. *On-Site Follow-Up*, during which work plans were designed to convert potential into real campaign income, and organization-wide strategies were identified to integrate resource development with other organizational goals.

"When local labor leaders ask me how to best represent their members, I answer, 'Ask them what they want and listen very carefully to their answers.' I can offer no better advice to United Ways that seek to help employers and employees."

—NADRA FLOYD, *Past Member, United Way of America Board of Governors*

CAN-DO quickly became a staple on United Way of America's consultation shelf and, by the end of the 1980s, had contributed to the ability of several hundred local United Ways to keep pace with the double-digit growth of inflation and the funding of the highest-priority agencies whose budgets had been reduced by federal and state governments.

SWEEPSTAKES AND GIFTS OF "RECYCLED" FURNITURE HELPED FILL INCOME GAPS

Thanks to the owners of Wegmans Food and Pharmacy, the United Way of Rochester, New York, netted $6 million over the four years in which an annual "United Give-A-Way" was conducted. "Wegmans' customers were asked at the checkout counter to qualify for a sweepstakes entry by donating

$1 to the United Way," according to Joe Calabrese, Rochester's United Way president.[25]

"Promotions ran for approximately six weeks each year. Weekly prizes were provided by Wegmans and their vendors, including a weekly grand prize of $10,000 worth of groceries. Wegmans paid all of the sweepstake costs; the United Way of Greater Rochester received all of the revenue." Wegmans' program served as a model for several local sweepstakes programs during the years ahead, including a subsequent program in Rochester for which General Motors donated several automobiles as prizes for individuals who registered for drawings during each year's campaign.

 "All United Way resources should focus on this one imperative: that every person counts."

—ELIZABETH G. GOWER, *Past Executive Director, Community Planning Council of Greenville County, South Carolina*

A unique program jointly sponsored by the United Way of the Bay Area and the United Way of Santa Clara matched the needs of local nonprofit agencies with a corresponding surplus in local corporations. Previously, in-kind contributions of products were commonly given to local United Way organizations by manufacturers, wholesalers, and retailers, but gifts of used furnishings had been limited to occasional windfalls. In a *Community* article titled "Recycled Furniture: Boon for West Coast Agencies," Sherry Norman described a ground-breaking program.

"The proverbial 'free lunch' may be a myth these days, but 'free furniture and office equipment' is an accessible reality for nonprofit agencies located in the San Francisco/Santa Clara area."[26]

By the time the program was a year-and-a-half old, over $100,000 worth of equipment and furniture had been "allocated to more than 500 nonprofit organizations. Agencies acquired needed equipment and furnishings, while donor corporations disposed of these items through one channel whose nonprofit status allowed contributors to write off depreciated values."

The 1980 West Coast creation proved to be of such great interest to corporations in the dozens of communities that emulated the San Francisco/Santa Clara approach that United Way of America created Gifts in

Kind, Inc. in 1983 to promote manufacturers' gifts of materials. At the outset, the national program supported local United Ways' direct involvement with manufacturers, but the volume of gifts and the need to collect and distribute them efficiently prompted the Gifts in Kind organization to become a national channel through which corporations could create maximum value to as many local United Way organizations as wished to participate in a national gifts-in-kind gift network.[27]

CONTROVERSY WAS PREEMPTED WITH THE FIRST "NONCOERCION GIVING" POLICY

As paternalism in families, schools, and workplaces faded away during the second half of the twentieth century, the practice of "required" (considered by some to be "coerced") giving to United Way fell out of favor. In most communities, however, the perception or fact that a small number of companies continued to require rank and file workers to give to United Way as a condition of employment continued to serve as an irritant to some people. Leaders of the United Way of Greater St. Louis found a way to speak to the subject in their community before it became a problem.

In a *Community Focus* article titled "Preparing for Controversy," Bob Hyland, regional vice president of CBS Radio and chairman of St. Louis' public relations committee, wrote, "When controversy comes, it's best to have a plan in mind for dealing with it."[28] His committee's "Policy Statement on Coercive Solicitation" served as a model for hundreds of local United Way organizations. Carefully worded, it didn't duck the issue, but it focused more on what the organization stood *for* than what it stood *against*:

> United Way of Greater St. Louis does not encourage or condone coercive solicitation in its annual fund-raising campaign. In fact, the basis of the existence of United Way is voluntarism. Therefore, the fundamental basis for giving to United Way is giving voluntarily. Threats of coercion of any kind should never become part of the solicitation process. All campaign volunteers are instructed to adhere to this principle.

As other communities dealt with this issue, the St. Louis model served as the standard on which they built their own positions. A number of communities went beyond the St. Louis position and offered to confidentially refund documented contributions of individuals who felt that they had been coerced to give to their local United Way. While reports noted that this provision of noncoercion policies was well received, no incidences that it was exercised were shared among United Way leaders. It must also be noted that in disseminating these policies, great care was taken to make it clear that United Way was privileged to be invited to participate in corporate campaigns and could only establish policies for itself and its agents, not for corporations or their employees.

CONTRIBUTIONS BEGAN TO BE USED TO PURCHASE SERVICES, RATHER THAN CONTINUING TO FUND DEFICITS

As government budget cuts sliced the service capacities of many local agencies, United Way allocation volunteers began to look more closely at agencies' abilities to operate programs and services rather than their line-by-line operating deficits, the basis of allocations for decades. *UWASIS*, the catalogue of program descriptions developed during the 1970s, and the *Standards of Accounting and Reporting* that had been developed shortly thereafter, served as common tools that community after community used in a movement-wide transition. Without exception, local United Way organizations moved from *deficit financing* to *purchase of service* agency funding without disrupting the flow of agency services.

Seattle's United Way was the first to report the use of "purchase of service" in a 1982 *Community* article titled "Project Transition: Seattle's Way of Dealing with the Cuts." Instead of reviewing the budget forms that documented income and expense for each agency service, volunteers gave substance to earlier changes in nomenclature that made them members of *allocation* committees, instead of *budget* committees. They set budget forms aside and focused on factors that Seattle called "Review and Advisory Guidelines":[29]

- The number of people being served.
- What kind of personal consequences people would suffer if they did not receive that service.
- What effect the government cuts had on that program/service area in both human and financial terms.

What began in Seattle as an effort to develop a rational system to replace lost government grants for programs and services that were judged to be of the highest priority in meeting individual and community needs became the "model heard 'round the field," according to Chuck Devine, then president of the Seattle United Way.[30]

RUNAWAY UTILITY BILLS SERVED AS THE "MOTHER" OF A COST-SAVING INVENTION: ENERGY AUDITS

Akron's YMCA director, Rick Hrnyak, couldn't figure out how he could continue to pay his agency's energy bills. They had tripled within two years, rising to nearly $42,000 in 1982. A *Community* magazine article titled "Akron's Energy Misers" told the happy ending of Hrnyak's 1983 budget year: "Thanks to the energy experts that the United Way had gathered to assist agency efforts to economize, the YMCA learned ways to shave $17,000 off of its utility budget."[32]

"The program recruits energy specialists from the area's major corporations and hospitals to serve as volunteers. By identifying energy problems and suggesting conservation strategies, they help agencies overcome financial problems created, in part, by high energy costs." To perform what Akron's leaders considered an effective energy audit, volunteers examined all portions of a building, including the walls, roof, and type of lighting used. Recommendations ranged from the insulation of heating pipes to the installation of timers on light switches.

Dozens of communities requested detailed information so they could initiate their own energy audit programs after reading of Akron's success.

A "CIRCUIT RIDER" SERVED SMALL ARKANSAS
UNITED WAY ORGANIZATIONS

When the United Way volunteers of Arkansas' newest and smallest United Way organizations called Leon Matthews, president of the United Way in Little Rock, he did his best to provide telephone advice. But that wasn't enough. They all wanted to know how to raise more money to help their communities' agencies offset high inflation and cuts in their government contracts.

Ideally, Matthews would have visited each of his callers' communities, but that was out of the question. Thanks to grants from the Levi Strauss and Winthrop Rockefeller foundations and additional financial support from United Way of America, a program was created to meet the need. "Project Circuit Rider" was described in the July/August 1983 issue of *Community* as "the crucial difference" to the 10 participating United Ways whose combined campaigns rose nearly 19 percent and whose fund-distribution programs were "totally revamped."[33]

Sam Highsmith, volunteer vice president of the United Way of Independence County in Batesville, Arkansas, recorded his observations so that all readers of *Community* could consider how they could make use of the lessons learned in Arkansas. "Today's circuit rider is a far cry from last century's minister on horseback. [Our] circuit rider is Patricia Lindeman, a United Way professional whose job it is to travel around the state logging more than 30,000 miles a year helping smaller United Ways in every aspect of their work, from fund-raising to allocations."[34]

NO STONE WAS LEFT UNTURNED AS LOCAL UNITED WAYS
REACHED OUT TO INVOLVE NEW CONSTITUENCIES

"Good folks always find ways to help their neighbors." That favorite expression of Louisville's long-time labor staff director, Charlie Clark, described the dozens of creative approaches tried by local United Way organizations as they beat the devils of "stagflation" and government cutbacks in human service funds from the doors of their communities.

- In 1980, Metro United Way volunteers in Louisville created a "10-K Run for the Roses" to kick off their 1980 campaign in the tradition of the Kentucky Derby. More than 2,100 runners from 12 states finished their foot race on the track at Churchill Downs. Many of the runners knew nothing about United Way until they read the informational banners that marked their course.[35] Similar events were reported shortly thereafter in Hartford, New York City, Washington, DC, and Little Rock. Not to be outdone, "a San Francisco runner named Frank Giannino ran the 3,103 miles to New York City in 46 days, 8 hours, and 36 minutes to break the record time by 41 hours. He stopped along the way to tell United Way audiences of the nationwide appeal of neighbor helping neighbor."[36]

"The most effective United Way advertising I have ever seen is advertising that invokes a deep response in the viewer about how United Way helps people in need."

—JOHN E. PEPPER, *Past Chairman & President, Procter & Gamble*

- Volunteers of the United Way of Central Ohio added "a half million" to the resources their allocation committee distributed to agencies in 1982. "Success hinged on how many cans of tuna fish and boxes of cereal the volunteers collected from Franklin County employees. Their goal," according to a *Community* article titled "To Feed the Hungry," was "500,000 food items for the area's 60-plus food pantries that supply nourishment to needy families."[37] Their "Operation Feed Drive" served as a model adopted by hundreds of local United Way organizations that followed Central Ohio's example of involving local Boy Scout and Girl Scout councils to provide people to help organize and carry out their programs.[38]
- In Singapore, the Community Chest decided to publish a children's magazine in order to convey their campaign and human service messages to parents. First published in 1985, *Sharity Magazine*, whose title played on the word "charity," featured a Malaysian ele-

phant named "Sharity." Stories portrayed "helping people in need" as a value that its readers should apply to their daily lives. By the end of the decade, *Sharity Magazine* enjoyed the highest circulation of any local magazine.[39]

"Aren't we lucky? Every day, we see the inner beauty of United Way people, from the children and the old folks who attend the centers we make possible . . . to the talented people who serve them . . . and the generous donors who make it all possible."
—CHARMAINE S. CHAPMAN, *Late President, United Way of Greater St. Louis, Missouri*

- In Memphis, public school Assistant Superintendent Sara Lewis shared her dream with staff Vice President Bill McQueen. She sought "a new generation of civic leaders who begin with the values I see when I volunteer at United Way."[40] Together, Lewis and McQueen led the development of a kindergarten-to-eighth-grade curriculum that "covered various aspect of voluntarism and was taught in approximately 10 days."[41] Training for teachers to use the new curriculum produced an unsolicited windfall for the United Way campaign in the form of quadrupled 1985 campaign gifts of Memphis City Schools employees.

AN INITIATIVE NAMED "SUCCESS BY SIX©"
CROWNED THE CREATIONS OF THE 1980s

As if 1980 volunteers wanted to leave a historical reminder of the reasons that local United Way leaders worked so hard to counteract the many barriers that challenged their communities, the United Way of Minneapolis Area introduced "Success by Six©." It was an initiative that sought to provoke the Minneapolis community to respond to its failure to prepare many of its young people to be responsible, productive citizens. Its theme stated its goal, "Unlocking the Door to Early Childhood Development."

"This story began with a vision: something could be done to correct the neglect in this society of thousands of young children who are not getting the care and nurturing they need to prepare them for fulfilling lives and productive citizenship," wrote Charles Mundale in his booklet "United Way of Minneapolis Area's Success by Six©, The Early Days."[42] "The failure becomes obvious in school, but it does not begin there," he wrote. "It begins in the womb. And it persists because, for the early childhood development system in this society, *no one is in charge.*"

"United Way must view the community as its primary customer, human services as its agenda, donors as its investors, and service organizations as its armed forces."

—DAN MACDONALD, *Past President, United Way of Central Indiana*

Success by Six© was a *model* of community organization and not an organization itself. "Institutional partners"—leaders of businesses, professions, education, and agencies—framed models of community action, spoke to the value of building on strengths that existed in the community, and encouraged increased effectiveness among organizations that were already at work. In every activity, it used the influence of three of its founders: Jim Ranier, chairman and CEO of Honeywell Inc., Minneapolis Mayor Don Fraser, and Minnesota State Senator Ember Reichgott. They gave witness to their personal belief in the importance of their goal by refusing to delegate the work on the program to deputies. "What you have to do as a business leader is lead," Ranier declared. "You have to find ways to make money already going into the problem more effective, and I'm going to use the position [as co-chair] and the chits I have in the community to get these things going."[43]

"Success by Six© was the first local community-building effort in which United Way of America placed staff within a local community to gain a working knowledge of an initiative to replicate on a national basis," according to Jim Morrison, former United Way of America Vice President. "We saw the kind of community organization being practiced in Minneapolis that our predecessors learned in schools of social work. The community created a plan of action that included activities such as 'improving access to services' and then got the people who could make things happen to see that it did," Morrison observed.[44]

With the encouragement of United Way of America and a $50 million, five-year grant from the Bank of America Foundation, "Success by Six©"

initiatives spread to over 350 cities throughout the United States and Canada. Its promise of success for children prompted optimism among volunteers, staff, donors, and agencies. Its *community organization* methods reminded local United Way organizations of their own capacities to initiate change in the lives of people.

"Whenever I view change in the movement and resistance to change, I think of the transition we were asked to make by the newly-named United Way of America to adopt the new name and Saul Bass logo in 1974. My Executive Director professed to never changing the name of our beloved United Fund and the Torch Drive. At least he kept to his promise until football season started in the Fall. That marked the beginning of the NFL United Way spots. Our name was changed to United Way within 90 days. Just goes to show that 'never' in United Way language can be a very short period of time."

—RAY HUMPHREY, *Past Campaign Director, United Fund of Chester, Pennsylvania, President, United Way of Riverside, California*

THE RATE OF CHANGE WAS DESTINED TO CONTINUE ITS SPIRAL "Peggy Sue Got Married" in the 1980s, but only half of the people who chose to live together did the same. This increasing phenomenon was redefining "the American family" and the human services that would be needed to support the alternative lifestyles that were becoming commonplace.

"E.T." called home, thanks to the imagination of Hollywood's screen writers, but cellular telephones and personal computers had grown from imagination to reality. Technological advances such as these were already re-shaping the ways in which local United Way organizations did business. Local United Ways were further shaped by United Way of America's use of the banking industry's term "full service" for affiliates whose "core strategies" and "supportive programs" were altered to fit the design mold introduced during the 1970s when Paul Akana predicted the shapes of future organizations.[45]

Lee Iacocca's autobiography and Miss Piggy's *Guide to Life* were best sellers. They supported the "me" generation's aspirations for power, wealth, and personal security. *Forbes'* list of the "400 richest people" became more important than its list of "500 largest companies." The United Way campaign role of "leadership giving" from communities' wealthiest individuals and families began to grow.

"Think globally, act locally" was heard at the board meetings of most national corporations as foreign competition required business leaders to restructure themselves to address multi-national or global markets. Calls for help in establishing United Way organizations in dozens of countries poured into the offices of United Way International.

Takeover mania had struck corporate America. Mergers and consolidations meant decreases in home-owned businesses in every city and "downsized" workforces. Larger campaign gifts were forthcoming from surviving companies and employees, but that string was sure to run out soon.

Tom Wolfe named the baby boomers the "splurge generation" as "shopping 'til you drop" was made possible with credit cards that filled the pocketbooks of the 20-somethings and 30-somethings who were less prone to delegating their charitable giving decisions to "well-schooled and impartial" allocation committees.

Talk shows became part of our lives. CNN filled the airwaves with news 24 hours per day, seven days per week. United Way leaders wished they could get more air time to share their news. It wouldn't be long, however, until they hoped that the broadcasters and journalists would stop talking about United Way.

Key Innovations in the United Way of Serving
Communities Between 1980 and 1989

1980	Noncoercion policy adopted	St. Louis, MO
1980	Goal to "double campaign results in five years" announced	Atlanta, GA
1980	5 percent pretax earnings requested	Detroit, MI
1980	In-kind gifts solicited to recycle used furniture	Santa Clara, CA and San Francisco, CA
1980	"Run" for United Way introduced	Louisville, KY
1981	United Way purchased agency services	Seattle, WA
1981	Alexis deTocqueville Society founded	Nashville, TN
1982	United Way led food drive	Columbus, OH

1982	"Circuit Rider" staff offered to small communities	Little Rock, AR
1983	Agency energy audits made available	Akron, OH
1984	Campaign challenge gift offered	Memphis, TN
1985	United Way curriculum adopted for grades K-8	Memphis, TN
1985	National children's magazine published	Singapore
1986	Minority leadership giving club organized	Indianapolis, IN
1987	Sweepstakes initiated	Rochester, NY
1987	"CAN-DO" campaign analysis begun	Vancouver, BC
1988	"Success By Six©" initiated	Minneapolis, MN

---

[1] Gardner, John W. Remarks on the occasion of the Alexis deTocqueville Award, United Way of America Volunteer Leaders' Conference, San Francisco, April 27, 1981.

[2] Common Cause was founded in 1970 as a citizens' advocacy group that aimed to make political institutions more open and accountable.

[3] Independent Sector was founded in 1980 to support hundreds of nonprofit groups nationwide.

[4] Among the "alternative funds" that sought access to workplace campaigns during this period were groups such as the National Black United Fund and the Women's Way.

[5] Cooper, Alan S. "United Way in a Competitive Fund-Raising Environment." George A. Shea Memorial Fellowship Lecture, 1985-1986. Presented to United Way of America's National Professional Advisory Council, June 17, 1986, Alexandria, Virginia.

[6] Gardner.

[7] Gardner. *Toward a Pluralistic but Coherent Society*. Aspen: The Aspen Institutes for Humanistic Studies, 1980, title page.

[8] Gardner, p. 15.

[9] "Revitalizing Community Problem Solving Within the United Way System—a Task Force Report." United Way of America, June 1984, p. ix.

[10] Drucker, Peter. Paraphrased by the author from *Managing for the Future: The 1990s and Beyond*. New York: Truman Talley Books, 1992, p. 191.

[11] McCan, Robert L. *An Outline of the American Economy*. Washington, DC: Center for Educational Services, Washington, DC, 1981.

[12] Copeland, James. "A Plan to Double Campaign Results in Five Years." Presented to the Board of Directors of the United Way of Metropolitan Atlanta, February 1980.

[13] Hudson, Joseph L. Jr. "The 5% Solution." Louis A. Baum Lecture, Detroit, 1979, published in *Community Focus*, June 1980, pp. 17-19.

[14] Independent Sector. "Give Five" program bulletin, 1987.

[15] NOTE: Permission was required because United Way of America, under the leadership of Mary (Mrs. William) Gates, had created and incorporated "The Alexis deTocqueville Society" in 1972. Its purpose was to "recognize persons deemed to have rendered outstanding service as volunteers in their own communities or nationally." The name was chosen, according to *People & Events*, "because of deTocqueville's admiration for the spirit of voluntary association and voluntary effort for the common good." The first annual award in 1972 was presented to entertainer Bob Hope at the April 25, 1977, United Way of America Volunteer Leaders' Conference.

[16] Stringer, Catherine. Correspondence with the author, August 20, 2003.

[17] "Contagious Commitment." *Community*, July/August 1984, pp. 15-17.

18 Wills, Edward L. Correspondence with the author, June 20, 2003.
19 "History of the Minority Key Club of Central Indiana." *Minority Key Club Directory*, 2001–2002, p. 3.
20 Plough, Abe. Conversation with the author, June 1984.
21 Plough to the author, November 1984.
22 Gardner, Thomas P., Ed.D. "Professionals Go the Distance." *Community*, May 1986, pp. 12-13.
23 Heiden, Dorothea, Group Vice President Resource Development, United Way of America. Introductory comments in *Resource Development On-Site Assessment* by Robert J. Meyers, Peter Ufford, and Mary-Scot Magill. United Way of America, May 2001, inside front cover.
24 Meyers. *Resource Development On-Site Assessment*, p. 3.
25 Calabrese, Joe. Correspondence with the author, September 12, 2003.
26 Norman, Sherry, Brenda Gibson, and Pat Vare. "Recycled Furniture: Boon for West Coast Agencies." *Community*, March/April 1982, pp. 5-6.
27 Corrigan, Susan. "Investment Vision." *Community*, Fall 1988, pp. 26-28.
28 Hyland, Robert F. and Robert G. Stipsits. "Preparing for Controversy." *Community Focus*, August 1980, pp. 17-19.
29 Mourer, Peter. "Project Transition: Seattle's Way of Dealing With the Cuts." *Community*, January/February 1982, pp. 8-9.
30 Devine, Chuck. Interview, 2002.
31 Matisse, Don. Correspondence, October 28, 2002.
32 Bradley, Connie. "Akron's Energy Misers." *Community*, April/May 1983, pp. 18-20.
33 Highsmith, Samuel C. "Project Circuit Rider: Professional Help for Small Communities." *Community*, July/August 1983, pp. 13-14.
34 Highsmith, p. 12.
35 "Running for United Way." *Community Focus*, January 1981, p. 17.
36 ibid, p. 18.
37 "To Feed the Hungry." *Community*, March/April,1982, pp. 2-4.
38 Foley, Deborah. "Campaigning for Food." *Community*, Spring 1988, pp. 21-23.
39 Laux, Evelyn. Conversation with the author following her visit to Malaysia, 1994.
40 Bennett, Cathy. "A Dime's Worth of Difference—Developing Student Leadership." *Community*, Volume 5, Number 6, 1985, pp. 21-24.
41 "Memphis Tennessee, Teaching a New Curriculum." *Innovations for a Second Century*, Volume 2, Number 4, April 1987, p. 3.
42 Mundale, Charles. "United Way of Minneapolis Area's Success by Six©, The Early Days." The United Way of Minneapolis Area, 1991, p. 28.
43 Mundale, p. 31.
44 Morrison, Jim. Correspondence, August 2003.
45 Akana, Paul and Bill Aramony. "The Second Century Full-Service United Way: Five Core Strategies and Eight Supportive Programs." United Way of America, 1986.

Chapter Nine

Technology and Vision Spur Change

1990—1999

Responding to Societal Forces With Transformational Concepts

Paul Akana, United Way of America's scholar-in-residence, hit the bull's-eye in his 1976 prediction of the United Way movement's focus in the 1990s. "We grew up town by town with local points of view, but the pervasive impact of national and multinational corporations, the power and influence of the federal government, the speed of communication, and our own increasing interdependence, are leading us inevitably toward a national perspective."[1]

 "In the early years of the Christian church, the people of Corinth asked Saint Paul, 'What is the ultimate in life, the things that are permanently important, that never change?' He gave an intriguing answer, 'The things you cannot see.' So, what are the things you cannot see? I think these are the things that signify the character of the United Way and the millions of people who participate in a leadership position or as contributors. You can't see justice; you can't see truth; you can't see honor; you can't see humility; you

can't see service; you can't see compassion; and you can't see love. I think United Way lets us see these things."
—President Jimmy Carter

National trends and issues required a nationwide perspective for the leaders of local United Way organizations. National and global corporations wanted single points of United Way contact, as opposed to more expensive, community-by-community interactions. Electronic advances made "on-line" transactions more affordable than face-to-face business. The times called for increased collaboration among local United Way organizations and even more system-wide innovation than had been achieved during the past two decades. But that wouldn't come to pass until local United Way leaders dealt with a national tragedy and its waves of aftershocks.

INAPPROPRIATE AND ILLEGAL BEHAVIOR BY UNITED WAY OF AMERICA'S PRESIDENT STIFLED INNOVATION

Beginning in February 1992, local United Way leaders winced as they read public reports of United Way of America President Bill Aramony's actions that appeared to reflect bad judgment on his part and that of the United Way of America Board of Governors. No one suspected that nearly three years later Aramony and two of his subordinates would be convicted "on conspiracy and fraud charges for bilking the charity of more than $1 million."[2]

The headline on the front page of the February 16, 1992 *Washington Post* ended months of speculation on how Pulitzer-Prize-winning reporter Charles E. Shepard would handle rumors of Aramony's improprieties. It read, "Perks, Privileges, and Power in a Nonprofit World; Head of United Way of America Praised, Criticized for Running It Like a *Fortune 500* Company."[3] The article described Aramony's compensation and questioned a number of his expenditures. On February 24, Shepard presented information that raised questions about Aramony's lifestyle and professional practices. *Wall Street Journal* reporters summarized the primary concern of local United Way leaders. They said, "Recent disclosures of United Way's excesses, capped by the abrupt resignation of its highly paid national president, have tarnished the organization's image and jeopardized future giving."[4]

Local volunteers were outraged and voted to withhold support of the national organization until all questions of alleged improprieties were resolved. Angered as well, local professionals expressed feelings of betrayal by the person who had helped shape their careers and organizations with his charismatic and effective leadership of the national organization. Press and media, locally and nationally, gave no quarter as they demanded information about compensation and management practices from hundreds of local United Way organizations.

In November, *Philanthropy Monthly* described issues that faced nearly every local United Way organization in North America. "What started out as 'the Aramony Affair' has now broadened to a full-cry media campaign (with a kernel of truth) castigating the 'excessive' salaries and perquisites of leaders of local or regional United Ways."[5] The article went on to offer an explanation for the entire affair. "At the first level, what went wrong was that governing boards (1) did not fulfill their responsibilities and (2) did not sufficiently understand public attitudes so as to protect the institutions they served."

In the months that followed, the United Way movement suffered its own "great depression." Energies that had previously been applied to community planning, fund-raising, and fund distribution were being dissipated on efforts to justify compensation of local United Way executives and assurances that board oversight was appropriate. Local leaders insulated themselves from criticism of their national association by disassociating themselves from it until its image and those of its leaders could be repaired. In doing so, they also distanced themselves from one another.

 "It is interesting to note that the United Way movement changed as the nation changed and as each community changed. It was, and still is, the community table around which local volunteers come to build a system of caring that they feel is best for their community."

—TOM VAIS, *Past President, United Way Retirees Association*

218

After more than a decade of nationally inspired innovation, the need and energy to create new approaches to United Way challenges had diminished or had been lost. Instead, resourcefulness was now being applied to distinguish local United Way leaders and organizations from their national counterparts. As actions were taken to insulate local campaigns from the national United Way scandal that consumed news media attention, local volunteers and staff hunkered down to the practice of the functions they had mastered during the 1970s and 1980s. When they met, they shared more information on the ways in which they were "surviving" than the ways in which they were innovating. All the while, the rates of social, economic, and technological changes around them were spiraling at a dizzying pace.

 "While I was always impressed at the quality of the volunteers in our business, I was just as impressed at the ability and flexibility of the United Way staff to constantly adjust, change, care, and create in ever changing environments."

—DELL RAUDELUNAS, *Past CPO, United Way of Union County, New Jersey*

Signs of the Times

IN THE NEWS

1991	Soviet Union dissolved.
1993	Apartheid ended in South Africa.
1993	Truck bomb exploded in New York's World Trade Center killing six and injuring 1,000.
1999	Dow Jones average broke through 10,000.

SOCIAL MOVEMENTS/GOVERNMENTAL POLICIES & PROGRAMS

1990	President Bush accelerated return of grant decision-making to states; "entitlement" drove grants to states, rather than local priorities.
1990	Congress approved the Americans with Disabilities Act (required physical access for disabled people).
1991	A Six Nations man in Ontario was the first to be allowed to make

a traditional native oath in Canadian courts, instead of swearing on a Bible.

ECONOMY/BUSINESS CYCLES AND THE WORKPLACE

1991   The longest North American economic expansion in history began, following an eight-month recession.

1992   U.S. unemployment hit 7.8 percent, the highest level in eight years.

1999   Unemployment reached 4 percent, the lowest level since 1957.

SCIENCE AND TECHNOLOGY

1990s   Electronics rapidly increased data storage and public, private, and personal communication.

1992   Health care costs hit $838.5 billion, or 14 percent of total economic output.

HUMAN NEEDS

1990   Welfare rolls reached record high of 14.3 million people.

1998   National welfare rolls fell to 8 million, a 30-year low.

1999   Number of divorced adults reached an all-time high of one in 11.

NINE FORCES RESHAPING AMERICAN SOCIETY AND THE UNITED WAY MOVEMENT WERE IDENTIFIED

The countdown to the twenty-first century for local United Ways was no less complex than it was for the society of which it was a part. Nine leading forces, according to United Way of America's environmental scan titled *What Lies Ahead,* were defining the boundaries within which United Ways and their communities would function during the 1990s and the century that followed.[6] When they were published, the leaders of local United Way organizations found these helpful in understanding many of the issues they were currently facing. Many also prepared local environmental scans by adapting United Way of America's publication as their first steps in developing their own strategic plans.

"United Way is at the heart of caring. It's not just a way to help others . . . it's also the way we help ourselves."
—MICHAEL J. MCLARNEY, *President and CEO, United Way of the Midlands, Nebraska*

To varying degrees, local United Way leaders found that the nine forces outlined in *What Lies Ahead* had direct bearing on their abilities to serve their communities.

- *The Maturation of America*—starting with the maturing of the baby boom generation and the "graying of America." Implications for local United Way organizations included the shift in the population of contributors from "hourly, payroll deduction" to "leadership level" to "former donors." The decline of manufacturing in most communities had resulted in the loss of large numbers of workplace contributors, i.e. those who participated in payroll deduction programs. Leadership giving programs such as the Alexis deTocqueville Society proved to be a ready resource for the cultivation of five- and six-figure gifts from established and new donors.

> *"United Ways across our great country, and now throughout the world, like the famed artist Henri Mattisse have created colorful masterpieces in the form of diverse communities with unique ways of caring for themselves."*
>
> —MICHAEL L. WILLIAMSON, *President, United Way of Aiken County, South Carolina*

- *The Mosaic Society*—reflecting increased ethnic diversity, a growing population of elderly individuals, and new definitions of households. Each of these factors provided its own set of challenges and opportunities.
    - In most communities, United Way boards of directors did not reflect the ethnic diversity of their communities. (NOTE: To a large measure, this was the result of the continuing leadership roles played by founders and large corporate and individual contributors, populations that seldom reflected the ethnic diversity of their communities.) Many local United Ways, after looking at how they measured up in this area, instituted minority leadership training and recruitment programs to meet their needs and those of direct service agencies. A smaller number created minority campaign giving programs.

- The growing number of older people in many communities presented the challenge of service needs and the opportunities to expand the ranks of volunteers. Inclusion of "care for the elderly" in campaign cases for giving increased, as did efforts to ask retired workers to continue their contributions. Efforts to recruit new volunteers from the ranks of the older population met with mixed results.

 "With an understanding of the past, modern community builders must envision a future that focuses on long-term gains, process as well as product outcomes, and a view of community with links to larger systems."
—NANCY M. FINDEISEN, *Executive Director, Community Services Planning Council of Sacramento, California*

- *Redefinition of Individual and Societal Roles*—blurring the boundaries among the public, private, and nonprofit sectors and the responsibilities of individuals versus institutions. Federal budget deficits meant reductions in funding for many local services. For-profit enterprise competed with nonprofits to capture client fees that produced income in excess of expense. Nonprofit organizations' services were often determined by their income sources instead of their missions. As United Way funds continued to shrink as a percentage of the total of nonprofit agency budgets, the role of United Way leaders changed. United Way planners, both professional and volunteer, adopted roles as "community problem solvers" and "community builders" as their roles shifted from "plan-makers" to "convenors." Instead of doing the planning for their communities, they sought to facilitate its doing.
- *The Information-Based Economy*—allowing business to increasingly operate through networks rather than under one roof, valuing information as a commodity, and using technologically enhanced communication in every field of human endeavor. If United Way organizations were to continue to enjoy close relationships with corporations, organi-

zations, individuals, and one another, they would need to maintain abilities to respond to the increasing variety of ways in which each of their constituents operated.

"United Ways must struggle to retain the discretion to make investment decisions based on evidence as well as emotion, on master plans for community improvement as well as marketing plans for particular programs."

—HUGH B. PRICE, *Past President, National Urban League*

- *Globalization*—moving products, capital, technology, information, and ideas around the world would continue to escalate. Increasingly, the decisions affecting local United Way organizations' campaign income were being made in other cities and sometimes, in other countries. Immigration, national and local, was placing different demands on community agencies and their requests for United Way financial support. Local United Way leaders saw increased relevance of the efforts of United Way International to establish national and local United Way organizations in countries hosting the many installations of global corporations. Not only would these new organizations help meet local needs, but they would serve as helpful allies in telling the United Way story to corporate leaders on behalf of the multiple locations of their employees.

"It seems there were as many reasons for our volunteers to become involved as there were volunteers . . . some wanted to improve the community, some wanted to improve a particular situation, some wanted to rub shoulders with key leaders, some wanted to impress their boss, and some wanted to feel needed. There were no 'bad' reasons. Our job was to do our best to help them satisfy their specific needs."

—GEORGE PFEIFFER, *Past President & CEO, United Way of Asheville & Buncombe County, North Carolina*

- *Economic Restructuring*—supported by increased information acquisition, management, and storage capacities, business could be done from anywhere in the world and by any size company. All organizations, large and small, profit-making and nonprofit, were subject to merger, acquisition, or obsolescence. The local corporate leaders involved with United Way organizations were increasingly subjected to relocation and repositioning. This required United Way staff capacities to refresh information and maintain external relationships, skills that had not been required in the past.

- *Personal and Environmental Health*—concerns about individual and public health were growing. "Global warming" affected entire populations beyond the reach of local United Ways. Cigarette smoking, substance abuse, and nutrition affected individuals who looked to community organizations to help them and their family members understand and deal responsibly with personal choices. Increasingly, United Way organizations looked for ways to increase the value they provided to growing lists of stakeholders.

- *Family and Home Redefined*—the functions that once were handled predominantly by families, such as meal preparation and child care, were increasingly offered by commercial concerns. These factors, as well as increasing divorce rates, single parenting, and same-sex relationships, were making dramatic changes in the patterns of health, recreation, and welfare services. Services such as those for divorced and single parents weren't new to United Way fund distribution committees. They adjusted their priorities based on changing local needs. Issues surrounding homosexuality prompted most United Way leaders to walk the fine line between the "for" and "against" positions that were commonly communicated by press, media, and advocates for differing approaches.

"For more than a century local United Ways have rallied volunteer spirit and focused energy to meet the highest priority needs, community by community."

—JOE CALABRESE, *President, United Way of Greater Rochester, New York*

- *Rebirth of Social Activism*—following a decade of concentration on business and economic growth, the public-agenda pendulum was swinging decisively in the direction of social concerns. Homelessness, lack of affordable housing, racial tensions, and extensive child poverty were some of the issues that were gaining increased attention. "Access" became the term that advocates for many causes used to express their overriding goal. They wanted access to information, services, and power to make decisions that would meet the needs of the people they represented. Given their involvement with information, services, and decisions, local United Way leaders searched for ways to respond to activists without going beyond the middle-of-the-road positions that allowed them campaign access to the majority of their supporters.

LOCAL VOICES RETURNED TO NATIONAL
DIALOGUES, BUT SLOWLY

Within this environment, local United Way leaders searched for opportunities that would allow them to reclaim the national center that had supported their abilities to meet day-to-day operating challenges. Their disenchantment with the forum that had served them so well for nearly two decades was compounded by the campaign bruises and questioned credibility brought to most communities by "the Aramony scandal."

"The processes and operations that positioned the United Way brand have had an unusual side effect. They have created the most astounding family of very diverse leaders who are miraculously connected in close friendships and alliances for life."
—VINEY POLITE CHANDLER, *President & CEO, United Way of Metropolitan Tarrant County, Texas*

One professional described it to his colleagues in late 1992 as "a time when our communities have moved us and our organizations from the list of good guys to the status of salespeople who have to prove themselves every time they knock on a door."[7] The Harvard Business School described the situation in a case study as one in which, "the governance system had grown distant from the voices of . . . those who had given it the right to govern."[8] In either case, the interaction that had generated individual-local and collaborative-national creativity reached a low ebb as local United Way leaders pulled back from one another and their national association.

Paula Harper Bethea, chair of the 1993 United Ways' Leadership Conference, and new United Way of America president, Elaine Chao, began the slow process of reestablishing trust among local leaders. They opened the national meeting by calling for a "renewed emphasis on the partnership that is so important to United Ways' success: volunteers and staff working as a team to help others help people in their communities."[9] Representatives of hundreds of local United Way organizations came together that year in San Francisco and discussed ways to "Change Today and Meet Tomorrow's Challenges."[10]

> *"United Way continues to promise opportunities for all of us . . . as donors, opportunities to make a difference to others and to our communities . . . as neighbors, opportunities to help people in need and sometimes, ourselves. I am thankful for the opportunity to help make the promise of United Way a real one in my community."*
> —MIKE DURKIN, *President, Mile High United Way, Colorado*

But the conference didn't generate the enthusiasm and ensuing creativity that had characterized the conferences of many preceding decades. The "best practices" that were shared reflected exceptional performance of ordinary approaches, not the exceptional programs that were needed to deal with the forces that were reshaping society.

Sparks of local creativity only flashed a few times during the 1990s. When they did, however, they reenergized a movement that had been anxiously awaiting breakthroughs that would transform United Way as much as forces were transforming society.

INNOVATIONS EMERGED THAT WOULD INCREASE
UNITED WAYS' CAPACITIES TO PROVIDE VALUE

While small in number, the few local innovations that emerged during the 1990s targeted system-wide needs and generated sea-changes in local United Way capacities:

- South and Central American, Asian, and European affiliates of United Way International opened doors to the gifts and volunteer talents of global businesses and their employees.
- Contributions were directed from programs and services to outcomes to respond to donors' insistence on "value."
- The groundwork was laid for local United Way organizations to document their "impact" on community conditions.
- Electronic tools were applied to campaign pledge processing.
- A nationwide "211" telephone system to make information about services easily available was born.
- Ways to make use of cutting-edge technology to consolidate "back room" functions were explored.
- First steps were taken to consolidate the "back room" operations of geographically distant United Way organizations.

UNITED WAY INTERNATIONAL (UWI) THOUGHT
GLOBALLY AND ACTED LOCALLY

Once the administrative shock waves of Bill Aramony's alleged inappropriate involvement with United Way International's governance had dissipated, UWI responded to requests of governments, corporations, and nongovernmental organizations for technical, volunteer, and financial support to create and operate national and local organizations like those in North America.

By the end of the decade, United Way International affiliates were operating in 40 countries. Their global mission was "Promoting the Voluntary Initiative Worldwide."[11] To varying degrees, they were providing the local community planning, fund-raising, and allocating functions for which their counterparts in North America were known. Consistently, they were building awareness among the leaders of global corporations that through the United Way they could meet their philanthropic needs. Consistent with the history of the United Way movement, United Way International sought to support local initiatives with global support.

"Since the earliest days of the Community Chest, committed volunteers have helped this nation navigate through good times and bad. Today, in the midst of world conflict and economic uncer-

tainty, United Way continues to be a constant beacon of hope for people in need."
—JACQUELINE S. MARTIN, *President, United Way of the Texas Gulf Coast, Texas*

Innovation by local United Way organizations affiliated with UWI, for the most part, dealt with cultural translations of established United Way practices and regulatory requirements unique to each country. One notable exception during this period was initiated by United Way International volunteers during the 1990 formation of Eröforrás Alapítvány, the United Way of Hungary.

"It was serendipity that brought the newly appointed Finance Minister of post-Soviet Hungary together with a creative American volunteer who was in Budapest to help community leaders form a United Way for their country and a dozen of its cities," according to *A Joint Venture in Human Services.*[12] Using as a model the provision by which American taxpayers can designate one dollar of their federal taxes to a presidential election fund, the volunteer helped leaders of Hungary's new government construct a choice by which Hungarian taxpayers would designate up to one percent of their federal taxes to a fund to be distributed by a national United Way-like allocation committee. Two years later, authors of a new tax code for Poland made use of the same technique, but doubled Hungary's allowable designation to 2 percent.

IN THE U.S., SERVICE "OUTCOMES" DEFINED
A MEASURABLE VALUE TO DONORS

Market research conducted in 1992 by the United Way of Central Maryland made it clear that Baltimore area residents wanted to know the results for which their campaign gifts were responsible. "They wanted to see a relationship between the money they gave to the United Way and changes in peoples' lives or conditions in the community," said Larry Walton, Baltimore's United Way president, when he shared his reflections on "outcome measurements" with United Way of America's National Professional Council.[13] "Some folks just wanted to know what happened. Others expected us to make problems go away," he added. In either case, Baltimore's concept led hundreds of local United Way organizations over a threshold that separated over 100 years of asking donors to support "services to people in need" from asking donors to pay for "outcomes" that people would experience as a result of receiving services. The rationale for requesting contributions and the basis of allocating funds to agencies took a giant step forward.

"Perhaps the most significant and rewarding aspect of our work is that each day you realize a life is changing because of what we do. Over my 28 years in this business that's a lot of people and a lot of lives that have made it so personally and professionally satisfying."
—CRAIG A. CHANCELLOR, *President, Triangle United Way, North Carolina*

Over the next few years, the definition of "outcomes" was sharpened and differentiated from programs, services, outputs, and results. As the use of outcome measurement as a factor in evaluating programs and determining agency allocations was initiated in local communities, refinements were developed and shared through a United Way of America project team. By the end of the decade, communities had produced a new vocabulary for describing the impact that United Way donors, volunteers, and agencies were making in their communities.

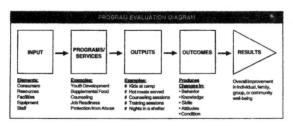

"Putting Outcomes in Perspective."[14]

BEYOND SERVICE OUTCOMES, COMMUNITY WORKS™ [15]
DEFINED RESULTS WITHIN SERVICE CATEGORIES
Beginning in 1994, the United Way of Minneapolis Area launched Community Works™, a comprehensive approach to deal with tough problems in the community by:

229

- focusing on achieving results, changing systems, and leveraging resources;
- bringing people from all over our local community to work together, defining and building the kind of community we all want;
- preventing problems before they take hold in peoples' lives; and
- focusing on collaboration, public policy, and public awareness in addition to program funding."[16]

The program focused all local United Way expenditures in one of six categories of results.

CommunityWorks™

increasing self sufficiency
United Way works to prevent hunger and homelessness and to help people become more independent, by providing for basic needs and access to education, employment and affordable housing. As a result, people can become active, contributing members of our community. Those who need food, clothing and shelter will receive it.

respecting diversity
United Way works to ensure all people can actively participate in and contribute to community life without discrimination. As a result, people of all backgrounds can interact with and support one another without racism, hatred or prejudice.

promoting health & healing
United Way helps people safeguard their health, prevent illness and recover from debilitating diseases, injury or abuse. This includes education on healthy life styles and on preventing and treating diseases such as cancer, heart disease, arthritis and diabetes as well as counseling for mental and chemical health. As a result, people are achieving physical and mental well-being.

strengthening families
United Way works to help people with the many problems and changes that can tear families apart — violence, drugs, job loss, divorce and death. United Way also helps reinforce and strengthen stable families. As a result, families are developing and maintaining secure and healthy relationships.

nurturing children & youth
United Way works to help children from earliest childhood through the teen years through good nutrition, parenting, health care, mentoring, education and youth development activities. As a result, children and youth are developing to their full potential, growing up in safe, healthy environments that promote learning.

supporting older people
United Way works to help older people live independently in their own homes, deal with chronic disease, overcome loneliness and remain secure, active, contributing members of our community. As a result, older adults are maintaining their economic, physical and social well-being.

With the establishment of visual connections between the use of donations and the anticipated results that would come from programs supported by the United Way, the groundwork was laid for the next major breakthrough in United Way technology—the allocation of contributions to achieve "visions."

"VISIONS" DESCRIBED THE WAYS IN WHICH RESULTS WOULD BENEFIT PEOPLE AND THEIR COMMUNITIES

Categories of results had been defined and visually described. Results had been articulated. But how would things actually look when all had been said and done? That question weighed heavily on the minds of Minneapolis' volunteers, staff, and agency representatives as they struggled with the challenges of measuring the impact of Community Works™.

"The transition year was 1993. Six vision councils were created simultaneously and vision plans, baselines, and milestones for measuring progress were developed and approved," according to the description of Minneapolis' innovations in *On the Road to Impact*.[17] Over the next few years, volunteers, agency representatives, and staff worked together to "identify and understand the most critical issues in the community, United Way resources, recent research, and best practices, and to learn about each vision area from a community perspective."[18]

Minneapolis and neighboring St. Paul worked closely to record their journey and learnings. When asked for suggestions that might help other local United Way organizations benefit from their experience, they responded, "Don't move too quickly. Communication from the start— involving all of the key players—is really important. Agency participation at every step of the way is critical. Everybody has to be on board. The reality is that it will take several years before there is a process that everyone understands and that it is doing what it's intended to do."[19]

As other cities emulated Minneapolis' approach by creating vision councils and identifying the ways their people and communities would appear when United Way dreams became reality, Minneapolis joined with St. Paul to experiment with a step beyond vision councils they called "impact planning councils."[20] These groups attempted to consolidate all United Way functions that planned, evaluated, prioritized, reviewed, and financed agency services within a single group whose point of view could be comprehensive, rather than piecemeal.

ELECTRONIC PLEDGE PROCESSING
WAS APPROACHED CAUTIOUSLY

As local United Way organizations and their corporate supporters increased their use of electronic information management systems, much thought was given to ways in which these new tools could be applied to campaign management. The first development along these lines was reported at the 1995 meeting of United Way of America's National Professional Council by Tom Ruppanner, president of the United Way of the Bay Area.

Ruppanner summarized the rationale in a *Wall Street Journal* interview when he said, "We had to make it easy for our customers to buy at our store."[21] From Ruppanner's point of view, the increased competitiveness of charitable organizations asking to be given access to workplace-based payroll deduction giving continuously required United Way organizations to prove their worth to corporate leaders. Use of electronic tools was just one more way to increase United Way's competitive advantage through the time and cost savings that machinery could offer.

In late 1994, the United Way of the Bay Area created a 30-employee computer subsidiary called Uniteq. By early 1998, Uniteq was receiving information from San Francisco's "largest corporate donors, especially those with several office and plant locations."[22] The early electronic systems did no more or less than the manual information management systems they replaced during those years, they just carried out functions with greater speed and accuracy than had been possible with nonelectronic systems.

"The United Way system has made its reputation by constantly meeting new challenges in human services and now our future depends on our ability to do this even better with new technology, customer service and a changing environment in all areas of service."

—LARRY WALTON, *President, United Way of Central Maryland*

In 1996, information management technicians at the United Way of Toronto, Ontario, under the direction of information systems manager Mike Rumack, found a way to get data from companies who were making use of electronic pledge processing to interact with Toronto's total campaign data base. By 1998, after the United Way had turned its pledge processing software development business over to Toronto-based Helix Data Processing Consultants Ltd., Helix introduced software that was designed to meet integrated data management needs common to nonprofit organizations. Known as "ANDAR for Fund Raisers," the software package dealt with a variety of information processing needs that included:

- Prospecting and soliciting
- Donor segmentation and cultivation
- Leadership tracking and recognition
- Campaign management
- Pledge and designation processing
- Web-based e-pledging
- Customer relationship management
- Volunteer matching
- Information and referral
- Allocations and outcomes[23]

Despite its proven effectiveness in cities that made early use of electronic information processing, especially campaign pledge processing, local United Way organizations were slow to make greater use of this aspect of technology. Costs were often prohibitive and risks of losing control of data without which campaigns could not be conducted made the use of electronic information processing a low priority for many local United Way organizations. Even when the United Way of America attempted to introduce an information system that could become available for all United Way organizations at reasonable costs, there was not enough interest to make the national effort viable.

"The United Way offers each of us the opportunity to serve others, and in the doing, enriches us all."
—ERIC D. DEWEY, *President and CEO, Greater Kalamazoo United Way, Michigan*

TECHNOLOGY MADE FOR EASY ACCESS OF COMMUNITY-WIDE INFORMATION & REFERRAL SERVICES: "211"

In Atlanta, as in most other cities, people who wanted to telephone for information or referral to helping services found numerous and diverse sources in the phone book: call-in lines, help lines, crisis lines, hot lines, and more. For people who sought information to help others, the choices of where to turn could be more confusing than helpful. For people dealing with stresses brought about by their need for information and referral services, the impact of so many phone numbers could be devastating.

Most local United Ways either operated or funded information and referral services that were available 24 hours a day, seven days a week. Many of these provided contractual support to more specialized call-in services that couldn't afford "24/7" operation. Still, none of them made it as convenient for people to get help with their human needs as it was to dial 411 for directory assistance or 911 for emergencies.

 "I never lose sleep over whether what I do professionally is worth my time and energy. Helping people in need, working with caring people and making our corner of the world a bit better for all of us is an outcome that gives me peace and pleasure."
—MARK LARSON, *President/CPO, United Way of Whatcom County, Washington*

In 1997, the United Way of Metropolitan Atlanta initiated 211, a single telephone service through which callers could find help getting food, housing, drug treatment, or crisis assistance.[24] The program proved to be so effective that dozens of local United Way organizations began to explore the idea. Together, in coordination with the United Way of America, United Way advocates for a national three-digit phone number for human services efforts undertook the task of convincing the Federal Communications Commission (FCC) to designate 211 nationally for that purpose. As the decade ended, the FCC had formulated plans to make 211 available nationally as a single phone number that people could call for help in getting social, health, and recreation services.

CONSOLIDATION OF "BACK ROOM" FUNCTIONS WERE EXPLORED

During the decade, several large cities and groups of large cities had established pledge processing centers or were developing plans to do so. Notable among these was a joint exploration of ways to consolidate the "back room" functions of pledge processing, accounting, payroll, purchasing, audit, and financial management for a number of cities. Under the leadership of Yvonne Gray, chief operating officer of the United Way of Greater Cincinnati, "the chief financial officers of United Way organizations located in Indianapolis, Louisville, Dayton, Columbus, and Lexington met to identify any and all ways to coordinate or consolidate internal functions to save time and money."[25]

"United Way is not an organization. Thinking of it that way is too limiting. United Way is the way a community manifests the strongest value in the human creed. Taking care of one another is the first responsibility of life."

—MARK O'CONNELL, *President, United Way of Metropolitan Atlanta, Georgia*

The first initiative of the group was an experimental program in which the Lexington United Way became an online client of the Cincinnati information management program. Following months of training and preparation, Lexington permanently terminated its own internal information management functions and received all of its information management service from equipment located in Cincinnati.

Winston Faircloth, president of the Lexington-based United Way, described the early experience of his organization in a report to the CEOs of the project's sponsoring United Ways. "Every morning when we turned our computers on at the United Way of the Bluegrass, machines lit up at the United Way in Cincinnati. After a while, we didn't care where the service was coming from: our basement, another state, or another country. The fact was that we were getting a higher quality of service by collaborating with others than we could afford to purchase for ourselves."[26]

A VISION OF A *UNITED WAY* BEGAN TO TAKE SHAPE

When, in 1976, Paul Akana shared his vision of "United Way—1996" with those in attendance at the National Staff Conference, he described the "united way" he loved in terms of its value to society. But, what he described was as much a way of doing things as it was an organization. "In a fundamentally pluralistic society," he said, "the value of the United Way system rests on the very simple proposition of centrism. By virtue of its centrist position, by virtue of its acceptability to all interests, the United Way is able to provide a workable mechanism for helping people— the charter, if you will, of social responsibility."[27] Akana's vision was different from those of the Federations and Councils of Social Agencies' leaders who had come together over a hundred years earlier. His forebears dreamed of the days when their agencies' capacities would be sufficient to meet the needs that confronted them. Akana articulated a *way* in which all members of communities could help people in concert with one another, a *united way*.

"The United Way has historically been the best vehicle in any community to organize people around an agenda to care for one another. I am proud to be leading our local United Way through its transformation from a Community Building to a Community Impact Organization empowering the next generation of families towards positive and lasting change."

—MARIA VIZCARRONDO-DeSOTO, *President/CEO, United Way of Essex and West Hudson. New Jersey*

As local United Way organizations flew into the twenty-first century on the wings of technology and visions of the ways their people and communities would appear when United Way dreams became reality, they fulfilled part of Akana's forecast. They had used what he termed their "centrist positions" to begin the development of sufficient agreement among all stakeholders to solve the problems that each stakeholder knew was keeping individuals, families, neighborhoods, and communities from achieving their full potential.

236

Key Innovations in the United Way of Serving
Communities Between 1990 and 1999

1990	Hungary secured option for taxpayers to direct tax dollars to charity	Budapest, Hungary
1992	Campaign sought contributions for "service outcomes"	Baltimore, MD
1994	Focus on "impact in community" devised by "vision councils"	Minneapolis, MN
1994	Electronic pledge processing offered	San Francisco, CA
1995	United Way appeared on the Internet	Santa Barbara, CA
1996	Volunteer and pledging opportunities offered online	Provo, UT
1997	"211" universal information and referral service established	Atlanta, GA
1998	Consolidation of "back room" operations explored	Cincinnati, OH, Columbus, OH Indianapolis, IN Lexington, KY Louisville, KY

---

[1] Akana, Paul. "United Way—1966." Address at the 1976 United Way Staff Conference, March 9, 1976, Boston.

[2] "Convictions of 3 Upheld in United Way Fraud Case." *The Washington Post*, July 19, 1996, p. D4.

[3] Shepard, Charles E. "Perks, Privileges, and Power in a Nonprofit World; Head of United Way of America Praised, Criticized for Running It Like a *Fortune 500* Company." *The Washington Post*, February 16, 1992, p. 1.

[4] Allen, Frank Edward and Susan Pulliam. "United Way's Rivals Take Aim At Its Practices." *Wall Street Journal*, March 6, 1992, p. 8.

[5] Suhrke, Henry C., Editor. "The Aramony Affair." *The Philanthropy Monthly*, November 1992, p. 5.

[6] United Way Strategic Institute. "What Lies Ahead." United Way of America, 1989, pp. 2-9.

[7] Sanders, Don. Memo to 10 Key Cities members, November 1992.

[8] Watson, Alison H. "The United Way of America: Governance in the Nonprofit Sector (B)." Harvard Business School, Publication 9-494-033, October 12, 1993, p. 2.

[9] Bethea, Paula Harper. "A Conference for a Time of Change." 1993 United Ways' Leadership Conference program, p. 5.

[10] 1993 Leadership Conference theme.

[11] Mulvaney, James F., Chairman, United Way International. "A Review of Eighteen Years of Accomplishment," March 1992.

[12] Aft, Mary Lu. "A Joint Venture in Human Services," January 1991, p. 4.

[13] Walton, Larry. Comments during a 1998 discussion of "outcome measurement" at a meeting of the United Way of America National Professional Council.

[14] "Putting Outcomes in Perspective." *Agency Guide to Outcome Definition*. United Way of Greater Cincinnati, 1998.

[15] Trademark of the United Way of Minneapolis Area, 1994.

[16] Community Works™, United Way of Minneapolis Area, August 18, 1994.

[17] "On the Road to Community Impact." United Way of America, 2002, pp. 86-89.

[18] ibid, p. 90.

[19] ibid, p. 94.

[20] ibid, p. 93.

[21] Veverka, Mark. "United Way Weights Pros and Cons of Centralizing." *Wall Street Journal*, January 7, 1998.

[22] Veverka.

[23] Helix Data Processing Consultants Ltd. Web site, October 6, 2003.

[24] "211 more than just the 411 on social services." *United Way Online LexisNexis News Feed*, September 20, 2002.

[25] Gray, Yvonne. "Report to the United Way Board of Trustees," November 1998.

[26] "Early Success." A presentation to the presidents of the United Way of Central Indiana, Metro United Way (Louisville), the United Way of Central Ohio (Columbus), the United Way of Greater Dayton, and the United Way of Greater Cincinnati, November 2000.

[27] Akana.

CHAPTER TEN

2000 and Beyond
"What Is Past Is Prologue"[1]

A Quaker expression drawn from Deuteronomy[2] gives context to the history of the United Way movement: "All of us have drunk from wells we didn't dig and have been warmed by fires we didn't light."[3] The shape of the United Way movement had been sculpted by thousands of people who had shared the best practices of hundreds of community organizations over more than a dozen decades. Now, it seemed, everything was new and different.

It wasn't the dawn of the information age, but people in nearly every local United Way office were awakening to a new era of practice and community service.

"Sometimes in a vision, I see a world of happy human beings, all vigorous, all intelligent, none of them oppressing, none of them oppressed. A world of human beings aware that their common interests outweigh those in which they compete, striving toward those really splendid possibilities that the human intellect and the human imagination make possible. Such a world as I was speaking of can exist if people choose that it should."
—BERTRAND RUSSELL, *Philosopher*

High speed, wireless, 24/7 Internet connections made "doing things differently" commonplace. Still, local United Way organizations that involved people from diverse backgrounds and points of view, maintained their capacities to hear the heartbeats of their communities. Their experience provided them with operating habits that give witness to Margaret Wheatley's observation, "In human communities, the conditions of freedom and connectedness are kept vibrant by focusing on what's going on in the heart of the community rather than by being fixated on the forms and structures of the community."[4]

In 1982, John Naisbitt forewarned that "The major industry in the future will be the information industry."[5] Faith Popcorn, another futurist, pointed out that this industry would be run by "free range children [a generation that had been raised with limitless access to information]."[6] They were right, but information no longer described an industry as much as it described an environment in which the wells were always full and the fires were endlessly fueled.

Signs of the Times

2000   Wall Street's Dow Jones Average hit an all time high.

2000   The number of children living on the threshold of poverty in working facilities surpassed 10 million after increasing throughout the 1990s.

2001   On September 11, terrorists flew hijacked jetliners into the World Trade Center and Pentagon.

2002   Publishers of the Encyclopedia Britannica estimated that new information sufficient to double the size of their publication is currently discovered every day.

2003   The slump in the world economy became the longest since World War II.

THREE THEMES DESCRIBED AREAS IN WHICH EARLY TWENTY-FIRST CENTURY CREATIVITY EMERGED

- *Using technology.* "United eWay" rolled out of Phoenix at the beginning of the century. It was billed as "the United Way movement's technology solution for corporate philanthropic programs." Its creators claimed that their product combined "advanced online giving with integrated pledge processing and fund distribution services with online reporting . . . a seamless, end-to-end solution."[7] Only part of the new system, the donor convenience called "pledge capture," was original. The United eWay computer software package incorporated state-of-the-art custom processing services that had been developed by the United Way of Tri-State (a cooperative, area-wide fundraising partnership of 31 local United Ways located in New York, New

Jersey, Connecticut, and Pennsylvania) and the electronic pledge distribution approach successfully operated by the national Charities Funds Transfer program (a United Way of America subsidiary whose mission is to simplify and speed the accurate disbursement of corporate, employee, retiree, and foundation donations from national and regional corporations to local communities.)

United eWay was typical of current technological innovations. If it had been a car, it would have been described as a 2001 body with a 2000 engine that had been built on a 1990 chassis. It was the best of all worlds when it was introduced, at least for the moment. But, as United Way of America's information management specialist, Phillip Walker, cautioned, "The life of specific technologies is so short these days that you can only hope that the things you correspond about today will still exist when your correspondence is read tomorrow."[8]

- *Reaching out with initiatives.* In early 2000, eight local United Way organizations shared the stories of their efforts to transform themselves into what they termed "community impact United Ways," local organizations whose internal structures and resources were aligned to create sustained changes in community conditions that improve people's lives."[9] The cities were Atlanta, Boston, Columbus, Louisville, Nashville, Pontiac (Michigan), and Portland (Oregon).

Each chose a different path in their undertaking, although, according to a report on their progress titled *On the Road to Community Impact,* "community initiatives are a common strategy for achieving community impact."[10] Their work together affirmed "guiding principles" that United Way of America adopted the following observations of the community-building initiatives of local United Ways.

- "Build on the strengths of local individuals, associations, and organizations.
- "Focus on specific actions and measurable results to improve community life.
- "Promote relationships among and participation of all races, genders, ages, and cultures.
- "Ensure local decision-making and ownership.
- "Draw on the resources of the total community.

- "Bridge all boundaries to develop healthy communities.
- "Share experience and knowledge to promote continuous community learning."[11]

• *Measuring impact.* Just as the Peat, Marwick, Mitchell and Company study of the community Fund and Council field in 1968 had called for a significant reorientation in the ways in which local community organizations approached their work, a late twentieth century study by United Way of America and its affiliated local United Way organizations did the same. *Strategic Direction for United Way, Charting a Path for Building Better Communities* challenged United Ways to change their definitions of themselves from organizations that:

- raised money
- funded agencies' programs and services, and
- served people

to organizations that:

- achieve measurable results, and
- change communities.[12]

Recent efforts to measure outcomes were identified as one of two legs on which local United Way organizations would stand to meet this challenge. "The United Way movement is striving . . . to find ways in which the results of diverse human service programs can be measured so that we know what services warrant the donor's contin-

At the 2004 United Way of America Leaders Forum, volunteers and professionals from hundreds of local United Way organizations received this refreshed symbol of their shared commitment to improve the quality of community life.

ued support and those which should either be terminated or redesigned."[13] The process by which local United Way organizations would change communities would build upon historical efforts conducted under the name "community building," but with a definition that went well beyond "solving community problems." "Community building," the new definition read, "is the process of engaging residents and other stakeholders in sustained collaborative efforts to strengthen and improve conditions in defined geographic areas . . . neighborhood focused, issue focused, or a combination of the two. Community building strengthens communities and develops healthy children and families."[14]

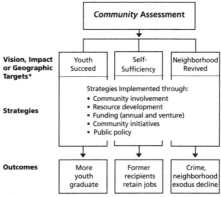

Community Assessment		
Vision, Impact or Geographic Targets*	Youth Succeed	Self-Sufficiency	Neighborhood Revived

Strategies Implemented through:
• Community involvement
• Resource development
• Funding (annual and venture)
• Community initiatives
• Public policy

Strategies

| **Outcomes** | More youth graduate | Former recipients retain jobs | Crime, neighborhood exodus decline |

* Strategies and desired outcomes are determined at this level.

Achieving United Way impact, according to the local volunteer and staff leaders who served as members of the United Way of America Community Impact Committee, would require a "new paradigm that integrates and aligns local United Way processes . . . into a seamless, *comprehensive, strategic* approach."[15] The new paradigm was built upon the Vision Council approach that had been developed during the preceding decade. It would focus all United Way tools and practices on a defined set of targets. The Committee illustrated its concept using terminology that was becoming commonly used in many cities, beginning with "Community Assessment" and concluding with "Outcomes" that illustrated change in communities.[16]

"The dignity that allows United Way leaders to stand tall reflects the backbone given to us by the cause we serve."
—VIRGIL H. CARR, *Late President & CEO, United Way Community Services, Detroit, Michigan*

United Way of America's president, Brian Gallagher, summarized the challenge of measuring impact during his comments at the 2003 United Way Leadership Forum. "It's a journey that begins with defining impact at a high level. And once you make the commitment to go, you have to go through the alignment process. You have to create an organization that can really deliver on the mission: *improving lives by mobilizing communities to create sustained changes in community conditions.*"[17]

"Any organization which is not changing as quickly as its environment is near the end of its existence."
—JACK WELCH, *Past Chairman & CEO, General Electric*

FUTURE LEADERS CAN DRAW PERSPECTIVE FROM
LOCAL COMMUNITIES' UNITED WAY HISTORY

To the extent that United Way is a *way* of leading or facilitating actions that improve communities and the lives of the people who live in them, leaders of any group or institution might learn from the experiences of United Way organizations in local communities. Those who choose to reflect on United Way history will observe three values that have defined local United Way organizations.

- *Take actions that are driven by principles and strategies.* On their best days, local United Way organizations have warranted words like those of President Herbert Hoover when, as Secretary of Commerce, he addressed the 1928 Citizens Conference of Community Welfare:[18]

The Community Chests have demonstrated their value and importance. They represent probably our greatest advances in the administration of charity through their great purpose of giving a large vision of the obligation of a whole city, of the integrity of charitable administra-

244

tion and of the overcoming of prejudice—all of these things have been brought about by the Community Chest.

The Community Chest has systematically spread the number of givers throughout the community. It has increased the interest of the communities in public charities themselves. It has eliminated the element of misguided sentimentality. It relieves the officers of charitable institutions of the time and the anxiety they must otherwise give to the gathering of funds for the support of these institutions and therefore releases to the communities the fine energy that must be used to attain the greatest good. It has tended to decrease the overlap. It gives the organizations a more measured and sounder basis of support. It protects against misrepresentation. It establishes each individual's responsibility to the community.

The growth of the Community Chest has been the growth and outcome of a desire for the efficient conduct of community work, just as we have efficient conduct of business. But charity does not lie entirely within the realm of efficiency. To become too logical is often to eliminate one of the great moral forces in our communities.

On their worst days, local and national United Way organizations woke to find that their leaders had not lived up to Hoover's description. It was at those times in the history of the movement that its principles served as the standards on which realignment could be achieved.

- *Provide return on investment.* Stakeholders of nonprofit organizations, like stockholders of profit-makers, expect value. They also ask questions to challenge those who lead nonprofit organizations; questions whose changing answers dictate the changing roles of the organizations in which they invest. In 1951, Donald Young, principal of the Russell Sage Foundation, in the Foreword of *Community Chest, A Case Study in Philanthropy,* articulated questions that should be asked often by the leaders of local United Way organizations, even though they may never be completely answered:
  - "How does one estimate the need for philanthropic dollars in a given community?
  - "What are the relative merits of the multitude of fund-raising techniques and gadgets commonly in use?

- "What do we know about fund-raising organizations and campaigns that may be helpful in guarding the interest of both the ultimate recipients of assistance and the general public, including the donors?

- "In short, what are the elements crucial to the success or failure in voluntary agencies of a community, not merely in terms of dollars, but with full regard for the needs and potentialities of all the citizenry and the community as a whole?

- "What return may one reasonably expect?"[19]

- *Maintain a focus on the future*, using history as a rudder, not an anchor. History books are filled with examples of defunct organizations and institutions that did things as they had always been done. Seldom have community problems and the needs of individuals and families responded to wishes for a return to the days before the problems occurred. Peter Drucker quipped, "Basing future goals on past performance is like driving a car while looking out the rear window." Who could have guessed just a few years ago the things that all of us know as fact today? "Twenty years ago," wrote the authors of *International Organizational Behavior* in 1998, "the year 2000 loomed like a colossus on the horizon. Futurologists speculated on what types of societies would evolve and wondered whether humanity would be better or worse off."[20]

Some envisioned a future of unlimited freedom and wealth; space travel would be common, poverty and disease would be eradicated, and happiness would abound. Others viewed the future pessimistically; overpopulation, environmental deterioration, war, famine, and alienation would pervade all civilizations.

The change that has affected most of the world's population the greatest is the increase in globalization of social, cultural, and economic activity. From the vantage point of 1998, it appears that globalization will continue and probably accelerate. Organizations are global. Business is global. Communication is global. Finance is global. Work is global.

Yet people live in local, not global, neighborhoods and communities. While many of their needs are global, adults and children are as individual and different as their families, their cultures, their economic position, and their friends. Together, people share what American social work scholar Charlotte Towle called *Common Human Needs*,[21] but none of them would consider their own needs to be identical to those of others. Children need to think that they are special. Families like to think that they are unique. Villages, towns, and cities are each different. United Way organizations have searched for similarities among these differences. They have focused on the future by seeing it through the eyes of groups of people who represent many points of view and are willing to meet long enough and think hard enough to identify common needs and solutions that will be commonly accepted.

"When United Way leaders truly lead, they seize or design initiatives that will create opportunities for citizens to take action on their own for others."

—RALPH DICKERSON JR. *Past President, United Way of New York City, New York*

UNITED WAY LEADERS HAVE LEARNED FROM ONE ANOTHER'S OCCASIONAL EXTRAORDINARY ACCOMPLISHMENTS

History illustrates that most organizations, like the people who lead them, are ordinary. Occasionally, they do extraordinary things. As serendipity shaped extraordinary approaches to common experiences, the news of their creation spread quickly among organizations of like needs and like values. Members of the United Way family rose together on the shared tide of their best practices. At the same time, they treasured the local autonomy that separated them from one another, thereby serving the particular needs of their communities as described in the *Encyclopedia of Social Work* as "the autonomous right to change or abandon current programs . . . to promote flexibility, to provide for unmet needs, to experiment with new services and approaches, and to demonstrate in unpopular matters of social concern."[22]

"Judge your predecessor's actions charitably; from where you sit, you can't see as much as they could."

—GORDON BERG, *Past President, United Way of Central Carolinas, North Carolina*

The United Way movement began in 1876 as agencies shared information on their clients and services in order to limit duplication and use limited funds efficiently. It grew as agencies pooled their efforts to plan services, then to raise money to meet their financial needs. It became the place at which community leaders fulfilled their social responsibilities to help people in need.

"Listen.

In every office
you hear the threads
of love and joy and fear and guilt
the cries for celebration and reassurance,
and somehow you know that connecting these threads
is what you are supposed to do
and business takes care of itself."

—PAULA UNDERWOOD SPENCER, *Native American storyteller*

The United Way movement is no longer young. But thanks to the ceaseless energy, idealism, and creativity of it constituents, it isn't old, either. Today, the United Way movement is a confederacy of local, national, and international organizations globally recognized as United Way and locally known as a *uniting* way.

---

[1] Shakespeare, William. *The Tempest*, Act II, Scene 1.

[2] Deuteronomy 6:10-11. "Then when the Lord your God brings you to the land he swore to your ancestors Abraham, Isaac, and Jacob—to give you large, excellent cities you did not build, houses willed with choice things you did not provide, hewn out cisterns you did not do, and vineyards and olive groves you did not plan—and you eat to your satisfaction."

[3] Smith, Robert Lawrence. *A Quaker Book of Wisdom: Life Lessons in Simplicity, Service, and Common Sense*. New York: Eagle Brook, 1997.

[4] Wheatley, Margaret J. and Myron Kellner-Rogers. "The Paradox and Promise of Community." *The Drucker Foundation: The Community of the Future* by Frances Hesselbein et al. San Francisco: Jossey-Bass, 1998.

[5] Naisbitt, John. *Megatrends: Ten New Directions Transforming Our Lives.* New York: Warner Books, 1982.

[6] Popcorn, Faith and Adam Hanft. *Dictionary of the Future: The Words, Terms and Trends That Define the Way We'll Live, Work and Talk.* New York: Theia, 2001, p. 84.

[7] Hassett, Brian. "United eWay Background."

[8] Walker, Phillip. Correspondence with the author, September 23, 2002.

[9] "On the Road to Community Impact." United Way of America, 2002, p. 5.

[10] Brennan, Michael. In United Way of America's letter transmitting *On the Road to Community Impact* to Chief Professional Officers of its affiliated local United Way organizations, September 12, 2002.

[11] *On the Road to Community Impact,* p. 8.

[12] "*Community Impact: A New Paradigm Emerging: A White Paper on Change in the United Way Movement.*" United Way of America, 1998, p. 2.

[13] ibid, p. 3.

[14] pp. 7-8.

[15] p. 4.

[16] p. 5.

[17] Gallagher, Brian. "*Community Impact Basics.*" Comments delivered at the 2003 United Way Leadership Forum, Nashville, TN, April 3, 2003.

[18] Hoover, Herbert. "The Human Welfare Responsibilities of Community Chests." Remarks presented at the Citizens Conference on Community Welfare, February 20–21, 1928, Washington, DC, pp. 3-4.

[19] Young, Donald. Foreword, *Community Chest, A Case Study in Philanthropy.* University of Toronto Press, 1957, p. vii.

[20] Francesco, Anne Marie and Barry Allen Gold. *International Organizational Behavior.* Prentice-Hall, 1998, p. xiii.

[21] Towle, Charlotte. *Common Human Needs.* National Association of Social Workers, 1945.

[22] Morris, Robert, et al. *Encyclopedia of Social Work.* National Association of Social Workers, New York, 1971, p. 1523.

INDEX OF INNOVATIONS

Introductory or Initial Application

Index of Innovations